The New Comedy of Greece and Rome

R. L. HUNTER

Fellow of Pembroke College, Cambridge

The right of the
University of Cambridge
to print and sell
all manner of books
was granted by
Henry VIII in 1534.
The University has printed
and published continuously
since 1584.

CAMBRIDGE UNIVERSITY PRESS

Cambridge

London   New York   New Rochelle

Melbourne   Sydney

Published by the Press Syndicate of the University of Cambridge
The Pitt Building, Trumpington Street, Cambridge CB2 1RP
32 East 57th Street, New York, NY 10022, USA
10 Stamford Road, Oakleigh, Melbourne 3166, Australia

First published 1985

Printed in Great Britain by the
University Press, Cambridge

Library of Congress catalogue card number: 84-29244

British Library cataloguing in publication data
Hunter, R. L. (Richard Lawrence)
The New Comedy of Greece and Rome.
1. Latin drama (Comedy)—History and criticism
2. Greek drama (Comedy)—History and criticism
I. Title
871'.01   PA6069

ISBN 0 521 30364 8 hard covers
ISBN 0 521 31652 9 paperback

Contents

Preface

Much of the material presented here was first collected for a series of lectures to undergraduate audiences. 'The book of the lectures' is a genre rightly regarded with deep suspicion in many quarters, and this particular example perhaps requires a brief explanation. I had no desire to produce an exhaustive treatment of Graeco-Roman comedy (a kind of updated *Daos*), and the time did not seem auspicious for such an undertaking. I am very aware that certain important topics, such as the differences between Greek and Roman comedy, do not receive their due in the chapters which follow, but my aim was to fill a gap in the existing literature by concentrating on what one might look for in watching and reading these plays and why such an exercise might be pleasurable. I am also acutely conscious of the fact that I have often simply stated my views on questions where more than one opinion may reasonably be held. This is intended to stimulate, rather than to suppress, discussion and dissent. I have also tried to restrict bibliographical notes to the absolute minimum, with the obvious result that in many places I have probably adopted the observation or argument of another scholar without explicit acknowledgement. I hope that those who find their work plundered in this way will not take it amiss. Where, however, I am aware that my debt is an extensive one, I have sought not to conceal the fact. I should like, moreover, to place on record a general acknowledgement to the two books from which I have learned most: Eduard Fraenkel's *Elementi Plautini in Plauto* and the commentary on Menander of A. W. Gomme and F. H. Sandbach.

In preparing this work for publication I have drawn heavily upon the goodwill of a number of friends and colleagues: William Arnold, David Bain, Eric Handley, Pauline Hire, Stephen Heyworth, Susan Moore and Malcolm Willcock all improved the typescript in various ways. I am particularly indebted to F. H. Sandbach for his pertinent criticisms of successive drafts; where I have rejected his advice, I have done so only with the gravest misgivings. I have received material assistance at various times from the British Academy, the Worshipful Company of Drapers and the Council of Girton College, and I wish to record my gratitude to these bodies. It is a great pleasure to be able once again to thank Pembroke College for its support and assistance. Without the help of my wife, Iris, the production of this book would have taken much longer than it has; she will probably not want to read it yet again, but I am deeply grateful for what she has already endured.

This book is dedicated to the memory of Alice Temperli, ποθεινῆς τοῖς φίλοις.

Cambridge   R. L. H.
January, 1985

References and abbreviations

1. *Menander*. Where no indication is given, references follow the numeration of F. H. Sandbach's Oxford Classical Text. The edition of Körte and Thierfelder (Leipzig 1959) is indicated by K–T.

2. *Other Greek Comedy*. The surviving plays of Aristophanes are quoted from Coulon's text. Where possible, I cite the fragments of Greek comedy in the text and numeration of R. Kassel and C. Austin, *Poetae Comici Graeci* (Berlin/New York 1983–), indicated by 'K–A', or of C. F. L. Austin, *Comicorum Graecorum Fragmenta in Papyris Reperta* (Berlin/New York 1973), indicated by 'Austin'. Where no indication is given, the numeration is that of T. Kock, *Comicorum Atticorum Fragmenta* (Leipzig 1880–8).

3. *Roman Comedy*. Quotations of Plautus and Terence generally follow the Oxford Classical Texts of W. M. Lindsay (Plautus) and R. Kauer and W. M. Lindsay (Terence).

4. Unless otherwise indicated, all translations are my own. They are intended to reproduce fairly closely the sense of the original, and where a translator must choose between idiomatic English and stilted literalism, I have generally chosen the latter. I have, however, occasionally signalled the presence of a pun in the original by including an English pun in the translation.

5. Modern works listed in the Bibliography are cited in the notes by author and date only.

6. The following abbreviations for periodicals and works of reference are used in the notes and the Bibliography:

A&A   *Antike und Abendland*
AJP   *American Journal of Philology*
BASP *Bulletin of the American Society of Papyrologists*
BICS *Bulletin of the Institute of Classical Studies*
CP   *Classical Philology*

CQ   *The Classical Quarterly*
GRBS   *Greek, Roman and Byzantine Studies*
HSCP   *Harvard Studies in Classical Philology*
ICS   *Illinois Classical Studies*
JRS   *The Journal of Roman Studies*
PCPS   *Proceedings of the Cambridge Philological Society*
Phil.   *Philologus*
RE   *Paulys Real-Encyclopädie der classischen Altertumswissenschaft* (Stuttgart 1893–)
REL   *Revue des études latines*
RFIC   *Rivista di filologia e di istruzione classica*
RhM   *Rheinisches Museum für Philologie*
SIFC   *Studi italiani di filologia classica*
TAPA   *Transactions and Proceedings of the American Philological Association*
ZPE   *Zeitschrift für Papyrologie und Epigraphik*

1

Introduction

This book is concerned with the comedies written by Greek poets in
the period between the death of Alexander the Great in 323 B.C. and
the end of the following century and with the Latin adaptations of
Greek comedies which were presented at public festivals in Rome
between 240 B.C. and 160 B.C. The chronological limits of the Greek
period must be interpreted flexibly. Although the death of Alexander
forms an obvious and convenient division in the history of the whole
Greek world, changes in literary and dramatic taste usually occur
gradually; of the five leading poets of the Greek New Comedy, as the
genre with which we shall be concerned is designated, two, and
perhaps three (Alexis, Philemon, ?Diphilos),[1] were writing plays
before Alexander's death. The creative phase of the genre continued
well into the second century B.C., but very little is known of these later
years and all of the leading poets belong to the period before 250 B.C.
The boundaries of the Roman period are rather easier to establish.
240 B.C. is the year to which ancient scholars assigned the first Latin
adaptation of a Greek play to be presented at Rome,[2] and 160 B.C. saw
the production of the last surviving play of the *comoedia palliata*
('comedy in Greek dress'), the *Adelphoe* of Terence. Roman poets
continued to write comedies long after this date,[3] but the truly creative
period of the genre was over by the end of the second century.

Our texts of Greek New Comedy may be divided into two broad
categories. The first consists of those texts which have been preserved
in the favourable climatic conditions of Egypt on the papyrus sheets
on which the plays were written out in antiquity. This source, which
has only been made available in the present century, has now yielded
a whole play of Menander (the *Dyscolos*), major parts of six others
(*Aspis*, *Epitrepontes*, *Misoumenos*, *Periceiromene*, *Samia* and *Sicyonios*)
and intelligible sequences of action from ten more. There is also a large
corpus of passages of New Comedy preserved on papyri which cannot
be assigned with certainty to a particular author.[4] The number of these
texts is constantly increasing as more and more papyri are pub-

I

lished, and it is thus almost inevitable that any modern discussion of this genre will be to some extent out-of-date even before it appears. This relative richness of material testifies to the enormous popularity of New Comedy with both spectators and readers throughout the Hellenistic and Roman worlds.[5] Despite this popularity, it seems that these Greek plays did not fulfil any of the conditions for survival in very late antiquity and in the Byzantine period;[6] among these conditions were continued use as a school text, linguistic purity, historical interest, moral rectitude and a fair share of good luck. As far as we know, no text of Greek New Comedy was copied after the dark ages of the seventh and eighth centuries, and we have no medieval or Renaissance manuscripts of these works. It will thus be clear to what extent the study of ancient comedy has been given new impetus by the advances in papyrology which the present age has witnessed.

The second group of texts of Greek New Comedy is a large body of fragments preserved in the work of other writers, both Greek and Latin. The reasons why moralists, historians and antiquarians quoted extracts from comedy are very diverse: passages are adduced for their literary value, their worthy sentiments, their value as historical evidence, their linguistic purity or oddity and so on. Extant fragments of this kind range from a passage of sixty-eight verses in which a cook explains his art in the language of abstract philosophy (Damoxenos fr. 2) to hundreds of single words quoted by lexicographers. These fragments must be used with very great care, as we are usually ignorant both of the scenic context and of the identity and character of the speaker, and literary appreciation is hardly possible without this information (cf. below p. 85). Nevertheless, these fragments sometimes provide invaluable illustration of much in our papyrus texts which would otherwise remain obscure, and I shall refer to them whenever they shed a helpful light on problems raised by our main body of texts.

We know the names of about sixty Greek comic dramatists who were active in the period which I have defined, but only five require special notice here. By far the most important, in terms both of what survives today and of the judgement of antiquity, is Menander,[7] who was born about 342 B.C. and died about 290 B.C. Menander was an Athenian citizen whose family was probably relatively prosperous; his first play seems to have been produced in the late 320s and at his death he left over one hundred plays. He won first prize at one of the two major Athenian dramatic festivals, the Dionysia and the Lenaia, eight times, and later antiquity considered this to be a scandalously low figure in comparison with his merits as a dramatist. Various ancient sources link him with Demetrios of Phaleron, who ruled Athens as a pro-Macedonian supervisor (*epimelētēs*) from 317 to 307 and whose literary and philosophical interests, as well as his political importance, make him one of the most interesting characters of the late fourth century; other sources also link Menander with Theophrastos, who took over the headship of Aristotle's school of philosophy just as Menander's career was beginning, and with Epicurus, who is said to have done his military service at Athens at the same time as Menander. None of these links is inherently implausible, and modern scholarship has been remarkably ingenious in finding traces of the ideas of these men in Menander's drama (cf. below pp. 148–51). In addition to the extant Greek texts, the following Roman plays are certainly based on Menandrian originals: Plautus' *Bacchides* (= *Dis Exapaton*, 'The Double Deceiver'), *Cistellaria* ('The Play about a Casket' = *Synaristosai*, 'The Ladies who Lunch Together'), *Stichus* (= *Adelphoi*, 'The Brothers'), and four plays of Terence which retained their Greek titles, the *Adelphoe* (based on another play with the same title as the original of Plautus' *Stichus*), the *Andria* ('The Woman from Andros'), the *Eunuchus* ('The Eunuch') and the *Heauton Timorumenos* ('The Self-Punisher'). It is not unlikely that other Plautine plays also are taken from originals by Menander (cf. below pp. 62–3), but only new evidence or arguments of a kind not yet foreseen will bring general agreement about this.

The four other leading poets of this period all came to Athens from outside, and were presumably attracted by that city's enormous prestige as the undisputed centre of Greek drama. The oldest of these poets was Alexis from Thurii in southern Italy, who is said to have written 245 plays in an extraordinarily long career stretching from the middle of the fourth century until well after Menander's death. Our sources link Alexis to Menander either as the latter's teacher or, less plausibly, as his uncle, and there is certainly nothing improbable in the idea of an older poet passing on some of the secrets of the dramatist's craft to a promising young man. In addition to a large number of fragments quoted by later writers, it is probable that the

Poenulus of Plautus is derived from *The Carthaginian* of Alexis.[8] The next poet is Philemon, who was a native of Cilicia, according to the geographer Strabo, or of Syracuse in Sicily, according to another tradition. He was probably born in the late 360s, and he too lived to a very old age, leaving behind at his death nearly one hundred plays. Philemon may have visited the court of the Ptolemies at Alexandria and have produced plays there;[9] if so, his career illustrates the gradual development of Alexandria as the centre of the Greek literary world in the Hellenistic period. Later authors quote over two hundred fragments (largely of a moralising or gnomic character) from Philemon and two plays of Plautus are certainly based on comedies by him, the *Mercator* (= *Emporos*, 'The Merchant') and the *Trinummus* (= *Thesauros*, 'The Treasure'); it is also not improbable that the *Mostellaria* ('The Play about a Ghost') is derived from Philemon's *Phasma* ('The Ghost').[10] Together with Menander and Philemon, the conventional triad of New Comedy poets to which later scholars referred was completed by Diphilos from Sinope on the Black Sea, home also of Diogenes the Cynic. Diphilos was a contemporary of Menander and wrote the originals of Plautus' *Casina* (= *Kleroumenoi*, 'Those who Draw Lots'), the *Rudens* ('The Rope', Greek title unknown) and perhaps also the fragmentary *Vidularia* ('The Play about a Little Trunk').[11] The final poet who deserves mention here is Apollodoros from Carystos in Euboea, a poet of the first half of the third century who seems to have been much influenced by Menander's work and from whom Terence took two of his plays, the *Hecyra* ('The Mother-in-Law') and the *Phormio* (= *Epidikazomenos*, 'He who Pursues his Claim in the Courts').

Whereas Greek New Comedy was almost entirely lost until this century, the fates were much kinder to the Latin adaptations. The works of Plautus and Terence have always been widely read and performed and have exerted enormous influence on the western dramatic tradition. I shall consider later in this chapter the ways in which the Latin plays differ from the Greek models (cf. below pp. 16–19), but it will be as well to introduce Plautus and Terence here before considering the history of comedy in our period.

Very little is known certainly about Plautus, except that the *Stichus* was produced at Rome in 200 B.C. and the *Pseudolus* in 191 B.C. Cicero (*Brutus* 60) tell us that Plautus died in 184 B.C., and there is at least nothing implausible in such a date. The dramatist's name itself, however, is a source of debate, and it is possible that some, if not all, of the three names by which he is usually known, Titus Maccius (or Maccus) Plautus, are theatrical jokes, perhaps translatable as 'Phallus, son of Clown, the Mime-Actor'.[12] Of the diverse ancient traditions about Plautus, the two most plausible are that he came from Sarsina in Umbria and that he worked as an actor before he turned to writing. It is certainly true that his plays reveal him as a man thoroughly acquainted with the possibilities which the stage offers and imbued with the spirit of popular entertainment. In the *Epistle to Augustus* Horace well captures the often frantic liveliness of his drama:

> aspice, Plautus
> quo pacto partes tutetur amantis ephebi,
> ut patris attenti, lenonis ut insidiosi,
> quantus sit Dossennus edacibus in parasitis,
> quam non astricto percurrat pulpita socco;
> gestit enim nummum in loculos demittere, post hoc
> securus cadat an recto stet fabula talo.　　　(*Epist.* 2.1.170–6)

> See how Plautus sustains the role of the young lover, the thrifty father, the tricky brothel-keeper; what a Dossennus he is among greedy parasites, how he runs across the stage with his slipper loose – he's dying to put the cash away in his chest and cares not whether the play falls or stands up straight.

Our manuscripts present twenty-one Plautine dramas, of which one (*Vidularia*) survives only in scanty fragments and five others have suffered varying degrees of damage in transmission (*Amph.*, *Aul.*, *Bacch.*, *Casina* and *Cist.*). A scholar of the second century A.D., Aulus Gellius, provides us with a fascinating account of how these twenty-one plays came to be chosen from the very large number which were extant in the middle of the first century B.C. Gellius begins by noting that Plautus' distinctive style is the best guarantee of authenticity:

We see Varro too using this criterion. For apart from the twenty-one plays designated 'Varronian', which he selected because they were not doubted and were agreed by everyone to be the work of Plautus, he also accepted and claimed for Plautus certain others on the grounds of their Plautine style and wit, even though they were already assigned to other poets... There are in circulation under the name of Plautus about one hundred and thirty comedies; but Lucius Aelius, a very learned scholar [of the first century B.C.], thought

that only twenty-five were by Plautus. However, there is no doubt that those which seem not to be by Plautus but are attached to his name were written by early poets and then revised and worked up by Plautus; that is why they have the Plautine flavour.
(*NA* 3.3.2–3, 11–13)

That our twenty-one plays are those picked out by Marcus Terentius Varro (116–27 B.C.) as being of unchallenged authenticity is beyond reasonable doubt.[13] As no play whose authenticity had been doubted survives, we are in no position to evaluate the worth of Varro's judgement in these matters, but Gellius' account ought to give us pause on at least one count. It is clear that by the end of the first century B.C. a very large number of scripts of doubtful authorship were known at Rome, and even as early as the 160s Terence was able to claim (*Eun.* 30–4) that he did not know that Plautus had translated Menander's *Colax*. Given this situation, it would be wise to keep at least an open mind about the authenticity of all twenty-one of the *fabulae Varronianae*, as the fact that no scholar before Varro had ever doubted them does not by itself amount to very convincing proof.[14] There is in fact no good reason to doubt the authenticity of any one particular play, but although we ought to respect the weight of ancient opinion which Varro synthesises, we should not give it our unquestioning assent, particularly as Plautus' comic style seems to resemble so closely that of other Roman comic poets of whom fragments survive.[15]

During the second and first centuries B.C. the plays of Plautus were often performed: some, if not all, of the prologue of the *Casina* was written for a production of that play at some time after Plautus' death (cf. vv. 14–15, 19), and our text of the *Poenulus* preserves two alternative endings, presumably written for different performances. During this period the plays were in the hands of producers and actors, for whom the need for successful entertainment was paramount and the preservation of the poet's original words very much a secondary consideration. Given this situation, we would expect our texts to show signs of additions and deletions by actors in the interests of holding their audience, and most scholars would agree that this is just what we do find. Often it is very difficult, perhaps impossible, to decide whether Plautus himself is responsible for the inconsistencies and loose ends in which the texts abound or whether later actors are responsible or perhaps even an ancient editor who has conflated two scripts originally prepared for separate performances. These issues are important for everyone who reads Plautus' plays, not just for the modern editor or textual critic, as they suggest that our texts present a living theatrical tradition and form merely the basic script for what was a complex popular entertainment. I shall return later to the nature of Plautine drama (cf. below p. 22), but the matter is raised here as it is one of the many ways in which our texts of Plautus differ significantly from the texts of the other Roman comic dramatist whose work has survived.

The six extant plays of Terence (Publius Terentius Afer) were produced at Rome between 165 and 160 B.C. Four are adaptations of plays of Menander (*Andria, Heauton Timorumenos, Eunuchus, Adelphoe*) and two are taken from Apollodoros (*Phormio, Hecyra*). In the extra-dramatic prologues with which Terence prefaced his plays (cf. below pp. 30–3) he tells us that three of his plays also contain material from a second Greek original which has been blended with the play which was his main model: thus the *Andria* has some material from Menander's *Perinthia* ('The Girl from Perinthos'), the *Eunuchus* from Menander's *Colax* ('The Flatterer') and the *Adelphoe* from the *Synapothnescontes* ('Those who Die Together') of Diphilos. This practice of adding a scene or character from one play to an adaptation of another, a practice to which modern scholars give the name *contaminatio*, is unlikely to have originated with Terence, who in fact claims, with how much truth we cannot tell, that he is merely following the precedents set by the great writers of the earlier generation, Naevius, Plautus and Ennius (*Andria* 15–21).

In addition to the six comedies of Terence, we possess also an ancient commentary on all of the plays except *Heauton Timorumenos*, ascribed to a grammarian and teacher of the fourth century A.D., Aelius Donatus (one of the teachers of St Jerome). Although the text of this commentary is rather badly interpolated and often corrupt, it does preserve much of value about Terence's dramatic technique and his use of his Greek models, along with much elementary grammatical information and naive moral exhortation. Transmitted with this commentary is a *Life of Terence*, derived from Suetonius' work *On Poets*. It is clear from this *Life* that scholars took an interest in Terence's life and works not long after his death. Unfortunately, this source proves disappointing both because of the limits inherent in

7

ancient biographical methods and also because the prologues attached to Terence's plays provided, as indeed Terence may have intended, an irresistible stimulant to speculation and gossip. What we are told, in outline, is that Terence was born in Carthage, became the slave of the Roman senator Terentius Lucanus who educated and freed him,[16] was later attached to some of the leading young men of the state (most notably Scipio Aemilianus and Gaius Laelius) and, after writing the six plays we now possess, disappeared from Rome on a trip to the East. One story which has a certain appeal for modern students of drama is that he died at sea on his way back to Rome with new translations of Menander in his possession.[17] Whatever the true facts of Terence's life may be, it is clear that in the ancient world he was the most read and studied Latin poet after Virgil; his continuing popularity in the medieval world and in the Renaissance is attested by the very large number of manuscripts of his work which survive. In comparison with Plautus, the text of Terence seems relatively free from actors' interpolations and conflations. This fact reflects not only the scholarly attention which Terence's plays received at a relatively early date but also the different nature of his comedy. In Plautus, repetition and the insertion by actors of jokes taken from other plays would be completely in keeping with the general comic style; in Terence, on the other hand, the importance of developed plot and character would make such buffoonery quite destructive.

The history of ancient comedy is the story of a continually evolving tradition and not of a series of discrete periods.[18] Aristophanes and Menander both competed as comic poets at the great Athenian festivals in honour of Dionysus, and ancient scholars assigned both poets to the same dramatic genre, while acknowledging also the changes which took place over time. In this book we will be concerned with the continuity of the comic tradition as well as with the new style which Menander and his contemporaries introduced, and it may be useful to indicate a few examples of this continuity before passing on to review the outstanding changes which our period witnessed. First, there is the comedy of character. Continuity here is most obvious in the case of stock characters: the absurd general Lamachos in Aristophanes' *Acharnians* looks forward to the many soldiers of the New Comedy (cf. below p. 66) and the parasites of the later age have as dramatic forebears the chorus of *The Flatterers* of Eupolis, a contemporary and rival of Aristophanes. Less obvious perhaps, but no less important, is the line we can trace from Philocleon, the obsessive juror of *Wasps*, to Cnemon in Menander's *Dyscolos*, whose obsession is with peace and quiet, or Euclio in Plautus' *Aulularia*, who is obsessed by real and imaginary threats to his beloved pot of gold. Secondly, there is the comedy of situation. As the slave Pyrrhias rushes onto the stage in the *Dyscolos* pursued, as he claims, by Cnemon, we are reminded of the hurried entry and exit of Amphitheos in the *Acharnians*, bringing peace treaties from Sparta and pursued by the angry chorus of grim charcoal-burners. In Aristophanes' *Frogs*, the slave Xanthias, now dressed as Heracles, receives an offer of entertainment far too good to refuse (*Frogs* 503ff.); so too in the *Menaechmi* of Plautus, the travelling brother succumbs to the exotic hospitality offered by a sexy lady whom he does not know and who mistakes him for his brother. Various themes are important in both Old and New Comedy: relations within families (cf. below pp. 83–109), for example, or between town and country (cf. below pp. 109–13). So also many comic techniques are common to both periods: puns, exploitation of tragedy (cf. below pp. 114–36), broad comedy and farce, disguise[19] and so on. This list is far from exhaustive, but it is, I hope, sufficient to counter any impression which the following pages may give that Old and New Comedy are related only in name.

In terms of form and structure, the most obvious difference between Aristophanes and Menander is that the drama of the later poet does not use a chorus and is characterised by very little rhythmical variety (cf. below pp. 42–5). The role of the chorus and the metrical richness which accompanies it are already much diminished in the last two extant plays of Aristophanes (*Ecclesiazousai* and *Ploutos*), and we can trace the decline of these aspects of comedy in the fragments which survive of the comedies written in the years between Aristophanes and Menander, in the period known as Middle Comedy.[20] Our papyrus texts of Menander are divided into acts by the word XOPOY (i.e. 'Performance/Song of Chorus'). At the end of the first act a character announces the approach of 'drunken revellers' or some other similar band; it is a reasonable assumption that this heralds the first entry of a chorus whose performance had nothing to do with the play taking place on the stage. Although there are no records of what these choruses did perform, their continued physical existence is attested by inscriptional evidence and would in any case have been surmised from the fact that the performance of the chorus was part of the religious ritual in honour of Dionysus and could not easily be dropped altogether. We do not know whether the chorus remained in the *orchestra* (cf. below p. 11) after its first entry or whether it left and returned for each act-dividing performance. It is not improbable that, together with the diminution in its dramatic importance, came a reduction in its size from the twenty-four members of an Old Comedy chorus, and we may even speculate that by the late third century B.C. there were less grand performances in towns and theatres outside Athens which dispensed with a chorus altogether.[21] The reasons for the decline in the importance of the comic chorus must remain obscure until we acquire much more evidence about the crucial period of change at the end of the fifth century and in the early years of the fourth.[22]

Not only is the structural and metrical range of Greek New Comedy greatly reduced from the heyday of Aristophanes, but so is the world in which the comic characters move. Aristophanes presents us with a world in which fantasy reigns, where everything is possible; Aristophanic heroes know no limits, just as Old Comedy knows no limits to the range of subjects with which it deals. Menander's canvas is a much narrower one. His plays deal, for the most part, with the private lives of a small range of characters drawn (except for slaves, cooks and so on) from the relatively prosperous middle- and upper-middle-class bourgeoisie of Athens and other Greek cities.[23] It would be nice to know whether the composition of Menander's audience differed significantly from that which watched the plays of Aristophanes, but unfortunately we can only speculate; many scholars have guessed that the fact that in Menander's day citizens were no longer subsidised by the state to go to the theatre resulted in a much higher proportion of the audience being drawn from the wealthier, propertied classes and that it is likely to be the values and aspirations of these classes which are reflected in our texts of Greek New Comedy.[24] There is certainly little social change advocated in these plays, and the common expression of sentiments about the duties of the rich to the poor (e.g. Men. *Dysc.* 271–87) and the equality of men, regardless of social station at birth (e.g. Men. *Samia* 137–43), need be no more than the conventional pieties with which a successful social class often satisfies its conscience. In one way, however, these characters are uneasy in their success. No theme is more persistent in these plays than the mutability of fortune and the external limits which are placed upon human action; characters are constantly urged to lower their sights and stay within the realms of the commonsensical and the obviously practical. In Aristophanes, characters know no such constraints; they make their own luck and forge their own world.

The greater realism of New Comedy is reflected too in the external circumstances of drama. At the end of the fourth century a permanent stone theatre was built at Athens; the essential plan of stage-area and *orchestra* (lit. 'dancing-area') was retained, but there were now regularly three openings in the stage-building. These openings functioned as the doors of the houses required by the play, although it seems that most Greek plays only used two openings for this purpose, the third either having no function or being used for a building of another kind, such as a temple or a cave (cf. *Dysc.*). From either end of the stage-building protruded enclosed areas, designated by modern scholars as *paraskenia*, which might have been used as stage-houses, but whose exact function is uncertain. The stage-area was usually imagined as being a city street, but could just as easily represent a place in the country (cf. *Dysc.*, *Rudens*, *HT*). Different locations (e.g. town or country) might be represented by painted panels, but gone for ever was the freedom which allowed the setting of an Aristophanic play to shift from the city to the country (as in *Acharnians*) or from heaven to earth (as in *Peace*): all plays of New Comedy broadly observe the so-called 'unity of place'. At a later date – the precise chronology is a matter of great debate[25] – the stage was raised to the level of the upper storey of the stage-building and supported on columns; drama had now completely divorced itself from its origins in the rituals of the *orchestra*. The costume of Greek New Comedy shows a similar shift towards realism. The grotesque padding and phallus of Old Comedy slowly gave way to a standard costume of a tunic (χιτών, the everyday wear of ordinary Athenians) worn over tights. Masks were still worn, but they were now more lifelike than those of Old Comedy. A gradual weeding-out of all but the masks which were most often used produced in the end a standard group of masks suitable for every play; to what extent a surviving list of comic masks compiled in the second century A.D. (Pollux 4.143–54) reflects the practice of Menander and his contemporaries is a fascinating question beyond the scope of the present book.[26] We do not know if characters of the same name in different plays tended to wear the same mask, but the existence of a stock repertoire of names and masks certainly gave poets a chance to exploit contradictions between an individual character and the expectations of the audience raised by that character's name and mask (cf. below pp. 66–9). In keeping with the changes in the theatre and the costumes, the plots and characters of Greek New Comedy are realistic and believable in a way in which those of Old Comedy are not. This must not be understood to mean that New Comedy is in any sense a faithful representation of 'real life'. It goes without saying that recognitions, comic misunderstandings and erotic melodrama do not represent life as it is lived, either in the fourth century B.C. or the twentieth century A.D.; the important contribution of escapist fantasy and harmless wish-fulfilment to Menander's drama must not be overlooked.[27] Nevertheless, it is clear that New Comedy characters are placed in situations which are within the possible experience of the audience, whereas those of Old Comedy are not; how successfully or 'realistically' Menander portrays the behaviour and psychology of his characters is, of course, a quite different problem and one on which disagreement is inevitable. In thus limiting the range of material which it used, comedy also lowered its sights. Whereas Aristophanic drama can fulfil the grandiose wishes of the whole state, in New Comedy the unit of solidarity is the family; when plays conclude with the promise of children to come (cf. *Dysc.* 842, *Mis.* 444, *Periceir.* 1013, *Samia* 727), it is the family, not the individual, which has triumphed. New Comedy offers no grand vision of a new world; the plays offer rather the comforting spectacle of the restoration of the status quo after disturbance caused by folly or ignorance.

Another facet of the narrowing of comedy's horizons is the almost total absence of explicit language about sex and other physical processes. The occasional vulgarity does turn up, but usually in the mouths of characters of low social class.[28] It is unlikely that in real life such language was restricted in this way, but New Comedy can be seen to stand at the end of a long process of increasing inhibition in all the public arts.[29] Already in Aristophanes' plays of the early fourth century we do not find extensive sexual humour in scenes where

12

we might have expected it (*Eccl.* 877ff., *Pl.* 959ff.). So too the almost total absence of homosexuality from Menander's surviving plays is probably determined more by the plots than by changes in public habits; Demetrios of Phaleron was himself said to have a keen eye for handsome boys, and it is a great pity that we do not know anything about the play of Diphilos entitled *The Paederasts*.[30] The relative rarity of references to contemporary persons and politics in New Comedy will also forcefully strike a reader coming straight from Aristophanes.[31] Poets no longer wrote only for the narrow interests of the Athenians, but for the Hellenic world at large, and this is reflected in the universal nature of the problems confronting the characters. Nevertheless, many passages of moralising sentiment that seem to us entirely apolitical will have been given a sharper edge by the events of the time; an obvious example is *Dyscolos* 741–6 (cf. below pp. 144–5), where Cnemon's appeal to the audience's utopian instincts may have struck a responsive chord in the hearts of many Athenians who were tired of the bloody politics which characterised the end of the fourth century. In one passage at least (*Sicyon.* 150–68), Menander also allows us to glimpse the tensions between different social classes that lie concealed beneath the usually shining surface of the society he depicts. Menander's picture of the legal and social structures of Athens is moreover realistic and convincing, but the generality of his drama appealed to audiences and readers throughout the Greek world for several centuries after his death.

Any account of Roman drama must begin with a famous story in Livy (7.2) that in 364 B.C., in an attempt to appease the gods who had sent a terrible plague upon the city, the Romans instituted public shows (*ludi scaenici*) and brought in dancers from Etruria to perform in the city; from these beginnings the various Roman forms of musical and dramatic entertainment evolved. Whatever historical facts may lie behind Livy's narrative, there is at least no reason to doubt that Plautus inherited a well-established Roman theatrical tradition. By the end of the third century B.C. half a dozen Roman religious festivals were preceded by days devoted to theatrical entertainments of various kinds, and other public gatherings, such as the celebration of victory in war or the games held in connection with the funeral of an aristocrat, also provided opportunities for large-scale popular entertainments. Many of the religious festivals seem to have been re-organised in the late third and early second centuries and new ones were instituted, so that by 190 B.C. it is likely that approximately seventeen days each year were given over to regular *ludi scaenici*, and this number will have been increased by non-recurrent celebrations and repetitions of festivals at which the ritual had not been properly performed (*instaurationes*).[32] The entertainments on offer at these *ludi* were widely varied: mimes, dancers, boxers, gladiators, different kinds of native and Greek farce (cf. below pp. 20–1) and drama, both tragedy and comedy. The spirit of these Roman festivals seems to have had much more in common with a medieval carnival than with the dramatic festivals of Athens. The prologue of the *Poenulus* captures much of the carefree relaxation of these festivals:

> scortum exoletum ne quis in proscaenio
> sedeat, neu lictor uerbum aut uirgae muttiant,
> neu dissignator praeter os obambulet
> neu sessum ducat dum histrio in scaena siet.
>
> dum ludi fiunt, in popinam, pedisequi,
> irruptionem facite; nunc dum occasio est,
> nunc dum scribilitae aestuant, occurrite.   (*Poen.* 17–20, 41–3)

No ripe whore is to sit on the front of the stage, no lictor[33] or his rods to make a sound, no usher to walk in front of spectators or show people to their seats while an actor is on the stage.

While the play is on, slaves, attack the bakery. Now's your chance, while the tarts are hot. Forward!

In 240 B.C., for the first time, a Latin adaptation of a Greek play was included on the programme at *ludi scaenici*. The translator was Livius Andronicus from Tarentum in Hellenised southern Italy. This innovation coincides with Rome's successful conclusion of the First Punic War and may in some way be connected with the exposure to the Greek theatrical tradition that Romans had enjoyed in southern Italy and Sicily during that war. Rome could, in any event, not have remained for long aloof from Athenian drama. The tragedies of Aeschylus, Sophocles and Euripides and the comedies of Menander and his contemporaries were recognised and performed as theatrical classics all over the educated world and there was no reason for Rome to shun this mark of civilisation and status. As, however, Latin was the language of the ordinary people and the ruling classes were unwilling to allow foreign influence to take too strong a hold, the plays were performed in Latin translations (although they were probably, at this early date, advertised and known by their Greek titles and the names of the Greek poets).[34] It may surprise us that, as time went on, Latin poets did not begin to write Latin comedies of this style which did not have Greek originals; here we should remember the power of theatrical tradition, an increasingly influential philhellenic element among the educated classes (cf. below pp. 30–3 on the prologues of Terence) and the existence of the *comoedia togata* ('comedy in Roman dress'), a kind of comedy about Italian life and manners which enjoyed considerable popularity in the second half of the second century.[35] The *togata* borrowed many themes and motifs from Greek and Graeco-Roman comedy and its existence must have partly checked any demand for a completely original *comoedia palliata* ('comedy in Greek dress'), as the genre of Plautus and Terence was designated. By 100 B.C. there was a large body of Roman comedy which had established itself as classical, and the golden period of the *palliata* was at an end.

The Romans kept some Greek theatrical traditions and discarded others. There was no permanent stone theatre at Rome until Pompey had one constructed in 55 B.C. In Plautus' day the stage[36] was a raised wooden platform specially erected for the festival; in front of the stage, where the Greek *orchestra* would have been, was an empty area where seats could be placed. The ancient evidence is conflicting as to whether masks were worn at the time of Plautus,[37] as they certainly were in a later period. It may be that practice in Plautus' day was not uniform, i.e. that some plays (or characters) used masks and others did not. In the Greek theatre the use of masks must have been an aid to the doubling of roles and, if this practice is allowed, Menander's plays seem to have been performable by three actors (together with silent extras). Roman comedy is certainly not bound by any such limitation, and we do not know how many actors the manager of a troupe had at his disposal.[38] Finally, we should note that the traditional separation of tragedy and comedy broke down at Rome. The first generation of Latin dramatists (Livius Andronicus, Gnaeus Naevius and then Quintus Ennius) were active in both fields, and Plautus seems to have broken new ground in restricting himself to comedy. A consequence of this is that the Romans did not preserve the sharp rhythmical distinctions that exist between Greek comedy and Greek tragedy, and this becomes important when evaluating the use of parody in Roman comedy (cf. below p. 114).

The most important evidence for Plautine methods in adapting Greek plays for the Roman stage is a passage of some sixty verses of Menander's *Dis Exapaton* ('The Double Deceiver'), first published in 1968, together with Plautus' version of this passage, *Bacchides* 494–560.[39] The situation in these verses is as follows. A young man, called Sostratos by Menander and Mnesilochus by Plautus, has written from overseas to his friend Moschos (or, as Plautus calls him, Pistoclerus) asking him to find and keep an eye on a courtesan (called Bacchis) with whom he has fallen in love. In fulfilling this task Moschos/Pistoclerus discovers that Bacchis has a twin sister with whom he then begins an affair. When Sostratos/Mnesilochus returns, he thinks that his friend has stolen his girl, a difficult situation as his slave has already told his father a tall story to allow them to keep a sum of money, which they had brought back with them, in order to purchase the girl. As our Greek text begins, Sostratos is urged by his friend's father and tutor to rebuke Moschos strongly for his lewd conduct. Sostratos, left alone on stage, expresses his anger in a jerky, almost incoherent monologue; to punish her and to protect himself from falling victim to her blandishments again, he decides to return the money to his father. When our text again becomes legible Sostratos and his father are in conversation; Sostratos tells his father that he can recover his gold. This presumably occurred in the subsequent act-break, after which the same two characters re-enter. Left alone again, Sostratos gives vent to his confused feelings:

καὶ μὴν δοκῶ μοι τὴν καλήν τε κἀγαθὴν
ἰδεῖν ἐρωμένην ἂν ἡδέως κενὸς
πιθανευομένην καὶ προσδοκῶσαν – "αὐτίκα"
φησὶν δ' ἐν αὐτῆι – πᾶν ὃ κομίζω χρυσίον.
"πάνυ γὰρ κομίζει τοῦτο καί, νὴ τοὺς θεούς,
ἐλευθερίως – τίς μᾶλλον; – ἀξίως τ' ἐμοῦ."
αὑτη δ' ἱκανῶς, καλῶς ποοῦσά γ', εὑρέθη
οἵαν ποτ' ᾤμην οὖσα, τὸν δ' ἀβέλτερον
Μόσχον ⟨◡◡–⟩· καὶ τὰ μὲν ἔγωγ' ὀργίζομαι,
τὰ δ' οὐκ ἐκεῖνον τοῦ γεγονότος αἴτιον
ἀδικήματος νενόμικα, τὴν δ' ἰταμωτάτην
πασῶν ἐκείνην.

                                                   (*Dis Exapaton* 91–102)

Now that I've got no money I'd like to see my fine and noble girl
sweet-talking me, her hopes of a large haul sky-high. She'll be saying
to herself 'Of course he's bringing it, I swear, just like the perfect
gentleman he is, and it's no less than I deserve.' She's just what I
once thought she was. Splendid! But I [...] that poor fool Moschos.
I'm angry all right, but I don't regard him as the cause of this
outrage; that shameless lady is to blame.

At this point Moschos enters and after a brief exchange Sostratos
accuses him of treachery. The structure of the corresponding Latin
script is, however, quite different. Sostratos/Mnesilochus' two monologues are combined into one (vv. 500–25) which borrows ideas from
both Greek monologues and which pads out the psychological realism
of the Greek text with a series of jokes:

> inimiciorem nunc utrum credam magis
> sodalemne esse an Bacchidem incertum admodumst.
> illum exoptauit potius? habeat, optumest.
> ne illa illud hercle cum malo fecit meo:
> nam mihi diuini numquam quisquam creduat,
> ni ego illam exemplis plurimis planeque amo.
> ego faxo haud dicet nactam quem derideat:
> nam iam domum ibo atque aliquid surripiam patri.
> id isti dabo. ego istanc multis ulciscar modis.
> adeo ego illam cogam usque ut mendicet meus pater.
> sed satine ego animum mente sincera gero,
> qui ad hunc modum haec hic quae futura fabulor?   (*Bacch.* 500–10)

I really don't know whether my friend or Bacchis is the greater
enemy. She wanted him, did she? Fine, she can have him. This is
sure going to bring a lot of trouble on – my head. For no one should
ever believe my sworn word again if I don't completely and
utterly – love her. I'll make her deny she picked the right man to
mock; I'll go home right now and – steal something from Father. I'll
make her a present of that. I shall have a thousand revenges on her.
I'll push her so hard that poverty overtakes – my father. But it's
hardly the act of a sane man to stand here babbling about the future.

Plautus has cut out the two scenes between the young man and his
father which fell on either side of the act-break in Menander's play;
Plautus' theatre had no chorus and his plays were performed continuously, without act-division (cf. pp. 37–40), and so the excision

of these scenes solved one structural problem for him. It also allowed him to concentrate on the confrontation between the two young men which, in his script, becomes a rather laboured scene of misunderstanding. In brief, we may say that the Plautine text is a mixture of close translation and free adaptation and is much more broadly and self-consciously comic than the original. Finally, it is to be observed that whereas the Greek text is entirely in what is the most prosaic, least poetic, ancient verse rhythm, namely the iambic trimeter, the Latin text is mainly in longer trochaic verses with Mnesilochus' monologue kept in iambic trimeters. Plautus' trochaics were accompanied by the music of the *tibia* (in Greek *aulos*), a reed instrument consisting of a cylindrical pipe (or more often a pair of pipes) with lateral holes, which may be compared to the modern oboe.[40] The far higher percentage of musically accompanied verses in Latin comedy compared with Greek is a striking difference between the two (cf. below pp. 45–6), and the importance of music in the former is reflected in the fact that the ancient notices concerning the occasion of performance which are attached to our texts of Terence's plays and of Plautus' *Stichus* name the composer (and probably also player) of the music and the type of instrument used.

The inferences which the *Dis Exapaton* papyrus allows us to draw about Roman methods of adaptation had in fact already been drawn, to some extent at least, on the basis of a general comparison of our Greek and Latin texts and some other ancient evidence. The most important pieces of this evidence[41] are the prologues of Terence's plays, Donatus' commentary on Terence, and a further chapter of Aulus Gellius (cf. above p. 5) in which that scholar compares certain extracts from the *Plocion* ('The Necklace') of Menander with the corresponding passages from the adaptation of that play by Caecilius Statius, a younger contemporary of Plautus. In this chapter (*NA* 2.23) we see the same preference for broad comedy, metrical richness – Caecilius turns an iambic narrative into a grandiose song – and verbal luxuriance which characterise all of our remains of Roman comedy until the era of Terence. The upshot of this is that many of the features which will strike any reader as most characteristic of Plautine drama seem indeed to have been added by the Roman poet to his Greek model.

Any explanation of why Plautus and his fellow poets so changed the form and nature of their Greek models will have to account for the fact that Roman tragedy also seems to have been far more musical than its Attic model. Moreover, although Plautus' plays all show the hallmarks of a common comic style, the proportion of song varies greatly from play to play. The *Casina* is elaborately polymetric, whereas the *Miles Gloriosus* is composed almost entirely of the two most common metres of conversation. It is reasonable to suppose that Plautus' mastery of the complicated rhythms of song grew firmer as his career progressed, but we do not know the dates of enough plays to confirm such a hypothesis.[42] It is in fact clear that, in order to understand the Roman transformation of Greek New Comedy, we would have to know far more about the theatrical history of third-century Rome than our present, very scanty, evidence allows us to see. Nevertheless, a survey of the various influences to which Plautus might have been exposed may suggest where we should look for an answer.

During the third century guilds of itinerant performers carried the classics of Athenian drama throughout the Hellenistic world. These prestigious troupes, the so-called Artists of Dionysus (οἱ περὶ τὸν Διόνυσον τεχνῖται),[43] contained not only actors, musicians and stage-hands, but also dramatic, dithyrambic and epic poets. It is reasonable to suppose that an early *collegium* of poets and actors in third-century Rome about which our sources give us tantalisingly little information was to some extent modelled on the Greek guilds, and most of the early actors at Rome of whom we know seem to have had Greek origins.[44] Unlike their counterparts in Menander's Athens, however, these Roman actors, being either foreigners or slaves, were held in little esteem, and the theatre never attained in Rome the honoured and respected position which it held in Greece. We know very little about how the 'Artists' performed, and it has been suggested[45] that our texts of Menander do not give an accurate impression of the Greek comedy which Plautus and his contemporaries would have witnessed in the theatres of southern Italy and Sicily or of the kind of Greek script from which Plautus would have worked. There may, for example, have been much more music than we now suspect in the Greek performances of the late third century, and such a hypothesis has been thought to be confirmed by the apparently Greek origins of many of Plautus' lyric patterns. There is, however, no reason why Plautus himself should not have introduced Greek patterns into his plays, and there is absolutely no evidence that a Greek comedy was ever performed 'after the Plautine fashion' in a public theatre. It is, of course, perfectly possible that Roman dramatists were influenced by less formal Greek performances than those of the guilds; we know, for example, that New Comedy shared certain themes with the sub-literary performances given by travelling entertainers (μῖμοι, 'mime-actors') at fairs and street corners.[46] It seems reasonable that such entertainers might refashion familiar scenes from formal drama after their own style, but this is still a long way from the full text of a Plautine play.

The most famous Greek writer of the literary version of these mimes was Sophron, a Sicilian writer of the late fifth century who is said to have influenced Plato's literary technique. From earlier in that century the strength of the Sicilian dramatic tradition is attested by the many extant fragments of the great comic poet Epicharmus, and a wonderful series of painted vases of the fourth century from Sicily and southern Italy illustrates that comedy continued to thrive in these areas.[47] On these vases we see masked and padded actors (or *phlyakes*), many with the artificial phallus, performing scenes both of a mythological character (often involving the parody of a tragedy) and also drawn from ordinary life – food, slaves and violence play a large part in these paintings. These performances were obviously far closer to broad farce than were the plays of the Greek New Comedy, and it is quite reasonable to suspect that this tradition has influenced the style of Roman comedy; Horace indeed tells us that some critics had connected Plautus and Epicharmus, although the exact inference to be drawn from his words is not clear.[48]

Also from southern Italy came a type of farce associated with the town of Atella in Campania. Atellan farces placed a small group of ridiculous characters, clowns (Bucco, Maccus), stupid old men (Pappus), greedy buffoons (Dossennus) in a variety of stock situations. There was clearly a great deal of improvisation and low humour, and as these farces were performed at *ludi scaenici* in Rome, the opportunities for cross-fertilisation with more formal drama were abundant. Plautus is directly linked with these farces not only by his name Maccus or Maccius (cf. above p. 5) but also by Horace, who likens Plautine parasites to Dossennus, the greedy buffoon of Atellan farce (*Epist.* 2.1.173, quoted above p. 5). It is indeed very likely that the bold colours of Plautus' characters, i.e. the fact that his parasites are so greedy and his old men so stupid, owe something to the unsophisticated humour of these farces.[49] Unfortunately, most of our information about the Atellan farce comes from the first century B.C., when Pomponius and Novius gave a literary form to these previously sub-literary improvisations.[50] When, therefore, we find similarities between the titles and fragments of Atellan farce and the remains of early Roman comedy, it is just as likely that the later farce is borrowing from comedy as that we have evidence for the influence of the *Atellana* on Plautus.

We have now identified a number of theatrical traditions which, in varying degrees, were probably influential upon the style of Roman comedy: the musical performances imported from Etruria, the Greek mime, the drama of southern Italy, the Atellan farce. We cannot, of course, go through our texts of Plautus assigning individual features to different influences, because theatrical tradition does not develop in this way. Forms of popular drama evolve slowly, almost imperceptibly, and draw inspiration wherever inspiration seems to offer itself. Even if we could melt down a Plautine play into 'constituent elements' we would find that the intermingling between those elements had been so complex long before the days of Plautus that anything like a complete analysis was impossible. What ought, however, to be clear is that, in the Graeco-Roman world of the fourth and third centuries B.C., there was a great richness of dramatic entertainment, of all grades of formality, and that our preserved texts are only one link, albeit a major one, in the chain of evidence for popular entertainment in this period.

Of importance also were the special factors surrounding the early years of formal comedy at Rome. Livius, Naevius and Ennius all adapted both comedies and tragedies, and so we cannot rule out the influence of tragedy on the metrical and linguistic structures of comedy. As far as we can tell, Hellenistic tragedy retained a greater lyric (if not choral) element than did Hellenistic comedy and this may have influenced the Roman adaptations of fifth-century classics. Unfortunately, although few problems of ancient literary history are as interesting as this one, very few are as bedevilled by lack of evidence.

Whatever may have been the formative influences upon Plautus, his plays present a rather mixed society. The world of the plays is basically Greek – the cities where the plays are set are Greek, the characters have (often exaggeratedly) Greek names, their dress is essentially Greek, the Romans are *barbari*, the world of the characters is full of Greek mythology. It is clearly part of the fun that the foolish characters we are watching belong to another society and this otherness is exaggerated in these obvious ways. Into this world, however, Plautus places significant Roman elements. These range from simple Graeco-Latin puns (cf. *Bacch.* 129, *Men.* 264–7), through extravagant lists of Roman food, to speeches such as the following in which an actor playing a Greek suddenly speaks as a Roman:

> tum isti Graeci palliati, capite operto qui ambulant,
> qui incedunt suffarcinati cum libris, cum sportulis,
> constant, conferunt sermones inter sese drapetae,
> obstant, obsistunt, incedunt cum suis sententiis,
> quos semper uideas bibentes esse in thermopolio,
> ubi quid subripuere – operto capitulo calidum bibunt,
> tristes atque ebrioli incedunt – eos ego si offendero,
> ex unoquoque eorum crepitum exciam polentarium.   (*Curc.* 288–95)

> Those damned Greeks with their cloaks, who walk around with
> covered heads, laden to the hilt with books and lunch boxes,
> runaway slaves who stand around to chatter and block your way or
> stroll along philosophising, the ones you can always see drinking in a
> bar when they've managed to steal something – they cover their
> heads and drink hot wine, then walk along looking serious and a bit
> the worse for drink – if I meet any of them, I'll knock the barley-fed
> wind out of every one.

The plays are riddled with references to Roman institutions and Roman legal practice. A man who is encouraging immoral behaviour can be ironically described as *senati columen* ('a pillar of the senate', *Casina* 536) and Menaechmus, a citizen of the Greek town of Epidamnus, tells us how he wasted a day pleading for one of his clients (*clientes*) before the aediles (*Men.* 588–95). Plautus clearly exploits every opportunity for humour: by emphasising the Greekness of his characters he can make his audience laugh at them all the louder, and by using material drawn from contemporary Rome he gives his audience the pleasure of recognition and identification. All the ingredients of his plays have only one test to pass: they must be 'theatrical' in all senses of the term.

The world of Terence's plays is a very different one from that of Plautus'. These plays seem to move in a pure Greek world – reference to things Roman is hard to find and in any case never stridently obvious[51] – but the Greekness of the world is also not exaggerated. Thanks to Donatus' commentary we can in fact identify certain places where Terence has removed specifically Greek references and replaced them with places and customs which are neither Greek nor Roman but 'international'. Thus we learn that in the Greek original of the *Phormio* it was a barber, who had cut a poor girl's hair (a standard Greek sign of mourning), who told Getas and his young masters about her; in Terence this duty is taken over by a rather mysterious young man (*adulescens quidam*) with no further role in the play. Donatus' explanation that Terence wished to eliminate from the play a non-Roman custom seems a reasonable one. Another example occurs at *Heauton Timorumenos* 63 where the generalised 'in this area' replaces a specific locality in Attica, which would have been quite obscure for a Roman audience. Despite these minor changes it is clear that Terence differs from Plautus in his presentation of a consistent, if unobvious, Hellenic milieu. It is likely that this is to be connected with an increasing demand in educated Roman circles for 'pure' reproductions of the classics of Greek culture. In this attempt to fossilise a genre whose life came from its contact with the changing demands of a popular audience we may perhaps see the seeds of the genre's decline.

2

The form of New Comedy

The comic prologue

The extant plays of Aristophanes may be broadly divided into those with a narrative prologue-speech (*Ach.*, *Knights*, *Clouds*, *Wasps*, *Peace*, *Birds*) and those (*Lys.*, *Thesm.*, *Frogs*, *Eccl.*, *Pl.*) in which the exposition is largely conducted through dialogue. Although the *Ploutos*, where the slave's opening monologue leads into an expository dialogue, suggests that firm dividing lines are difficult to draw, the extant plays do seem to fall into two clear groups. It is striking that these groups reflect the chronology of Aristophanes' career; Aristophanes seems gradually to have moved away from reliance on a formal narrative prologue, although we must always remember that the preserved selection of comedies may not reflect accurately the development of his technique. Within the first group of plays a sub-division may be made which points towards the situation we find in New Comedy. In *Knights*, *Wasps*, *Peace* and *Birds* the prologue is delivered by a character who has already appeared in a short opening scene (cf. below p. 27). In *Knights*, *Wasps* and *Peace* this character is a slave, who breaks off his banter with a fellow-slave to tell the audience the λόγος or πρᾶγμα ('plot'). In *Birds*, Euelpides too turns to address the audience and explains why the two Athenians are looking for birds in the wilderness (v. 30). In *Acharnians* and *Clouds*, however, the play begins with a narrative by the major character of the comedy; Dicaiopolis and Strepsiades explain their troubles to the audience without explicitly addressing them or acknowledging that they are acting in a play. We find a very similar technique at the end of the New Comedy period in the monologue of Micio with which Terence's *Adelphoe* begins. Here we can see the strength of theatrical tradition in the form, as well as the substance, of ancient comedies.

The question of 'audience address' in prologue-speeches is worth following a little further as it points towards the ancestry of the New Comedy prologue. New Comedy makes great use of both human and

24

divine prologists, in both the initial and postponed positions; our present body of texts indeed suggests that most Greek plays had a formal narrative prologue. The probable influence of Euripidean tragedy upon this feature of New Comedy has long been noted; already in the fifth century Aristophanes parodied, and hence gave prominence to, the stereotyped prologues with which Euripides began his plays. Although the audience is nowhere explicitly addressed in Greek tragedy,[1] there are many places in the prologues of Euripides where the distinction between direct address to the audience and a manner of speech which the audience could interpret as addressed to itself is of no importance in the practical circumstances of theatrical performance. Into the latter category fit not only the frequent use of deictic pronouns by Euripidean prologists (a technique which is hilariously parodied at Ar. *Thesm.* 855ff.), but also the phrases with which the prologists articulate their material, as in the following instances: *Hippolytos* 9 δείξω δὲ μύθων τῶνδ' ἀλήθειαν τάχα ('I shall show the truth of these words at once'); *Helen* 22–3 ἃ δὲ πεπόνθαμεν κακά | λέγοιμ' ἄν ('I shall reveal the ills I have suffered');[2] *Telephos* fr. 102.8 Austin καὶ πόλλ' ἐμόχθησ', ἀλλὰ συντεμῶ λόγον ('Many were my troubles, but I shall be brief'). It is thus clear that in the late fifth century the tragic prologue was well on the way towards becoming an extra-dramatic speech addressed to the audience, and here, as elsewhere, it was Euripidean technique which was decisive in determining the directions in which later drama moved. In New Comedy, prologists, both human and divine, freely address the audience,[3] but Menander at least seems to have given his human prologists some apology for the delivery of a long and undramatic narrative. In the *Samia* Moschion explains that, being at leisure, he has got plenty of time to give a lengthy account (vv. 19–20),[4] and in the *Cistellaria* of Plautus (= Menander *Synaristosai*) the old bawd introduces her narrative by noting that too much wine has made her talkative (vv. 120–2).[5] These 'excuses' are not the result of any embarrassment which the poet feels at the prologue convention, but are rather a device for sophisticated humour. The audience knows perfectly well that these characters deliver 'unrealistic' narratives precisely because that is their function as prologists; it is thus amusing when the poet, with his tongue firmly in his cheek, offers a 'realistic' motivation for a conventional technique.

In Roman Comedy we find, as well as prologues delivered by divinities or by characters from the play, prologues delivered by a *prologus* ('prologue-speaker') who has no further part in the play and who does not pretend to be a god or a specific human character (Plaut. *Asin.*, *Capt.*, *Casina*,[6] *Men.*, *Poen.*, [*Pseud.*], *Truc.*, ?*Vidularia*, Ter. *Andria*, *Eun.*, *Phormio*, *Ad.*); the prologue to the *Heauton Timorumenos* and to the third performance of the *Hecyra* form a special group as they were written for delivery by Ambivius Turpio, the actor-manager in charge of the troupe which performed those plays. There is no evidence that this practice of using an impersonal prologist was anticipated in Greek comedy,[7] and it is not improbable that the Roman practice arose from the need to introduce a play and its actors to a rowdy audience who had not had the benefit of the Greek *proagon* '(preliminary contest') in which the plays to be performed at the festival had been introduced.[8] The Roman *prologus* therefore fulfilled something of the function of the fairground barker. Two further features of this technique may lend some support to this hypothesis about its origin. In the first place, there is no example in which the speech of an impersonal *prologus* appears in the postponed position (i.e. after the opening scene of the play). Secondly, it is broadly true that impersonal *prologi* have more to say about the audience and the conditions of performance than do prologists with a specific identity (cf. esp. *Capt.*, *Casina*, *Men.*,[9] *Poen.*). The most significant exception here is Mercury's prologue in the *Amphitruo* where, however, there are reasons for seeing a deliberate anticipation of an important comic element in that play (cf. below pp. 79–81); the chatty opening of Palaestrio's postponed prologue in the *Miles Gloriosus* (vv. 79–87) also suggests that very firm distinctions cannot be drawn in this matter. Nevertheless, the evidence, such as it is, points in the direction that I have indicated. It need hardly be said, however, that prologists of all types use similar jokes and devices to capture the goodwill of the audience. As illustration, I offer two examples from different periods of comedy of the device in which a prologist 'on stage' comments upon the reactions of the audience:

οὐκοῦν ἂν ἤδη τῶν θεατῶν τις λέγοι
νεανίας δοκησίσοφος· "τὸ δὲ πρᾶγμα τί;
ὁ κάνθαρος δὲ πρὸς τί;"   (Ar. *Peace* 43–5)

Some smart young man in the audience will now be saying, 'What's this play[10] about? What's the beetle for?'

26

sunt hic inter se quos nunc credo dicere:
'quaeso hercle, quid istuc est? seruiles nuptiae?
seruin uxorem ducent aut poscent sibi?
nouom attulerunt, quod fit nusquam gentium?'

(Plaut. *Casina* 67–70)

I think that there are people here now saying: 'Heavens, what's all this? Slaves getting married? Are we going to see slaves marrying or claiming wives? This is new, and it certainly happens nowhere in the world.'

Comic prologue technique differs from that of tragedy most radically in the use of postponed prologues. The advantage of grabbing an audience's attention by beginning with a striking or puzzling scene rather than with a lengthy narrative is obvious. In the *Aspis*, for example, the audience is presented with a comedy which opens with a lament by a slave for the death of his master; most of the audience will have guessed that this grief is premature, but they will be curious to learn the actual nature of the misapprehension. In the *Miles Gloriosus* the opening scene is devoted to a vivid portrayal of the absurd soldier, and in the *Peace* to the rare sight of two slaves preparing fodder for an enormous dung-beetle. We are naturally tempted to ask whether the New Comedy examples are direct descendants of the Old Comedy technique. Two factors perhaps count against such a supposition. One is that there is no Aristophanic example in which a postponed prologue is delivered by a character (whether human or divine) who has not appeared in the opening scene as well, like Palaestrio in the *Miles Gloriosus*,[11] and secondly the scene or scenes preceding the postponed prologue are much fuller in New Comedy than in Aristophanes. Perhaps, therefore, the New Comedy examples are merely the result of a successful experiment by one poet. It is clear from the rather unusual prologists that we find in New Comedy and from novelties such as the split prologue of the *Cistellaria*, where the duties are divided between a human and a divine speaker, that poets sought various remedies against the monotony to which the stereotyped prologue inevitably leads, and the postponed prologue as we find it in New Comedy may have been one such remedy. It is, however, very likely that even if we had a large number of fourth-century comedies, we could not discern an obvious line of development: a constant, almost imperceptible, process of change and re-emphasis is a much more probable hypothesis.

Although we know that some lost plays of Old Comedy used divine prologists, it is very hard not to see in New Comedy's use of this device the influence of Euripidean drama; this influence will have stemmed both from Euripides' general importance for the development of dramatic technique after his death and, more specifically, from the popularity of tragic and mythological burlesque in the fourth century. A fragment from the prologue of Antiphanes' *Aeolus*, which probably burlesqued Euripides' tragedy of the same name, shows us the transitional stage between tragedy and complete adaptation to the comic idiom:[12]

> Μακαρεὺς ἔρωτι τῶν ὁμοσπόρων μιᾶς
> πληγείς, τέως μὲν ἐπεκράτει τῆς συμφορᾶς
> κατεῖχε θ' αὑτόν. εἶτα παραλαβών ποτε
> οἶνον στρατηγόν, ὃς μόνος θνητῶν ἄγει
> τὴν τόλμαν εἰς τὸ πρόσθε τῆς εὐβουλίας,
> νύκτωρ ἀναστὰς ἔτυχεν ὧν ἐβούλετο.   (Antiphanes fr. 18)

Macareus, struck by passion for one of his siblings, for a while
controlled his misfortune and kept himself in check. Then one day
he took wine as his general, wine which alone leads men's
recklessness in front of their prudence; rising up at night he
achieved his desires.

On what principles a poet decided whether or not to use a divine prologist is a question to which reasonable, if inevitably uncertain, answers may be given, although the situation is complicated by the fact that the lost Greek models of most, if not all, of Terence's plays and of at least some Plautine dramas probably had divine prologues which the Roman adapters have omitted.[13] Most obviously, divine prologists can convey information that none of the human characters would have been able to give without abandoning all pretence of realism. Thus, for example, we learn from Tyche in the *Aspis* that Cleostratos did not really die in Lycia, and this information, not known to any of the dramatic characters (except Cleostratos), allows us to enjoy the actions of the characters from a position of superior knowledge. In particular, plays which are to end with the revelation of the real identity of certain characters (so-called 'recognition plays') require a divine prologist if the audience is to have full knowledge of the facts and therefore be able to enjoy the effects of dramatic irony which this knowledge allows the poet to create (cf. *Periceir.*, *Sicyon.*, *Phasma*, *Cist.*, *Rudens*). Moschion in the *Samia*, Charinus in the *Mercator* and Palaestrio in the *Miles*, however, do not exceed the knowledge of past events which is 'realistic' for their character.[14] It is noteworthy that in these plays with human prologists there is no recognition and the misunderstandings are entirely of the characters' own creation. We must not assume, however, that divine prologists were only used when the complications of the plot demanded it. The dramatist's first duty is to entertain the audience, and comedy had always enlisted the aid of the gods in this task. A very good example of this is Pan's prologue in the *Dyscolos*. In this play the only expository information which could not have been revealed by a human character was that it was Pan who made Sostratos fall in love with Cnemon's daughter in order that she might be rewarded for her piety (cf. the Lar's concern for Euclio's daughter in the *Aulularia*). More generally we might say that Menander has constructed his play in such a way that, at the beginning of the action, only a god could possess full information about the two families whose contact is to form the subject of the play. Cnemon and Gorgias have apparently had no previous contact with Sostratos' family, although the latter's father owns a farm in the vicinity and is known by repute to Gorgias (vv. 773–5). In these circumstances we should note that Pan's prologue is as much devoted to entertaining the audience in a witty and chatty style as to the passing on of information. Pan's influence is certainly recalled at various stages in the play (the dream of Sostratos' mother, Sostratos' amusing self-congratulation at vv. 862–5), but there is no reason to view the play as a morality drama. Pan does not say that he intends to punish Cnemon and, when at v. 639 the cook Sicon exults after Cnemon has fallen down the well 'there are gods, by Dionysus' and proceeds to suggest that the Nymphs have taken their revenge upon the old man, we may well attach more importance to the unpleasant and ludicrous character which Sicon here reveals than to the moral justice of what he has to say. More explicitly theological than the *Dyscolos* is the *Rudens*, in which the prologue-speech of the star Arcturus firmly sets the action of the play within a scheme of divine rewards and punishments.

The influence of the abstract divinities of New Comedy (Tyche, Agnoia, Auxilium,[15] Luxuria[16]) on the actual events of their plays is an area where critical disagreement is almost inevitable, but there is at least no reason to think that poets were always unduly concerned to tie the identity of the prologist very closely to the subject of the play in which he or she appeared. A striking and novel prologist would have been theatrically at least as important as one whose identity was closely bound to the events which were to unfold.

In the history of the comic prologue, the prologues of Terence occupy a special position. Terence chose not to use a lengthy narrative prologue to put the audience fully in the picture, preferring rather to release gradually the information necessary to an understanding of the situation. This preference has caused endless trouble for modern scholars who seek to separate the Greek and Roman elements in Terence's plays, but the importance of Terence's technique for the development of Western drama is obvious. In place of narrative, Terence used the impersonal *prologus* or the manager of the acting troupe (cf. above p. 26) to conduct a war of words with certain of his fellow poets about tradition and originality in comedy, about the appropriate way of adapting Greek plays for the Roman stage and, particularly, about the propriety of the practice which modern scholars call *contaminatio*, that is the addition of material from a second Greek play to the adaptation of another (cf. above p. 7). Whether Terence was the first Roman comic poet to use the prologue in this way we do not know,[17] but the practice has an interesting literary history which deserves a moment's attention.

It has long been observed that the substance of the Terentian prologues may in part be paralleled from the prologues and parabases of Aristophanic comedy.[18] These are the two parts of Old Comedy where the rapport between actors and audience was closest and where the 'dramatic illusion', defined as 'the uninterrupted concentration of the fictitious personages of the play on their fictitious situation',[19] was weakest. That similar jokes should turn up in prologues and parabases is hardly surprising,[20] but we find also similar literary concerns expressed in these places. In the parabasis of the *Clouds* Aristophanes complains of the lack of success of the first version of the play and stresses the absence in this play of vulgarity and low humour (vv. 537–44). So too in both the prologue and the epilogue of the *Captivi* Plautus emphasises the novel sobriety of the play:

> profecto expediet fabulae huic operam dare:
> non pertractate facta est neque item ut ceterae:
> neque spurcidici insunt uorsus inmemorabiles;
> hic neque peiiurus leno est nec meretrix mala
> neque miles gloriosus. (*Capt.* 54–8)

This play will certainly repay attention; it is not written in the old, hackneyed style of all the rest. There are no obscene verses which ought not be repeated; no ungodly brothel-keeper, wicked harlot or boasting soldier.

> spectatores, ad pudicos mores facta haec fabula est,
> neque in hac subigitationes sunt neque ulla amatio
> nec pueri suppositio nec argenti circumductio,
> neque ubi amans adulescens scortum liberet clam suom patrem.
> huius modi paucas poetae reperiunt comoedias,
> ubi boni meliores fiant. (*Capt.* 1029–34)

Spectators, this is a chaste play: no sex, no loving, no changelings, no fraud, no young lover freeing some tart without Father knowing. Poets find few such plays where the good get better.

In the *Casina* we see this *topos* put to a new and witty use:

> ea inuenietur et pudica et libera,
> ingenua Atheniensis, neque quicquam stupri
> faciet profecto in hac quidem comoedia.
> mox hercle uero, post transactam fabulam,
> argentum si quis dederit, ut ego suspicor,
> ultro ibit nuptum, non manebit auspices. (*Casina* 81–6)

Casina will turn out to be chaste and free, the daughter of an Athenian citizen, and she won't have sex with anyone – at least during the play. But afterwards, as I have reason to believe, if someone were to come up with the money, she'd 'marry' him like a shot; she won't wait for the formalities.

In the prologues of Plautus and of post-Aristophanic Greek comedy we do not, however, find literary polemic on a scale comparable to that of the Aristophanic parabasis or the Terentian prologue. The two passages which are most often adduced in this context provide no real precedent for Terentian practice. The speaker of a fragment of Antiphanes' *Poiesis* (fr. 191) complains ironically (cf. below p. 65) of how easy it is to write tragedy compared with comedy, and it is very likely that this passage comes from the prologue of that play.[21] In tone and style, however, this passage is far removed from the Terentian prologues and has nothing to say about Antiphanes' rivals. The second passage is an unfortunately fragmentary divine prologue, possibly delivered by Dionysus (Adesp. 252 Austin). The speaker lays stress upon his identity as a god, presumably to contrast himself with the abstract divinities that very frequently delivered the prologues of New Comedy, and he attacks the long-windedness of prologising gods,[22] an attack which is nicely ironic when set against his own prolixity. The speaker's easy rapport with his audience is reminiscent of the prologues of both Aristophanes and Plautus and, in particular, of Auxilium's self-conscious attitude to the role of prologue god in the *Cistellaria*. Once again there is no support here for believing that Terence had direct precedents in Greek New Comedy for his use of a polemical prologue. If we move outside comedy, we note that orators had long used the *prooemium* of a speech to establish the difficulties of their position and the pressures which they faced; the fact that Terence's prologues are written in an elaborately rhetorical style[23] and are characterised by deceptive argumentation and glaring omissions may well be thought to indicate a debt to the style and techniques of the law-court. Furthermore, the use of polemical and programmatic material to introduce poetic works is a well attested feature of Hellenistic literature, most familiar to us in the surviving proem of Callimachus' *Aetia* (fr. 1 Pfeiffer) in which the poet replies to his opponents and defends his literary practices, and it is interesting to speculate on the possible influence of this field of literature on Terence.[24] Nevertheless, whatever other influences may be seen at work here, it is very difficult when reading the Terentian prologues not to be reminded of the spirit of Aristophanes, and I wish to examine the similarities a little further.

The link between Aristophanes and Terence goes beyond the fact that both poets lay stress upon the novelty of their characters and plots and that both provide us with a glimpse into the world of theatrical rivalries and feuds. Like Terence, Aristophanes seeks to defend himself against διαβολή, 'slander' (cf. *Ach.* 380, 502, 630). Like Terence too, Aristophanes seeks to commend to the audience a play (*Clouds*) which had 'failed' at an earlier performance. He does this by flattering the audience for their intelligence and stressing the vulgarity of the rival plays which defeated his own (*Clouds* 520–44). In a similar situation with the *Hecyra*, Terence too turned to flattery (cf. *Hec.* 31–2) and to accusations that his performance was ruined by rowdy elements who came into the theatre in order to see vulgar entertainments such as rope-dancers and gladiators (*Hec.* 33–42). We do not know why the *Clouds* received only third prize and we ought not to accept too quickly Aristophanes' reasons for this result. So too it would be rash to assume that the prologues of the *Hecyra* give a full account of the history of that play – an impartial observer may have seen things quite differently.[25] It is, indeed, possible that Terence and his rivals consciously modelled their theatrical in-fighting on the rivalry between Aristophanes and his fellow comic poets; even the charges of plagiarism and joint composition which we find thrown backwards and forwards in Old Comedy (cf. Ar. *Clouds* 551–9, *Wasps* 1017–22, Eupolis fr. 78, Hermippos fr. 64) resurface in Terence. In the prologue to the *Adelphoe* Terence neatly sidesteps the accusation that he has received help in the composition of his plays:

> nam quod isti dicunt maleuoli, homines nobilis
> hunc adiutare adsidueque una scribere,
> quod illi maledictum uehemens esse existimant,
> eam laudem hic ducit maximam quom illis placet
> qui uobis uniuorsis et populo placent,
> quorum opera in bello, in otio, in negotio
> suo quisque tempore usust sine superbia.   (*Ad.* 15–21)

As for what his enemies say, that grand men constantly help the poet in his writing, they think that this is a mighty reproach, but he considers it the greatest praise that he has won the favour of those who have the favour of you and all the people, men whose assistance every one has used when needed in war, in peace, in daily commerce, and been thought none the worse for it.

As we cannot recover the facts which lie concealed behind the rhetoric of Terence's prologues, we must be content that we can at least identify the theatrical tradition in which these prologues belong.

An expository device which may strike the modern reader as particularly unconvincing is the use of one or more characters in the opening scene who convey or listen to information which the audience needs to know and who then disappear from the play. Ancient scholars referred to such characters as 'protatic' or preliminary (πρόσωπα προτατικά). Such characters appear throughout the history of ancient comedy: in Aristophanes, one of the pair of slaves with which *Knights*, *Wasps* and *Peace* open does not reappear, and the use of a protatic slave recurs in the *Epidicus* and *Mostellaria* of Plautus and the *Phormio* of Terence. The soldier's parasite, Artotrogus ('Bread-nibbler'), does not reappear after the opening scene of the *Miles Gloriosus*, and with this parasite may be compared the absurd Chaireas who enters with Sostratos in Menander's *Dyscolos* but soon finds a reason for tactical retreat in the face of the threat from Cnemon (vv. 129–34) and who is thereafter not mentioned again in the play. It is noteworthy that in the *Epidicus* and the *Miles* Plautus explains the absence of the 'protatic' characters later in the play (cf. *Epid.* 657–60, *MG* 947–50) and thus shows a greater concern than does Terence to preserve some pretence of 'realism' in the use of this device.[26] Terence uses protatic characters in the *Hecyra* (Philotis and Syra), the *Phormio* (Davus) and, most remarkably, in the *Andria* where the old man Simo gives his freedman Sosia a lengthy account of his son's life and urges him to keep an eye on the son and his slave to see what they are planning. Sosia does not, however, reappear, nor is he mentioned again. We happen to know, thanks to Donatus' note on v. 14, that in Menander's *Andria* the father delivered a monologue and in the *Perinthia*, the other Menandrian play which Terence used in his *Andria*, the play began with a conversation between the father and his wife. It may be that Terence felt that an expository conversation between a master and his freedman was both more effective and more realistic than either of Menander's techniques, but whatever the reasons for his choice, it seems likely that a reader feels the awkwardness of this device more strongly than a spectator. Moreover, although Sosia's role is limited to the briefest of reactions to Simo's monologue, he is given enough scope to establish an interesting and amusing character. His sententiousness (vv. 40–5, 60–1, 67–8, 141–3) sits pleasantly with his exaggerated responses to the shifts of Simo's narrative (cf. vv. 73, 105–6, 127) to suggest a character both pleased with his upward social progress and very eager to keep on the good side of his patron. So too this opening conversation reveals Simo to be *iustus* and *clemens*, and this is important preparation for the play's exploration of the relationship between father and son (cf. below pp. 101–2). In short, Terence's use of the protatic character is already here very skilful.

Finally, one further aspect of expository technique may be mentioned. When necessary information is conveyed to the audience through the dialogue of two characters on stage, it is conventional that one of the characters may be told things which he or she would 'in real life' probably already know. This situation is particularly common where a play begins with a conversation between a master and his slave or retainer, as in the case of the *Andria* which we have just discussed; similar instances are found in the *Ploutos* of Aristophanes and the *Curculio* and *Pseudolus* of Plautus. The Plautine cases are particularly striking as they involve the standard theatrical pair of a lovesick young man and his cunning slave, and in this situation the slaves ought to be *au fait* with their masters' emotional entanglements. They are, however, made ignorant for the sake of the audience, and this is a convention which can be very readily accepted by any audience. As with so many conventions, poets could poke fun at the lack of realism upon which drama relied in this case. This is clear in the following extract from the conversation between Phaedromus and his slave Palinurus with which the *Curculio* begins; Phaedromus has left his house late at night and Palinurus has followed:

> PAL.   nam quo te dicam ego ire? PHAED. si tu me roges,
> dicam ut scias. PAL. si rogitem, quid respondeas?
> PHAED. hoc Aesculapi fanum est. PAL. plus iam anno scio.
>
> (*Curc.* 12–14)

> PAL.   Where shall I say you're off to?
> PHAED. If you asked me, I'd tell you.
> PAL.   If I asked, what would the answer be?
> PHAED. This is a temple of Aesculapius.
> PAL.   I knew that more than a year ago.

The five-act structure

In our texts of Menander the elaborate structures of Aristophanic comedy have given way to a simple pattern of five acts separated from each other by the word XOPOY ('choral performance'), which is most plausibly interpreted as indicating that a chorus performed, presumably with song and dance, in these breaks but that the performance had no necessary connection with the play which was being enacted and was not specially scripted by the poet (cf. above p. 9).[27] It is a reasonable guess that this pattern was almost universal in Greek New Comedy, although the fishermen of Plautus' *Rudens* will represent a survival of the older, more involved choruses, if indeed Diphilos and not Plautus is responsible for them.

In Menander the breaks between acts can, but need not, mark the passage of dramatic time. Within the limitations imposed by a highly conventionalised drama, Menander arranges the timing of events on stage with a keen sense of order and propriety. When a character leaves the stage for a short trip to the immediate vicinity, he may return quickly (cf. *Dysc.* 573–611, *Mis.* 237–59), but a longer trip, for example to the market (cf. Parmeno in *Samia* Acts II–III) or to another locality in Attica, is spread over at least two acts.[28] The action of most plays is imagined to take place within the space of a single day, a fact to which characters on stage often call attention (cf. *Dysc.* 186–8, 862–5),[29] but it is improbable that this was a 'rule' of Greek comedy; the action of Terence's *Heauton Timorumenos* covers the evening of one day and the following day, and there are no good reasons for believing this to be a Terentian change to the Menandrian model.[30] Events which must take place within one of the houses represented on stage either fall between acts or are 'covered' by monologue or dialogue on stage, and it is again noteworthy that Menander does not stretch the audience's willingness to accept convention too far. Thus Cnemon's rescue from the well takes place during a long monologue by the cook Sicon (*Dysc.* 639–65), and Demeas' impetuous haste to throw Chrysis out of his house in the *Samia* is marked by the brevity of his absence from the stage at vv. 360–8. We must, of course, seek to judge such matters with the eyes and ears of a spectator in the theatre rather than with the eyes of a reader. Gesture and movement are as important to the length of a speech as the simple number of verses. There may be a nice illustration of this in the *Periceiromene*. At v. 310 Moschion sends the slave Daos inside for the second time to prepare the way for his own entry; Daos' absence is covered by a short monologue from Moschion, and on the slave's return he narrates a dialogue between himself and Moschion's mother which occupies as many verses as Moschion's 'covering' monologue.[31] Although no ancient dramatist or audience would have worried about this timing, two factors contribute to the realism of the scene. One is the fact that the mother's reaction is angry and excited and her hasty dismissal of the slave (v. 323) helps to explain his rapid reappearance. Secondly, it is not improbable that Moschion drew out his rehearsal of what to do once inside the house (vv. 312–15) by imitative and extravagant gestures, thereby making Daos' absence longer than might appear to those merely reading the text.

As Greek comedy seems to have used a regular pattern of five acts, it is natural to wonder whether there was also a standard relationship between this pattern and the forward movement of the comic plot. Here we have the evidence not only of the plays themselves but also of ancient theory. Aristotle thought of a dramatic plot in terms of tying (δέσις) and untying (λύσις) a knot,[32] and in as much as most comedies concern the solution (< *soluere* 'to untie') of a problem, this image is a not inappropriate one. Hellenistic theorists refined the Aristotelian dichotomy into a tripartite pattern of *protasis* ('proposition' sometimes seen as coincident with the first act), *epitasis* ('tightening') and *katastrophe* ('conclusion'), and this scheme is still very influential in modern discussions of Menander's drama. In practical terms, however, such a pattern is no real advance upon Aristotle's observation that a unified and complete drama has a beginning, a middle and an end (*Poetics* 1450 b26). Menander uses the division of his plays into five acts to achieve a creative tension between the movement of the plot and the regular pattern of four pauses; he does this by placing major structural breaks within, rather than between, acts (cf. below pp. 44–5). Moreover, any simple analysis of the structure of a play is bound to be defeated by the complex reality of the play as it unfolds. Exposition, for example, covers the revelation of character as well as of plot, and this cannot be bound within the confines of certain acts; in the *Dyscolos* for example, Gorgias, who is to have a major role in the play, does not appear in person until the second act.

Roman comedy dispensed with the irrelevant chorus of Greek comedy and with it the division of plays into five acts. Ancient scholars imposed divisions upon their texts of Plautus and Terence as early as the first century B.C., but the act-divisions which are reproduced in modern editions of Plautus were first placed there at the beginning of the sixteenth century. Donatus (cf. above p. 7) complains of the difficulty of dividing into acts plays from which Terence has deliberately removed act-divisions,[33] and the extraordinary variety of results produced by modern attempts to reconstruct the act-divisions in the Greek models of Plautus and Terence confirms Donatus' observation. For a play divided into acts the Roman dramatists substituted continuous, uninterrupted performance, although we cannot rule out the possibility that at some places no longer marked in our texts the *tibicen* ('player of the *tibia*', cf. above p. 18) entertained the audience during a brief break in the stage action. Unfortunately, the one place where such an interlude is marked in our texts does not tell us a great deal. At *Pseudolus* 573 Pseudolus tells the audience that he is going into the house to concoct a plan and that during his absence they will be entertained by the *tibicen*. He re-emerges at 574 with a grandiose Plautine song for a triumphant slave, and his absence from the stage has no bearing on the course of the play. Plautus may have devised this interlude as a way of getting Pseudolus off-stage in order to exploit the dramatic effect of an exultant, lyric entry and, at the same time, give his actor a rest in the course of a very demanding part,[34] but we cannot deduce from the slave's announcement in v. 573 anything about the frequency of such musical interludes. It is, however, worthy of note that the passage with which *Pseudolus* 1.5 concludes (vv. 546–73) is full of references to the action on stage as 'a play', cf. vv. 552, 562–5, 568–70, and so the 'illusion-breaking' involved in the reference to the *tibicen* in v. 573 is stylistically integrated and less surprising than it would be in many other contexts.

As in Menander, off-stage action in Roman comedy is normally 'covered' by speech on stage, but the absence of act-division increases significantly the number of places where the timing of events seems highly contrived. The *locus classicus* in this regard is *Bacchides* 526–9 where Pistoclerus' short entry speech covers Mnesilochus' trip to return the gold to his father; thanks to a chance papyrus find, we happen to know that this particular instance is due to Plautus rather than to Menander (cf. above p. 17), and this may be thought to be suggestive for Roman comedy as a whole. Two instances from the *Menaechmi* may illustrate further typical cases. The splendid banquet which Erotium gives to the wrong brother (cf. v. 476) is 'covered' by

Messenio's brief exit-monologue (vv. 441–5) and Peniculus' entrance-monologue (vv. 446–65); here the convention is used easily and without obvious awkwardness. More problematic are vv. 876ff., where the old man's trip to fetch the doctor, which has involved a great deal of waiting (vv. 882–3), is 'covered' merely by the five verses of Menaechmus' exit-monologue. Whether there was a musical interlude after Menaechmus' departure at v. 881 cannot be determined, but, in brief, it appears that in Plautus there is no necessary relation between the length of a speech and the action which that speech is imagined to cover.[35] Conventional drama does not, after all, need act-breaks; the audience is regularly invited to accept much more outrageous things than the unrealistic passage of time.

Three particular situations which may be connected with the absence of a chorus in Roman comedy deserve special notice. First, we find a number of places where no stage-action or speech separates the departure of a character from his or her re-entry (cf. Plaut. *Cist.* 630–1, *Trin.* 601–2, Ter. *HT* 873–4).[36] This technique is extremely rare in Greek drama,[37] and it seems very likely that some at least of the Roman instances are to be explained on the hypothesis that in the Greek plays there was a choral performance during which the imagined off-stage action took place. In the three instances listed above, as was the case at *Pseudolus* 573–4, the scene preceding the character's departure is spoken and that following the re-entry is musically accompanied, and this fact makes not unlikely the guess that the *tibicen* filled the short pauses with music and then continued to play when the character returned. Secondly, there are instances of highly contrived timing. At *Casina* 758 Lysidamus and his bailiff enter their house and at v. 759 Pardalisca emerges to tell the audience how the women and the cooks in the house are making fools of the ridiculous duo. A momentarily vacant stage after v. 758 is inevitable, and the *tibicen* may well have continued the music which he was supplying for the conversation of Lysidamus and the bailiff for a brief period to suggest the passing of time. The music will have stopped for Pardalisca's spoken narrative. This can be no more than a guess, but it is clear that Pardalisca's vivid narrative in the present tense suggests that hers is not an account of past events but a commentary upon what is happening behind the stage as she addresses the audience. A related example occurs in the opening of Act V of the

Trinummus. At v. 1114 Stasimus leaves the stage and at v. 1115 Lysiteles enters, overjoyed at the good news that he has just heard from Stasimus (cf. v. 1120). Here again there is a real problem of staging only for a theatre which was less ready to join in the comic spirit than was Plautus', but again it is worth noting that between v. 1114 and v. 1115 there is a shift from a non-musical to a musical mode of delivery. Finally, we may note *Curculio* IV.I. At v. 460 the pimp goes into his house to get the girl whom he is to release and they emerge together at v. 487. The intervening verses are devoted to an entertaining 'Guide to Rome' by the *choragus* or stage-manager of the performing troupe. Whatever is imagined to have happened at this point in the Greek model of the *Curculio*, the speech of the *choragus* does suggest that performances of Roman comedy were not marked by the same formal regularity as was Greek comedy.[38] Breaks in the action could be filled in a variety of ways. The flexibility of Plautine comic structure may be seen by comparing the interlude which I have discussed in the *Pseudolus* (cf. above p. 38) with the opening sequences of the *Persa*. At v. 52 Toxilus, like Pseudolus, enters a stage-house to think up a plan, re-emerging with his plans laid at v. 81. The intervening period is taken up with an entrance monologue of the parasite Saturio. Here the plot does not advance (except in so far as Saturio is just the man Toxilus needs for his scheme), but the monologue is a witty and entertaining piece in the best style of comic parasites. Plautus so structures his drama that independent pieces of comedy may be inserted or dropped at will, and from performance to performance.

I wish now to consider how comedies end, and how poets structured the denouement of their often complicated plots.

Our present evidence suggests that in Menander the central dramatic climax often occurred during the fourth act, and that by the end of that act a settlement of sorts had been reached. In *Misoumenos*, *Periceiromene* and *Sicyonios* the relationships of the main characters are sorted out in the fourth act, although the soldier does not actually get his girl until the fifth act. In the *Dyscolos* the two main strands of the drama, Sostratos' efforts to win Cnemon's daughter and the presentation of Cnemon's character, finally come together in the fourth act, at the end of which Sostratos has achieved his object and we have heard Cnemon's defence of his lifestyle. The fifth act takes us in a quite new direction when the subject of the marriage of Gorgias is raised. Similarly in the *Samia*, the confusion which gives the plot its momentum is sorted out during the fourth act and the words with which that act closes, χάριν δὲ πολλὴν πᾶσι τοῖς θεοῖς ἔχω | οὐθὲν εὑρηκὼς ἀληθὲς ὧν τότ' ᾠμην γεγονέναι, 'I am very grateful to all the gods that there was no truth in all that I had imagined' (614–15), have a strong sense of finality. After the act-break, however, comes a surprise. Moschion decides to punish his father for his suspicions by pretending to set out for mercenary-service in the East (cf. below p. 104). Here again the play is given a new momentum in the final act. So too in Roman comedy the dramatic and emotional climax often, but by no means invariably, falls a little before the end of the play.

If the main problem of a play is solved, or nearly solved, four-fifths of the way through, then the final scenes are often concerned with the celebration and reward of the victors and the punishment of those who have stood in the way of victory. Variations of this basic pattern may be discerned throughout the history of comedy.[39] Reward and punishment lie at the heart of the conclusion of *Acharnians* and *Knights*, and of the fifth act of the *Dyscolos*; in that play Gorgias is rewarded for his noble assistance by marriage to Sostratos' sister, and Cnemon is punished for his unsociability. Gorgias' acceptance of polite, bourgeois society emphasises Cnemon's rejection of it. So too, the mockery of Smicrines in the final act of *Epitrepontes* is the verbal equivalent of the rude treatment which Cnemon receives. In Roman comedy punishment is often meted out to old men, soldiers and pimps who have obstructed romance (cf. *Asin., Casina, Curc., Merc., MG, Persa, Poen., Phormio*), and reward often takes the form of a celebration (cf. *Asin., Persa, Pseud., Stichus*). It has long been seen that there is a continuous thread binding the whole comic tradition in this regard. Aristophanic heroes celebrate with culinary, alcoholic and sexual excess; the first two are still visible in plays such as *Persa* and *Stichus*, and the happily drunken Pseudolus (vv. 1246ff.) may well remind us of the triumphant hero of Aristophanes' *Acharnians*. Sexual celebration, however, is confined in New Comedy to plays involving slave-girls or *hetairai* (*Asin., Persa, Stichus*). In other plays this motif has been formalised and 'purified' into the betrothals and wedding-preparations with which the action so often concludes. The transvestite farce at the end of the *Casina*, however, shows how an inventive poet can breathe new life into an old convention such as that of the final wedding. There are many other detailed points of contact between the ends of Aristophanic plays and New Comedy,[40] but I wish to note only one further matter which has wider significance for the genre as a whole. The *Lysistrata*, *Thesmophoriazousai* and *Ploutos* of Aristophanes illustrate the power of comedy to effect reconciliation among warring states or individuals. So too New Comedy draws together families which have split apart (*Epitr.*, *HT*, *Hec.*) and lovers who have parted through misunderstanding (*Mis.*, *Periceir.*). This healing power is also manifested in the forgiveness which is extended to 'villains' (*Casina*, *Merc.*, *Rudens*, *Eun.*[41]), a motif which balances those plays which end with the defeat of a troublesome character (e.g. Ar. *Ach.*, Men. *Dysc.*, Plaut. *Persa*). Both kinds of play show the triumph of a sort of 'virtue', but plays of reconciliation take a look into the future as well.

By no means all comedies reach their climax before the end of the play,[42] and already in the fifth century plays as diverse as *Thesmophoriazousai* and *Frogs* show that no one scheme will fit the dramatic movement of all comedies. *Thesmophoriazousai*, indeed, never seems to reach a real conclusion at all, and Euripides and the women seem to make peace simply because the play has got to have an ending. On the other hand, we can see that *Knights*, *Clouds*, *Birds* and *Frogs* reach their fitting end (their τέλος) as the play closes: the humiliation of Cleon, the burning of the think-shop, the wedding of Peisetairos and Basileia, and the resurrection of Aeschylus are the dramatic moments towards which the whole action of these plays has been moving. In New Comedy both patterns, that of the semi-independent tailpiece and that of the climactic finale, live on. It is perhaps noteworthy that, as a group, the plays of Terence conform more to the latter principle than do those of Menander and Plautus; in this, as in so many other ways, it is Terence who points most clearly towards the future.

Rhythmical structures

In this and the next section I wish to consider the various means by which comic poets varied the rhythm and pace of the stage action. I begin with metrical variety, which is probably the aspect of ancient drama most difficult for the modern reader and spectator to appreciate.

The predominant metre of Menandrian comedy is the iambic

trimeter, a metre which was not accompanied by music and which Aristotle describes as the metre most closely approximating to ordinary speech (*Rhet.* 3.1404 a32, cf. 1408 b33, *Poetics* 1449 a24–6). Of the best preserved plays of Menander, *Epitrepontes* and *Misoumenos* use no other rhythm than this. The remains of these plays are, nevertheless, striking for the richness and variety of their action, and it is thus clear that, in these plays at least, rhythmical variation was not for Menander a major dramatic weapon. The only other metre which Menander used with any frequency is the trochaic tetrameter, which Aristotle characterises as quick and lively (*Rhet.* 3.1409 a1, *Poetics* 1449 a23), but which appears in a wide variety of emotional contexts and whose 'colour' cannot be too narrowly defined. We do not know whether this metre was normally accompanied by the music of the *aulos* (cf. above p. 18), but it is not unlikely.[43] Nevertheless, the matter of some scenes in this metre does not differ significantly from that of trimeter scenes (cf. *Sicyon.* 110–49). In the *Periceiromene*, the trochaic tetrameter is used for a very lively and comical scene which opens the second act: Daos escorts his master Moschion back to his house with the news that Glycera has fled inside for shelter and, while Daos goes inside to prepare the way, the ridiculous[44] Moschion muses on his good fortune in finding, as he falsely believes, that Glycera has come to him as a mistress and not, as is the case, as a sister. When Daos discovers that Moschion is far from welcome in the house he has great difficulty in avoiding punishment and persuading Moschion to let things settle for a few days. As Moschion leaves the stage, the soldier's batman returns, bringing the more usual iambic trimeter back with him. The lively trochaics are thus here limited to one scene of farcical misunderstanding. The *Samia* and the *Dyscolos* present rather more complex patterns, but before considering these plays it may be helpful to say a word about the concept of 'a scene' in the context of Menandrian drama.

It will be clear that although it is very useful for the critic to divide each act into a number of 'scenes' for the purposes of analysis and discussion, such a division may completely misrepresent the spectacle with which an audience is presented. It may be argued that when, as often happens in Menander, different parts of an act are divided by a momentarily vacant stage as one set of characters leave and another enters,[45] it is perfectly legitimate to speak of separate 'scenes'. So it may be, but we must also recognise that there are many other sequences of action where the stage is not vacant but where clearly defined units are recognisable (e.g. *Aspis* 149–249, where Daos converses first with Smicrines and then with the cook). The 'scene' thus has no consistent identity in the context of Menandrian drama, but I shall continue to use the term as an obviously useful critical tool.

The first three acts of the *Samia* are all written in the iambic trimeter, but the third act, in particular, is one of highly varied action. After Demeas' lengthy account of how he has come to suspect that all is not well as far as Chrysis' child is concerned, we are offered comedy of a quite different sort with the by-play between a slave and a cook and with the traditional confrontation of a slave and his threatening master; then follows another monologue from Demeas and the affecting scene in which he throws Chrysis out of his house, a scene saved from unrelieved pathos by the presence of the absurd cook (cf. below p. 88). The act ends with another comic set piece, the entry of the humble Niceratos with a rather poor specimen of a sheep with which to celebrate the coming wedding. By contrast, the action of the fourth act is all pitched at roughly the same level of emotional excitement, reaching a farcical climax in Niceratos' wild ranting and the amusing way in which Demeas has to calm him down with mythological parallels to his daughter's fate. The whole of this act is written in trochaic tetrameters, and this reflects the unity of the action in the act. The final scene of *Samia* is also written in trochaic tetrameters which begin at v. 670 where Moschion, intent on his charade (cf. below p. 104), has summoned all his courage to face Demeas, whom he expects to emerge from the house but, contrary to his and our expectations, his slave Parmenon comes out and changes the metre to trochaic tetrameters; the change both marks Parmenon's high spirits (cf. vv. 673–4) and signals the climax of the play. In this scene, however, the metre accommodates both the farce of Moschion's charade and the seriousness of Demeas' monologue of self-defence (cf. below p. 105), and it is again clear that in Menander the trochaic tetrameter is not inevitably linked to farcical action. As for the *Dyscolos*, it is broadly true that a farcical third act which centres around traditional comic characters and slapstick humour divides two more 'serious' acts, although it is to be noted that both Act II and Act IV end with a brief scene of traditional comedy, which contrasts with the rest of the act. Menander thus avoids a monotonous coincidence of breaks in the action with act-breaks.[46] The final act falls roughly into two parts which are quite distinct in metre and tone. The fourth act contains three long speeches: two addresses to the audience in iambic trimeters by Sicon and Sostratos are directly juxtaposed, and then Cnemon's self-defence, the content of which I have discussed elsewhere (cf. below p. 144), is in trochaic tetrameters. Unfortunately we do not know whether the change of metre coincided with the start of Cnemon's speech, but as this is the first time that we have heard anything in this play other than the iambic trimeter, the speech is clearly marked off as different in tone from what has gone before. The speech itself is a very individual mixture of irony and pathos (cf. below pp. 144–5), and here it is the rhythmical change which is more important than any particular 'meaning' which the trochaic tetrameter might convey. It is also important that Menander does not limit this rhythm to Cnemon's speech but continues it to the end of the act, encompassing within it the humour of the arrival of the hungry Callippides. More remarkable, however, than these trochaics are the musically accompanied iambic tetrameters in which Sicon and Getas tease and abuse the helpless Cnemon in the final scene of the play. This lively rhythm was very common in Old Comedy and is much used by Plautus and Terence, but there is no other certain example in Menander and only two other examples can be found in the present corpus of New Comedy fragments.[47] Menander may, therefore, have used a slightly old-fashioned rhythm for an amusing and farcical scene not far removed in ethos from the Old Comedy. The scene ends with Getas exclaiming κρατοῦμεν ('we are victorious'), and vv. 959–69 which conclude the play are a kind of coda in unaccompanied iambic trimeters as Getas calls for wreaths and a torch and offers a prayer to the goddess Victory; the change of iambic length, strongly marked by the cessation of musical accompaniment, signals the victory of the slave and the cook and Cnemon's resignation to his fate.

It is clear that metrical variety takes second place in Menandrian drama to variations of tempo and emotional intensity. The melodramatic is set off against the farcical and traditional (cf. *Dysc.* 381ff., *Mis.* 259ff.) and lengthy monologues against scenes of lively action (e.g. the third act of *Samia*, the fourth of *Sicyonios*). In Plautus we find the same techniques, but also a metrical richness which transforms his drama into a quite different type of performance.

Plautine verses fall into three broad categories: iambic trimeters, or

45

senarii as they are more usually called in Latin verse,[48] which were not accompanied by music; tetrameters of various rhythms (trochaic, iambic, anapaestic) which have counterparts in Greek drama and which were accompanied by the music of the *tibia*; lastly, songs in a mixture of lyric metres or series of bacchiac ($\cup$ – –) or cretic (– $\cup$ –) verses which have no real parallel in Greek comedy. Our manuscripts, however, make a division only between the *senarii* and everything else, and it is entirely unclear how the delivery of the tetrameters differed from that of the lyric metres. On the analogy of Greek drama, it is usual to describe the three types of verse as speech, recitation and song, but it is disputed whether trochaic tetrameters, Plautus' favourite verse, were the only recited verses, everything else being sung, or whether the field of recitation was a larger one. What is clear, however, is that iambic *senarii* and trochaic tetrameters (or *septenarii* as they are usually called) account for about two-thirds of all Plautine verses; so too, about two-thirds of the verses are musically accompanied, although the proportion varies enormously from play to play. We can, therefore, readily appreciate how different Plautus is from Greek New Comedy, even if we cannot really understand how the change of rhythm affected delivery of the verses. This ignorance means that we must not assume that a change of rhythm necessarily signalled a new dramatic movement or a new 'scene' (cf. above pp. 43–4), but with due caution Plautus' use of his metrical structures as dramatic tools may be analysed.

Most commonly in Plautus song is preceded by speech and gives way to recitation;[49] song is also almost always initiated by an entering character,[50] a technique which may suggest that Plautine drama was very episodic, as single scenes are marked off from each other both by changes of mode and by the entry and exit of characters. This is particularly striking in the early, expository parts of a play. In the *Mostellaria*, for example, a spoken dialogue between the town-slave and the country-slave is followed by a long monody by the lover Philolaches; Philolaches then remains on stage to eavesdrop upon the conversation, in iambic tetrameters, between his girl-friend and her maid. The mode changes again at v. 313 with the drunken, lyric entry of Callidamates and Delphium. Recitative, but this time trochaic tetrameters, returns with Tranio's excited entry at v. 348. Here we can appreciate just how varied a dramatic experience Plautus offered his audience. Even those scenes which share a mode of delivery are sharply contrasted in tone and mood: Philolaches' elaborate aria, which compares a growing young man to a house, is set off against the purely farcical entry of his tipsy friend, and the female wisdom of Philematium and Scapha contrasts wittily with Tranio's haste and despair. Rather similar is the *Casina*, where the opening abuse between the two slaves, conducted in spoken *senarii*, gives way to a sung duet between the two wives; this is followed by the entry monologue of the old lecher Lysidamus in anapaestic tetrameters and then by a sung duet between husband and wife. In contrast to these cases, rhythmical structure and dramatic structure often move to quite different patterns, and Plautine practice again varies widely from play to play. Changes of rhythm are more often than not linked to exits and entrances, but often too a new character will continue the rhythm of the preceding scene. A few examples will indicate the range of options available to Plautus.

The *Menaechmi* presents a fairly regular pattern of speech – song – recitative, but within this scheme variations of technique emerge. At v. 225 Erotium re-enters her house and her cook leaves the stage, and the clear break in the action is marked by the change from recited tetrameters to the spoken *senarii* with which the travelling Menaechmus and the faithful Messenio enter. At v. 445 the latter leaves the stage after his master has all too willingly followed Erotium into her lair. The new entrant is the parasite Peniculus, who continues the trochaic *septenarii* of the preceding scene; iambics return with Menaechmus' emergence from the courtesan's house at v. 466. Here we may wish to argue that the continuity of rhythm over the break at vv. 445–6 emphasises the close link between events in Erotium's house and Peniculus' hopes and fears, but in other instances no such explanations are at hand. In the *Pseudolus*, the slave who gives his name to the play is left alone at v. 395 to think up a winning stratagem. His monologue is in spoken *senarii* in contrast to the recited trochaics of the previous scene; when he is joined on stage by the two old men at v. 415 the *senarii* carry on. At v. 667, however, another such link-monologue is not differentiated rhythmically from what has gone before. It is thus clear that, although the dramatic movement was an important factor in Plautus' choice of rhythm, there were other factors also, and it is these to which we now turn.

Although no exhaustive list of the contexts in which *senarii* are used is possible, we may note that certain types of material usually appear in this rhythm: plot narrative, whether in the prologue or elsewhere (cf. *Amph.* 463–98, 861–81, *Casina* 759–79), and expository dialogue are usually spoken, although *Epidicus*, *Persa* and *Stichus* begin with sung duets and the *Cistellaria* with a lyric trio. Scenes of complicated plotting or reasoning are often spoken, as are 'recognition' scenes in which the identity of a character is deduced (cf. *Cist.* 747–73, *Poen.* 930–1173). At *Curculio* 635 the soldier Therapontigonus changes the rhythm from trochaic *septenarii* to iambic *senarii* as he starts to explain the origin of the vital ring which has brought about the recognition. So too, letters are set off from their rhythmical context by being read out in spoken *senarii* at *Bacchides* 997ff., *Persa* 501ff. and *Pseudolus* 998ff. These documents were presumably considered particularly prosaic within the general poetic context. Purely farcical characters such as cooks and rustic slaves also rarely sing, and this is particularly true of soldiers and parasites.[51] It may be that Plautus felt that the verbal wit and fantasy which characterises the language of these characters was better appreciated when delivered in iambic trimeters or trochaic tetrameters rather than in the more complex and musical rhythms. It is, however, not true that low social status is generally associated with absence of song in Plautus, as the leading slave-roles in a number of plays clearly illustrate, nor that minor characters more usually speak than sing. Plautus indeed seems to have had a special fondness for creating elaborate lyrics for the one appearance of a minor character (cf. Phaniscus in *Mostellaria*, Cyamus in *Truculentus*, Ptolemocratia in *Rudens*, the doorkeeper in *Curculio*).

A consideration of Plautus' use of song may begin with plays which contain only one or two examples. In the *Curculio*, the only lyrical scene is the entry of the doorkeeper in pursuit of wine and the subsequent farcical exchange which results in Phaedromus' song to the door (96–157); here the 'Dionysiac' atmosphere suits the use of lyrics and we may compare the unusually musical ending of Menander's *Dyscolos* (cf. above p. 45), in which wine also has a role, and the drunken bacchiacs (an appropriately named rhythm) of *Mostellaria* 313–19 and *Pseudolus* 1246ff. In the *Mercator*, the only lyrics are found in the anguished monody of the young lover at vv. 335–63, where the heightened delivery reflects his mental turmoil. Young men in similar distress to that of Charinus often deliver elaborate lyric complaints in Plautus, and Plautus' characteristic verbal devices of alliteration, repetition and imaginative metaphor are particularly well suited to the representation of such mental anguish, cf. *Cistellaria* 203ff., *Mostell-aria* 84ff., *Trinummus* 223ff. An interesting example is the song of the lovesick slave Toxilus with which the *Persa* begins; here Toxilus imitates the behaviour and language of free men in Plautus who are unhappy in love, much as the lovesick Daos in Menander's *Heros* is an amusing imitation of the free-born comic lover.[52] So too the only lyrics in the *Asinaria* are the brief passage 127–37 in which a spurned suitor pours out his anger against the bawd who has thrown him out.[53] Sometimes we find lyrics associated with particular characters in a play. In the *Poenulus*, for example, the only lyrical exchanges are vv. 210–60, which mark the entry of the two sisters, and vv. 1174–1200, which mark their return from the festival of Venus; here these rather exotic young ladies are given musically more interesting entrances than the other characters. In the *Menaechmi*, the entrances of the two brothers are distinguished for most of the play by mode of delivery: the brother resident in Epidamnus enters with lyrics at v. 110 and v. 571, whereas his travelling brother always enters with *senarii* until v. 1050, where he berates the slave Messenio in trochaic tetrameters. It may not be too speculative to suggest that this distinction is a device to help the audience keep the two characters quite separate in their minds.

Song in Plautus can be a mark of emotional excitement of various kinds: Pardalisca's pretended terror (*Casina* 621ff.), Philippa's real distress (*Epid.* 526ff.), Halisca's anguish at having lost the box of recognition tokens (*Cist.* 671ff.) and Palaestra's lonely anxiety (*Rudens* 185ff.) are all expressed in song. Excited delivery of this kind obviously suits the emotions of distressed females, at least as comedy saw such characters. A different kind of excitement is seen in Sosia's battle narrative in the *Amphitruo*. The preparations for battle and the declarations of both sides are described in iambic tetrameters (vv. 203–18). For the description of the battle itself, a description which draws heavily on the high poetry of Roman epic and tragedy,[54] Sosia changes to sung cretics and trochaics (vv. 219–47). When Mercury speaks aside at v. 248 in iambic tetrameters again, the enemy is now in flight and Sosia can finish his account in the less excited metre (vv.

250–62). Here the changes in delivery not only help to break up a very lengthy account into smaller units but also reflect the emotional changes in the substance of what is being narrated. In the closest Menandrian parallel to Sosia's narrative, Daos' account of a battle in the *Aspis* (vv. 23–82), the remarks and questions of the greedy Smicrines perform the same function of breaking up the speech and providing variety. In Blepes' long messenger-speech in the *Sicyonios* the same effect is achieved by the alternation of narrative and reported speech and the interplay between the central characters and the reactions of the crowd to what it hears. These three scenes well illustrate some of the differences between Menandrian and Plautine poetry: the one is lively, sparse and colloquial, the other fantastically rich, verbose and musical.

Song in Plautus is not simply an ornament scattered over the drama at random, but a functional and meaningful dramatic weapon. In the *Rudens*, for example, song enters the play with the first female character; at v. 185 the spoken *senarii* give way to the excited entrance-song of the shipwrecked Palaestra. At v. 220 Palaestra's companion Ampelisca enters; she too is shipwrecked and alone, but her worries are much simpler and more down-to-earth than Palaestra's complaints about divine justice (complaints made ironic by what Arcturus has told us in the prologue), and this difference is reflected in the contrast between Ampelisca's regular anapaestic tetrameters and Palaestra's excited song. The difference in rhythm also reflects their physical separation. They are looking for each other, and when contact is renewed the different rhythms give way to a sung duet in metrically and verbally matched phrases (vv. 229–38):[55]

> PAL. quoianam uox mihi prope hic sonat?
> AMP. pertimui, quis hic loquitur prope?
> PAL. Spes bona, opsecro, subuenta mihi.
> AMP. †eximes ex hoc miseram metu.†
> PAL. certo uox muliebris auris tetigit meas.
> AMP. mulier est, muliebris uox mi ad auris uenit.
> PAL. num Ampelisca opsecro est? AMP. ten, Palaestra, audio?
> PAL. quin uoco ut me audiat nomine illam suo?
>   Ampelisca. AMP. hem quis est? PAL. ego Palaestra.
> AMP. dic ubi es? PAL. pol ego nunc in malis plurimis.

(*Rudens* 229–38)

PAL. Whose voice sounds nearby?
AMP. I'm frightened! Who is speaking nearby?
PAL. I beseech you, kindly Hope, help me!
AMP. Save me from my fears!
PAL. I definitely heard a woman's voice.
AMP. It's a woman; I heard a woman's voice!
PAL. It can't be Ampelisca, can it?
AMP. Is that you, Palaestra?
PAL. Why don't I call out her name so that she can hear me? Ampelisca!
AMP. Ah. Who is it?
PAL. Me, Palaestra!
AMP. Where are you?
PAL. In the most terrible trouble.

The technique may seem to us naive, but we should see this as one further example of Plautus' delight in pushing the conventions of his theatre almost to breaking-point. When Xanthias and Dionysus are reunited on the other side of Charon's lake in Aristophanes' *Frogs* (vv. 271–2) they take only two verses to find each other despite the 'darkness and muck'; Plautus would not have passed up such an opportunity.[56]

The rhythmical and metrical practice of Terence[57] stands in sharp contrast to that of both Menander and Plautus. The six plays of Terence contain only three short songs in the lyric metres so familiar from Plautus. Two are in Terence's earliest play, the *Andria*: at v. 481 the midwife Lesbia enters with a brief song in the course of the lively scene in which Davus fools Simo into disbelieving what is in fact the truth (cf. below pp. 77–8). The sudden break from spoken *senarii* marks the new entry very strongly, and we ought perhaps to remember that we have been told that the midwife is rather fond of drink (vv. 228–33); a 'heightened' delivery well suits such a character.[58] The two other Terentian lyrics are both expressions of anguish by young men who believe themselves to be unhappy in love (*Andria* 625–38, *Ad.* 610–17). Apart from these three short passages, Terentian verse may be divided into three categories: spoken iambic trimeters, series of uniform accompanied tetrameters like those of Plautus, and songs composed of mixtures of various iambic and trochaic lengths. In contrast to most Plautine verse, however, the latter two categories freely blend into each other in Terence, so that any impression of rhythmically distinct scenes disappears. Moreover, in sharp contrast to both Menander and Plautus, Terence regularly changes the metrical pattern one or more times within a scene and, indeed, within a speech. A scene may, for example, consist of relatively short sections of alternating trochaic tetrameters and iambic tetrameters. It is far from easy always to identify the reasons for the change or the difference in tone between one rhythm and another; the fact of the change may be more important than its nature. This technique must, to some extent at least, be an attempt to represent the emotional shifts in the course of a scene, and in some cases it seems possible to give a critical account of this without succumbing to the temptations of over-interpretation.

In the first act of the *Andria*, Simo and Davus converse in iambic tetrameters, but Simo inserts three trimeters (vv. 196–8) when he delivers a solemn threat to the slave (indicated in the translation by italics):

> SIMO nempe ergo aperte uis quae restant me loqui? DAVVS sane quidem.
> SIMO si sensero hodie quicquam in his te nuptiis
> fallaciae conari quo fiant minus,
> aut uelle in ea re ostendi quam sis callidus,
> uerberibus caesum te in pistrinum, Daue, dedam usque ad necem,
> ea lege atque omine ut, si te inde exemerim, ego pro te molam.
>
> (*Andria* 195–200)

> SIMO Presumably you want me to say the rest of what I have to say quite plainly?
> DAVUS Yes please.
> SIMO *If I find that you are trying any tricks today to stop this marriage or wish to give a demonstration of your cleverness*, I'll have you whipped within an inch of your life, Davus, and sent to the mill, on the firm undertaking that if I release you I'll take over the grinding myself.

Here the shift into and out of trimeters calls attention to Simo's earnestness and throws emphasis both on what Davus must not do and the fate that awaits him if he disobeys. After Simo has left, Davus remains on stage and, continuing in the tetrameters of his conversation with Simo, exhorts himself to face the danger bravely. He changes, however, to spoken trimeters to relate to the audience the story about Glycerium's parentage that he has heard that Pamphilus has made up, returning again to tetrameters to pronounce his reaction to the story and announce an entering character (vv. 213–27). Here spoken trimeters are used for simple narration and the longer verses for more emotional and subjective speech. *Mutatis mutandis*, we may compare the alternation between recitation and song in Sosia's battle narrative in Plautus' *Amphitruo* (cf. above pp. 49–50). Another interesting case is the parasite Gnatho's lengthy monologue in the *Eunuchus* (232–64). Verses 232–54 are in trochaic tetrameters: Gnatho tells of his encounter with a wretched man who had lost his property and he relates the subsequent conversation in which Gnatho outlined the art of parasitism. Verse 254 is a remark interposed by Parmeno who is listening to Gnatho's monologue. When Gnatho starts again in v. 255 he has switched to iambic tetrameters and to a narrative of events in the market which is in sharp contrast to the dramatic style of the earlier part of his speech. Here the change seems merely to be for the sake of variety and is eased by Parmeno's interposed remark. My final example is the confrontation of Micio and Aeschinus in IV.5 of the *Adelphoe*. Micio enters at v. 635 with the trochaic tetrameters of Aeschinus' preceding monologue; the pair change to spoken trimeters when they first address each other and the tetrameters return at v. 679 when Aeschinus breaks down and Micio drops his charade. Here the two halves of the scene are distinct: the first half is marked by argument and opposition, the second by affection and openness. This distinction is reflected in the metrical variation.

An explanation for Terence's metrical technique is hardly possible in the poor state of our knowledge about the development of Roman comedy in the first half of the second century. If the virtual elimination of lyric from his plays was part of an attempt to produce a more Hellenised type of drama, it is interesting that he felt no compulsion to reproduce the simplicity of the Greek metrical structures. Perhaps his plays reveal an attempt at compromise between the two styles, or perhaps he wrote what his own compositional powers best fitted him to write.

Some comic techniques

The most obvious way for a comic poet to achieve variety in his drama is to juxtapose comedy of different types. This may be done either by creating a single scene which encompasses more than one comic style or by setting off a scene of one type against one of another, as we have already seen Menander do (cf. above pp. 44–5). A common form of the mixed single scene involves a farcical character who interposes ridiculous remarks and questions during a 'serious' (in comic terms) conversation between two other characters. Such characters, known by modern scholars as βωμολόχοι ('clowns'), are familiar from Old Comedy (cf. Dionysus in the second half of *Frogs*, Euelpides in *Birds*), and the technique lives on in the later period. Sceparnio in the opening scene of the *Rudens*, the cook who interferes in the emotional scene between Demeas and Chrysis in the third act of the *Samia*, and Stasimus who tries to make his master see reason in *Trinummus* II.4 all carry the major comic weight of their scenes and prevent the tone of these scenes from rising too far above the comic level.

In the *Dyscolos* the burden of the farcical comedy falls upon Getas and Sicon. They enter at the end of the second act: Sicon comes first (v. 393) with a troublesome sheep, and this ridiculous cook with his punning language[59] makes an immediate contrast with the 'high' comedy of the meeting of Sostratos and Gorgias. Sicon is followed by another figure of traditional comedy, the complaining slave laden with equipment, a character most familiar from the figure of Xanthias in the opening scene of Aristophanes' *Frogs*. Two points are worth noting about Menander's technique here. First, his light touch. Cook scenes were often carried to extraordinary lengths, as we know both from the fragments of Greek comedy and from the Roman plays (cf., e.g., Plaut. *Pseud.* III.2), but Menander does not labour the humour here. Secondly, curiosity is a stock trait of the comic cook, but here Menander has used this characteristic as a functional device to elicit expository information from Getas about Sostratos' mother's dream. It is likely that a cook's curiosity performed a similar dramatic function also in the opening scene of the *Epitrepontes*. Getas and Sicon are not reunited[60] until the final scene of the play (for which cf. p. 45 above), but before that we see them first in parallel 'borrowing' scenes with Cnemon and then in separate actions. In the third act Getas plays the traditional role of a slave concerned with his stomach (vv. 563ff.) and he then taunts the distressed Simiche; in the fourth act Sicon taunts the distressed Simiche and then appears as the traditional boastful cook (vv. 639ff.). In deploying these two characters, Menander has found a way of satisfying both the need for *uariatio* and the obvious advantage in concentrating the main comic interest in one character at a time: hence Getas dominates the third act and Sicon the fourth.

Plautus' use of farce and broad humour hardly requires lengthy illustration, as these are among his most obvious and potent comic weapons: Euclio's pursuit of the cook (*Aul.* 406ff.), Sosia's confrontation with Mercury in *Amphitruo*, the wedding-scene in the *Casina*, Messenio's gallant rescue of the wrong Menaechmus (*Men.* v. 7) and the punishment of Pyrgopolinices (*MG* v. 1) are truly memorable examples of Plautine theatre. Plautus is often less concerned in these scenes with dramatic realism or the preservation of consistent character than with the immediate comic moment. It may, for example, be hardly realistic that the suspicious Euclio should twice reveal to the whole world and, in particular, to an eavesdropping slave the place where he has hidden or is going to hide his gold (*Aul.* 608–81), but the first occasion gives rise to a scene of splendid slapstick humour (628–60) and the second is demanded by the plot. The central scenes of the *Rudens* offer several enlightening examples. In III.2 Trachalio rushes out of the temple to seek help for the girls inside who are in danger from the pimp, but despite the urgency of the situation he has time to swap jokes with Daemones for over ten verses before he gets down to telling him the situation and asking for his help. After the girls have fled from the violence of the pimp, like Cassandras fleeing from the sacrilege of Ajax, they and Trachalio offer prayers (liberally sprinkled with puns) to Venus. Daemones and the pimp then emerge for a series of confrontations in which the pimp attempts to seize the girls but is kept at bay by a pair of slaves armed with clubs. This central section stands in sharp contrast both to the opening scenes and to the recognition-drama which concludes the play; these central scenes are characterised by repetitiousness[61] and farce of the most obvious kind (cf. esp. 780ff.), but knockabout humour was never meant to be subtle. It is interesting that one of the two clear examples of such broad humour in Terence is *Adelphoe* II.1 in which Parmeno hits the pimp Sannio and Aeschinus takes Ctesipho's girl from him (cf. below p. 72). Terence tells us (vv. 8–14) that he has taken this scene from a play of Diphilos, who also wrote the Greek original of the *Rudens*. The parallels between the *Rudens* and the *Adelphoe* may thus be traced back to Diphilos, but there is no reason to regard

Terence's inclusion of the scene as a 'sop to public taste', any more than is any other scene of the play (for an interpretation of this scene cf. below p. 72). The other major scene of broad humour in Terence is the siege of Thais' house in the *Eunuchus* (IV.7) by Thraso and an army of slaves, a scene which serves to characterise Thraso as a ridiculous coward and which marks his removal from the play as a serious threat to Phaedria.

A dramatic technique used by comic as well as tragic poets is the repetition of scenes and motifs at critical points in the play. The repeated scenes of borrowing in the *Dyscolos* (vv. 456–521) with their reprise at the end of the play have obvious point in the deflation of the pompous cook and the comic vengeance which is extracted from Cnemon. The use of repetition and echo in the *Samia* is particularly marked.[62] Chrysis is thrown out of on-stage houses in both the third and fourth acts, but by different men and from different houses; the two fathers in the play are victims of similar misapprehensions and react with similar 'tragic' outbursts to the situations which they have misunderstood (vv. 325–6, 495–6). It is a mark of the difference between them that Demeas' anger soon gives way to calmer reflection, whereas Niceratos' anger and frustration merely vents itself in farcical action. In Plautus' *Bacchides* the echo of the seduction of Pistoclerus in the first act by the seduction of the two old men in the final act points clearly to the major idea of the play: the power of the Bacchis sisters. This catalogue of repeated scenes could be much extended, but I add only the *Menaechmi* where the confrontations between the travelling brother and his brother's acquaintances are arranged to form a neat chiasmus. After Peniculus' opening monologue we see the brother resident in Epidamnus together with first Peniculus and then Erotium, who then converses with her cook. After their entry, however, the travelling brother and his slave confront first the cook, then Erotium and finally Peniculus. As we watch the play we may not be consciously aware of this patterning, but it lends a richness to the texture of the play, which thus avoids the obvious and amuses by the element of surprise; it is also satisfying that the travelling Menaechmus should first encounter the ridiculous cook rather than the seductive Erotium. We see him getting used only slowly to the strange happenings at Epidamnus.

It has long been recognised that ancient comic poets of all periods were not more concerned with the coherence and consistency of a drama as a whole than with the effectiveness and 'theatricality' of the individual scene. Of the three poets with whom we are concerned, it is above all Plautus in whose drama the essential unit of humour is the individual scene or pattern of action, and we have seen in this chapter how Plautus exploits a wider range of rhythmical options than do the other two in order to create a series of effective and semi-independent scenes. In this situation it is hardly surprising that dramatic loose ends should appear when Plautus' plays are closely analysed. The gathering of improbabilities and inconsistencies which arise in Plautine drama is, however, a large and dispiriting task, and so I choose merely two cases from the *Bacchides* to illustrate a widespread feature of these plays. At v. 169 Pistoclerus and his old tutor Lydus enter the house of the Bacchis sisters, and they give way to Chrysalus who greets his homeland on his return from abroad. After Chrysalus' monologue, Pistoclerus emerges from Bacchis' house promising to return forthwith; Chrysalus' monologue has fore-shadowed Pistoclerus' entry (vv. 175–7) but it is curious that, unlike most characters who speak back into the house as they leave (cf. Pisto-clerus again at vv. 526–9),[63] he gives no indication of why he leaves. After a conversation with Chrysalus he returns into the house, and the next to emerge is Lydus at v. 368 who can bear the degradation inside no longer. Here clearly we must view the play with the eyes of a spec-tator and not the mind of a reader. It is necessary for Chrysalus and Pistoclerus to meet to exchange information and it is also dramatically effective that the absurdly moral Lydus should be brought face to face with the events *chez* Bacchis; no one but Lydus could give such a prurient account of what goes on there (vv. 477ff., cf. below p. 96). Once Lydus leaves the stage at v. 169 he is out of sight and out of mind until he re-enters; we do not wonder what he is doing while Pistoclerus and Chrysalus converse. My second example is on a much smaller scale. At v. 500 Mnesilochus is left alone on stage to reflect upon what he believes to be Pistoclerus' treachery. The first part of his monologue (quoted on p. 17 above) contains a series of jokes which seem quite inappropriate to this character in his present situ-ation. We happen to know that Plautus rather than Menander is re-sponsible for these jokes (cf. above pp. 16–17), but we do not know whether the movements of Lydus and Pistoclerus in the earlier scene were in Menander's play just as they are in Plautus. Each spectator and each reader will have a different scale of improbability and inconsistency, and it is clear that modern criticism has too often sought to impose quite unrealistic standards upon ancient comedy,[64] but what must be stressed is that each dramatist is to be assessed on his own terms and not with an eye on some arbitrary critical notion of dramatic propriety.

3

Plots and motifs: the stereotyping of comedy

To a very considerable extent New Comedy relied upon stereotyped plots and stock characters; in a genre as productive as this (cf. above pp. 2–4) it would indeed be surprising if this were not the case. Modern popular entertainment (westerns, detective novels etc.) provides many parallels for this phenomenon. We must remember also that in antiquity literary originality was thought to reside in the creative reworking of material that was common to all. No poet 'owned' a plot; what mattered was not *what* happened, but *how* it happened. In classical tragedy, for example, poets based their plays upon myths which, at least in their broad outlines, were familiar to the audience, and yet when we can compare the treatment of the same myth by different poets (as we can with the stories of Electra and Philoctetes), we find that the plays are entirely different. *Mutatis mutandis*, the situation is similar in New Comedy. As an illustration I choose a case where two plays by different poets are quite unlike, but where a simple plot summary would make them appear very much alike.

The *Epitrepontes* of Menander concerns a young man called Charisios who is informed by his slave that his wife, Pamphile, has given birth to and subsequently exposed a child. As they have not been married long enough for the child to be his, Charisios takes off to a neighbour's house where, in the arms of a courtesan, he tries to forget his troubles. The play shows us how, through the efforts of this courtesan, Charisios comes to discover that he himself had raped his wife before their marriage and that his treatment of her has been unjust. The exposed child is saved through the lucky chance of being awarded in the arbitration which gives the play its name to a slave of Charisios' friend and neighbour. Very similar in outline is the *Hecyra* ('The Mother-in-law') of Terence, which is an adaptation of a play by Apollodoros, a poet of the early third century. In this play we learn from the slave, Parmeno, that his master, Pamphilus, was forced by his father's persistent nagging to give up a beloved courtesan and to marry their neighbour's daughter. So strong, however, was his attachment to the courtesan that for two months after the marriage Pamphilus did not sleep with his wife but continued his visits to the courtesan, whose name is Bacchis. His feelings for his wife eventually deepened, however, and after a while he began to live a normal life with her. While he is away overseas to collect an inheritance, his wife refuses to have anything to do with her mother-in-law and finally returns to her parents' home. When Pamphilus returns he discovers his wife in the process of giving birth to a child and, as he believes that the child cannot be his, he refuses to take her back on the pretext that she does not get on with her mother-in-law. With the help of Bacchis, however, it is discovered that he had raped his wife and made her pregnant before their marriage and so all ends happily. There are certainly striking similarities between these two plays. The two courtesans perform similar functions, although Habrotonon in the *Epitrepontes* has a much larger and more active role, whereas Bacchis is rather an instrument of good fortune – when she goes to see Pamphilus' wife and mother-in-law to assure them that she has no further interest in Pamphilus she happens to be wearing the ring which he had snatched during the rape and which he had then given to her. It is also very likely that both Greek plays had a postponed divine prologue which enabled the audience to enjoy the characters' confusion from a position of superior knowledge.[1] Nevertheless, the differences between these plays far transcend the similarities and are by no means restricted to differences of detail.[2] Menander's play has a wide and very comic canvas. The cook Carion, the slave Onesimos and the miserly Smicrines are all vivid, traditional characters; Habrotonon is a particularly memorable example of her class (cf. below pp. 89–90), and in the arbitration-scene we meet two wonderful characters from the lower half of society: Daos, the simple, straight-talking shepherd is confronted with the grandiose and amusing rhetoric of a charcoal-burner who draws his arguments from the law-courts and the theatre (cf. below pp. 134–5). The scene with which our text ends has Onesimos, now confident and aggressive, taunting Smicrines with quasi-philosophical conundrums; this is very close to farce and quite unlike in tone and feeling to anything in the *Hecyra*. At the centre of the *Epitrepontes* stand the problems of the young couple, Pamphile and Charisios. Particular force is given to Charisios' realisation of how he has wronged his wife (cf. below p. 86), as this coincides with what was probably his first entry in the play (v. 908). Until that point we have seen his dilemma through the eyes of the other characters; his violent entry at v. 908 ends a self-imposed exile behind the stage and vividly symbolises his emergence from maudlin self-pity into clarity and decisiveness.

The *Hecyra* lacks the many colours and sharp contrasts of the *Epitrepontes*. The cast of central characters is smaller and our interest is much more narrowly focused. In the *Epitrepontes* Pamphile had forcefully proved her loyalty to her husband by defending him in the face of her father's attempts to persuade her to leave him, but in the *Hecyra* we do not see the young wife at all as she is fully occupied in giving birth. We do, however, see and hear a lot of her husband. His dilemma is indeed a difficult one because he is well aware that the new child could easily be passed off as his own (vv. 392–3, 531); he refuses to do this, despite his love for his wife (v. 404), and the Greek audience will not have had to be told that he could not even contemplate bringing a bastard into his family and his clan.[3] Terence's play becomes a question of what course of action is *honestum* and what *humanum* (cf. vv. 403, 499, 553). We see a sympathetic young man forced by social and moral pressures to inflict pain upon those he loves, both his wife and his parents. Pamphilus, however, never takes the decisive step of questioning the validity of those pressures and the inequality in the position of the sexes which they impose. His attempted solution is simply a web of deception, which only gets him into worse trouble but which we recognise as the sort of thing human beings do. The characters of the *Epitrepontes* are, by way of contrast, more obviously comic and their actions are grander and more colourful; in a word, they are theatrical.

When we move from the overall conception of plays to individual scenes and motifs, the repetitiveness of New Comedy becomes even more striking. The mere fact that Roman dramatists could insert a scene from one Greek play into their adaptation of another play, not necessarily by the same author, is a clear indication of the extent to which comedy relied upon stock scenes and characters (cf. above p. 7). This phenomenon was by no means new. Old Comedy too relied upon repeated scene-types and plots. The main features of *Frogs*, for example, the descent to the underworld to retrieve a great figure from the past and the literary debate between two poets, may both be paralleled from other plays and other comic poets.[4] Poets protested that their ideas were novel and those of their rivals stale,[5] but the protest itself became a standard *topos* of the genre. If the sameness of New Comedy strikes the modern reader with greater force than the sameness of Old Comedy, this is presumably the result both of our greater evidence for the former and also of the fact that, whereas New Comedy seeks, to some extent at least, to reproduce the familiar patterns of normal social behaviour, in Old Comedy fantasy reigns: anything is possible in Aristophanes – one can ride to heaven on a dung-beetle or make private peace treaties with hostile states.

If two scenes which survive on unidentified papyri or in Latin adaptation are very alike, we must ask whether this is because two poets were working independently within a common tradition, or because one poet has borrowed from another, or because both scenes are by the same Greek poet, or (in the case of scenes preserved only in Latin) because the two scenes have been adapted by the same Latin poet. In some cases we can feel fairly confident. The *Asinaria* of Plautus, for example, seems to echo so many other plays that it is likely that the Greek original was a play of late New Comedy in which the poet borrowed freely from the 'classics' of the genre.[6] Happily, the result is a highly entertaining farce. Another case upon which many scholars now agree is that of the striking similarities between the *Aulularia* of Plautus and Menander's *Dyscolos*: in both plays a desired marriage is achieved after the obstacle of the girl's outrageous father has been removed. In Plautus the father is a miser and in Menander a misanthrope; in both plays the girl is rewarded for her piety to the god who speaks the prologue. There are various coincidences of detail between the two plays, such as the violent manner in which the two old men treat their servant women, and we can also point to similarities between scenes of the *Aulularia* and scenes of Menander from plays other than the *Dyscolos*.[7] It is thus a quite reasonable guess that the Greek original of Plautus' play was a play of Menander. In many cases, however, there is less scholarly agreement because more of the evidence is ambiguous; to illustrate this, I consider now the case of the *Truculentus* of Plautus.

There are close parallels between the *Truculentus* and certain scenes in Menander and the Roman adaptations of Menander. The change of heart of the rustic slave in the *Truculentus*[8] is paralleled by the behaviour of Demea in the *Adelphoe*, who changes, or pretends to change, his attitude to people and life after a lengthy review of his past behaviour (cf. below pp. 107–8); so too in the *Bacchides* (= Men. *Dis Exapaton*) Pistoclerus, like the *truculentus*, is seduced from the narrow path of virtue by an experienced courtesan (cf. below pp. 96–7), and we may compare the 'fate' of the two old men at the end of that play; in the *Eunuchus* of Terence (= Men. *Eunouchos*) it is the young man from the country, Chremes, who is changed by a little wine and the charms of the slave-girl Pythias from suspicious hostility to compliance with the plans of Thais.[9] It is in fact the parallels between the *Truculentus* and the *Eunuchus* which attract particular attention. In both plays a courtesan asks one of her admirers temporarily to take second place to a soldier, although for widely differing reasons, and in both plays this lover enjoys a special relationship with the courtesan (*Truc.* 387–8, 435ff. ~ *Eun.* 127–8). In both plays the lover and the soldier compete with gifts for the courtesan's favour, and *Truculentus* II.7, in which the lover's servant conveys gifts to the courtesan under the eyes of the soldier, finds a close parallel in *Eunuchus* III.2, in which Parmeno conveys the false eunuch to Thais and in the process confronts Thraso. In the *Truculentus* the soldier presents Phronesium with two Syrian slave-girls (v. 530) and in the *Eunuchus* the lover offers, in addition to the eunuch, a slave-girl from Ethiopia (vv. 165–6, 471).[10] So too, the division of the courtesan's favours at the end of Plautus' play bears a certain similarity to the ending of the *Eunuchus* (cf. below pp. 93–4). Whether or not these parallels go beyond the similarities of technique and motif observable in so many comedies is a question on which disagreement is almost inevitable. Was Menander the author of the Greek original of the *Truculentus*,[11] or was it someone either deeply influenced by Menander's work or influential upon it, or are we dealing with two poets working independently within the same tradition? Unfortunately, only new evidence (probably in the shape of a papyrus) will allow us to answer these questions.[12]

A skilful dramatist can exploit the fact that his repertoire of scene-types and characters is limited. He may do this, for example, by treating the audience to a novel version of a familiar theme. Thus, for example, at the start of Plautus' *Cistellaria* (= Menander's *Synaristosai*) we see a young girl suffering the torments of ill-starred love rather than the unhappy young man who is so familiar. Our selection of plays often shows us two or more different ways of using the same basic idea. As an illustration I choose the theme of the 'locked-out lover'. The *Curculio* of Plautus opens with an expedition by the young lover and his servant to the house of his beloved (a courtesan in the charge of a brothel-keeper). The lover achieves his desire by bribing the doorkeeper with wine to allow his girl out onto the stage. The lover before a locked door is a theme very familiar from Hellenistic epigram and Roman elegy, but it has particular force in drama as the door which represents the barrier between lover and beloved is also, for the audience, the division between seen and unseen. The visual clarity with which the lover's problem is presented in drama can hardly be reproduced in poetry designed solely to be read. In Terence's *Eunuchus* the lover Phaedria has been 'excluded' and then recalled, and so is toying with the idea of voluntarily staying away in order to punish his cruel mistress. Like so many of the young men of comedy, however, he does not have the strength of character for anything so self-denying. We do in fact find such self-denial at the opening of Menander's *Misoumenos*. We see the soldier Thrasonides shutting himself out of his own house, despite the filthy weather which is traditionally associated with locked-out lovers, and refusing to take sexual advantage of a young girl whom he has captured in war, although it would be perfectly possible for him to do this. This scene was very famous in later antiquity,[13] and the novelty of Menander's conception must have been at least partly responsible for this. In these three scenes we see also the slaves of the lovers behaving in different ways; admonitory and mocking in *Curculio* and *Eunuchus*, comforting and concerned in *Misoumenos*. It is thus clear that the use of stock scene-types does not necessarily lead to sameness or lack of invention.

There are other ways too in which comic poets exploited the repetitiveness of the genre. If an audience expects something to happen it has the pleasure of anticipation as well as the pleasure of watching the actual event or of realising that it has been fooled if its expectations are cheated. Menander's *Dyscolos* provides a number of examples of this phenomenon. At vv. 181–5 the young lover Sostratos resolves to fetch his slave Getas to help him to win Cnemon's daughter:

ἔχει ⟨τι⟩ διάπυρον καὶ πραγμάτων
ἔμπειρός ἐστιν παντοδαπῶν· τὸ δύσκολον
τὸ τοῦδ' ἐκεῖνος ⟨‿‿⟩ ἀπώσετ', οἶδ' ἐγώ.   (*Dysc.* 183–5)

He's burning with ideas and experienced in all sorts of things.
He'll get rid of this fellow's grumpiness, that's for sure.

Here the audience is invited to expect that Getas will play the role of the scheming slave who assists his master's love affairs; in the event, however, Getas is not involved at all in the romantic plot and indeed finds the whole trip to the countryside rather a bore. When Sostratos returns at v. 259 he informs the audience that he could not find Getas because his mother had dispatched the slave to hire a cook for a sacrifice and party which she is planning. Here the simple mention of a cook will have been enough to make the audience look forward with pleasure to the broad humour and verbal wit which the comic cook traditionally brought with him. A third example comes at the end of the third act. The old servant Simiche rushes out with the news that she has dropped a bucket and a mattock down the well; Cnemon comes out, threatens the old woman with a beating and then laments the fact that he will have to climb down the well to retrieve his equipment. Here Menander has devised a very effective way of holding the audience's interest over the act-break, as it is not difficult to guess that poor Cnemon will meet with disaster at the bottom of the well. For an ancient audience this guess was reinforced by the knowledge that the poet was using a traditional motif attested by the existence of play titles like *Into the Well*.[14] The suspicion is confirmed at once when the fourth act opens with the scream of the old servant, τίς ἂν βοηθήσειεν; ὦ τάλαιν' ἐγώ, | τίς ἂν βοηθήσειεν; ('Help! Help! O alas! Who will help?').

Rather similar is the way comic poets cheated the audience's expectations of the behaviour of familiar stock characters. Comedy used stock names and stock masks for commonly occurring character types such as slaves, young men, old men, cooks and so forth.[15] In a famous passage of the Middle Comedy poet Antiphanes, a character complains that comic poets have to invent the stories which they use, whereas tragic poets use stories already well known to the audience and can thus leave out details which the audience will fill in for itself:

> ἂν ἕν τι τούτων παραλίπηι
> Χρέμης τις ἢ Φείδων τις, ἐκσυρίττεται,
> Πηλεῖ δὲ ταῦτ' ἔξεστι καὶ Τεύκρωι ποεῖν.   (Antiphanes fr. 191.20–2)

If a Chremes or a Pheidon leaves out any of these details, he's booed off the stage, but Peleus and Teucer get away with it.

The point of these verses is not simply that Chremes and Pheidon are everyday names which are likely to turn up in a comedy; they are in fact stock names for comic characters and turn up in play after play. If anything, Teucer and Peleus are far more 'individual' and 'real' than Chremes and Pheidon. There would also be a further level of wit in this passage if the speaker of these verses was himself called Chremes or Pheidon, but unfortunately that is quite uncertain.[16] A related example occurs in Plautus' *Bacchides*, where the slave Chrysalus ('Goldie') boasts of his trickery:

> non mihi isti placent Parmenones, Syri,
> qui duas aut tres minas auferunt eris.   (*Bacch.* 649–50)

> I don't care for those Parmenos and Syruses who steal two or three minae from their masters.

Parmeno and Syrus are stock names for comic slaves and so Chrysalus' reference here is to comic tradition as well as to 'real life' (cf. below pp. 74–7); there is also the irony that in the Greek original of the *Bacchides* the slave whom Plautus calls Chrysalus was himself called Syrus.[17] Whether many more people than just Plautus himself appreciated this joke, we have no way of telling. This example also illustrates Plautus' fondness for 'speaking' or 'significant' names (cf. *Bacch.* 240 *opus est chryso Chrysalo*, 'Goldie needs gold'). Some of Plautus' most memorable names belong to soldiers – Therapontigonus in the *Curculio* and Pyrgopolynices in the *Miles Gloriosus* are two familiar instances – and I wish now to consider how comic poets rang the changes in their use of this traditional character.

The comic soldier appears already in the *Acharnians* of Aristophanes in the figure of the general Lamachos, but the roots of this character may be traced much further back in Greek literature.[18] Although the most extreme examples are found in Roman comedy, it is a reasonable supposition that this character was fully developed as a stock type in the period of Greek Middle Comedy. It was during the fourth century that a large growth in the use of mercenary soldiers would have made such professional warriors with their marvellous tales of exotic places a familiar phenomenon. Menander could therefore play off the audience's expectations against the reality of the individuals whom he presents. Menander's soldiers do have 'significant' and rather bellicose names (Bias, Polemon, Thrasonides, Stratophanes) and are given to a colourful,[19] and occasionally boastful,[20] manner of speaking, but the ones about whom we know most prove to be far removed from the

the Plautine *miles*. Thrasonides in the *Misoumenos*, whose name is connected with words meaning 'bold' or 'confident', is anything but bold in his approach to the girl he loves, and this ironic contrast is clear in the following speech in which he prepares to face the girl's father:

εἰ μὴ γὰρ οὗτος δοκιμάσει με, κυρίως
δώσει τε ταύτην, οἴχεται Θρασωνίδης·
ὃ μὴ γένοιτ'. ἀλλ' εἰσίωμεν· οὐκέτι
τὸ τοιοῦτον εἰκάζειν γάρ, εἰδέναι δὲ δεῖ
ἡμᾶς. ὀκνηρῶς καὶ τρέμων εἰσέρχομαι.
μαντεύεθ' ἡ ψυχή τι μου, Γέτα, κακόν.
δέδοικα.   (*Mis.* 262–8)

If he doesn't approve of me and give her to me as my wife, it's all up with Thrasonides. May that not happen! But let's go in: it's time we stopped guessing and found out for sure. I tremble and shake as I go in! Getas, my spirit forebodes some ill. I'm afraid!

In the *Periceiromene* we meet Polemon, who hacked off his beloved's hair in a fit of misplaced jealousy after being informed that the girl had been seen conversing with a strange man. In the scene which immediately follows the postponed prologue of Agnoia ('Misapprehension'), the soldier's batman describes his master's present state:

ὁ σοβαρὸς ἡμῖν ἀρτίως καὶ πολεμικός,
ὁ τὰς γυναῖκας οὐκ ἐῶν ἔχειν τρίχας,
κλάει κατακλινείς. κατέλιπον προούμενον
ἄριστον αὐτοῖς ἄρτι, καὶ συνηγμένοι
εἰς ταὐτόν εἰσιν οἱ συνήθεις, τοῦ φέρειν
αὐτὸν τὸ πρᾶγμα ῥᾶιον. οὐχ ἔχων δ' ὅπως
τἀνταῦθ' ἀκούσηι γινόμεν' ἐκπέπομφέ με
ἱμάτιον οἴσοντ' ἐξεπίτηδες, οὐδὲ ἓν
δεόμενος ἀλλ' ἢ περιπατεῖν με βούλεται.   (*Periceir.* 172–80)

Our swaggering soldier of a moment ago, our war-hero, the one who won't let women keep their hair, is lying down in tears. When I left, lunch was being prepared – his friends have rallied round to help him bear his distress. He's got no way of knowing what's going on here and so he has dispatched me to fetch a town-cloak, but really he just wants me to wear my legs out.

The rough sarcasm of his speech (with the joke on Polemon's name in v. 172²¹) suggests that Polemon's emotions are quite beyond the understanding of his servant. The play will make abundantly clear the depth of Polemon's affection for Glycera, and his real distress becomes clear even to the batman:

πάλιν πέπομφε τὴν χλαμύδα φέροντά με
καὶ τὴν σπάθην, ἵν' ἴδω τί ποιεῖ καὶ λέγω
ἐλθών. ἀκαρὲς δέω δὲ φάσκειν καταλαβεῖν
τὸν μοιχὸν ἔνδον, ἵν' ἀναπηδήσας τρέχηι –
εἰ μή γε παντάπασιν αὐτὸν ἠλέουν.
κακοδαίμον' οὕτω δεσπότην οὐδ' ἐνύπνιον
ἰδὼν γὰρ οἶδ'. ὢ τῆς πικρᾶς ἐπιδημίας.   (*Periceir.* 354–60)

Another expedition! I've got to bring back his travelling-cloak and his sword so that I can spy on her and report back. I almost feel like saying that I found her lover in the house so that he'll come running – but in fact I pity him a great deal. I know I've never even dreamed of seeing my master so unhappy. What a bitter homecoming!

Moreover, Polemon's rival Moschion, whom the audience know to be in reality Glycera's brother, is such an absurdly comic figure that it 'wants' Polemon to get the girl. In this play, therefore, the soldier is anything but a figure of fun. As for Stratophanes in the *Sicyonios*, we learn already in the prologue that he is a 'very good and wealthy soldier' and, as far as the remains of the play allow us to judge, his part was an entirely honourable one. It is, of course, very likely that not all of Menander's soldiers were sympathetic characters. It is a great pity that we do not have a clear picture of Bias in the *Colax*, the character who may have contributed a great deal to Thraso in Terence's *Eunuchus* (on whom cf. below pp. 93–4), and the only soldier to appear in a Plautine play which certainly derives from a Menandrian original, Cleomachus in the *Bacchides*, figures in only one scene, in which he is characterised by violent and colourful language (vv. 847–9, 869) and his inclination to use physical force is bought off with little trouble. Nevertheless, there is more than enough evidence to show that Menander was interested in exploring beneath the surface of the stock type, and the charm of his soldiers comes very largely from the contrast between our expectations, which have been shaped by a knowledge of theatrical tradition, and the reality of the characters whom he presents.

The great period of Roman comedy coincided with widespread Roman military success and imperial expansion. It is therefore hardly surprising that Roman comic poets elaborated the comic soldier into one of their most memorable dramatic creations.[22] The freedom with which Roman comedy exploits the language and earnestness of military decrees, inscriptions and formulae is an important aspect of comedy's ability to amuse its audience by departing from the normal patterns of social behaviour: slaves become generals and an atmosphere of topsy-turvy liberty prevails. Plautus, however, sought to introduce novelty and variety, as well as farcical humour, into his treatment of the soldier. In the *Epidicus*, for example, a boastful soldier meets his match in the shape of old Periphanes, who has his own deeds of valour to report. The soldier enters in search of Periphanes:

PERIPHANES adulescens, si istunc hominem quem tu quaeritas
                tibi commostrasso, ecquam abs te inibo gratiam?
MILES uirtute belli armatus promerui ut mihi
                omnis mortalis agere deceat gratias.
PE. non repperisti, adulescens, tranquillum locum
                ubi tuas uirtutes explices ut postulas.
                nam strenuiori deterior si praedicat
                suas pugnas, de illius illae fiunt sordidae.
                sed istum quem quaeris Periphanem Platenium
                ego sum, si quid uis. MI. nempe quem in adulescentia
                memorant apud reges armis, arte duellica
                diuitias magnas indeptum? PE. immo si audias
                meas pugnas, fugias manibus dimissis domum.
MI. pol ego magis unum quaero meas quoi praedicem
                quam illum qui memoret suas mihi. PER. hic non est
                    locus;
                proin tu alium quaeras quoi centones sarcias.

                                  (*Epid.* 440–55)

PERIPHANES Young man, if I show you the man you're after, will I
                get any gratitude from you?
SOLDIER By my courage in armed conflict I have earned the right
                for everyone to be grateful to me.
PER. Young man, this is no quiet spot for recounting your
                great deeds, as you'd like to do. For if a lesser soldier

> tells of his achievements to a better, the comparison
> makes them mean. But I am that Periphanes Platenius
> whom you seek: I am at your service.
>
> SOLDIER You mean the one who is said to have served with kings
> when he was a young man and to have won great riches
> by his armed skill in warfare?
>
> PERIPHANES If you heard about my deeds, you'd flee off home as fast
> as you could.
>
> SOL. I want someone to tell my exploits to, not vice versa.
>
> PER. You won't find him here. Better look for someone else to
> patch up your rags for.

This exchange both subverts the soldier's traditional function and, by apparently placing Periphanes in a position of dominance, prepares for this character's heavy fall in the following scene in which the soldier reveals that the old man has been tricked by his slave. In assuming the characteristics of the *miles gloriosus*, Periphanes also takes over the role of dupe which the soldier usually plays. A second Plautine example of this subversion of the stereotype occurs in the *Truculentus*. In this play the soldier Stratophanes enters with the following words:

> ne exspectetis, spectatores, meas pugnas dum praedicem:
> manibus duella praedicare soleo, haud in sermonibus.
> scio ego multos memorauisse milites mendacium:
> et Homeronida et postilla mille memorari potest,
> qui et conuicti et condemnati falsis de pugnis sient.
> non placet quem illi plus laudant qui audiunt quam qui uident.
> pluris est oculatus testis unus quam auriti decem;
> qui audiunt audita dicunt, qui uident plane sciunt. (*Truc.* 482–90)

> Spectators, don't expect a long account of my battles: I prefer to
> give an account of myself in war with my hands, not with my
> tongue. I am well aware that many soldiers have told lies – there is
> Homeronides and thousands of others one could think of who have
> been convicted and condemned for battles which they never fought.
> I have no liking for the man who is praised more by those who have
> heard than those who have seen. One witness with eyes is worth ten
> with ears. Those who have heard report what they've been told,
> those who have seen really know.

The soldier rejects the behaviour usual in comic soldiers in favour of the doctrine that 'seeing is believing'. In fact, however, his behaviour in the following scene with the courtesan who pretends to have had his baby suggests that he differs very little from the stereotype of his breed (cf. esp. vv. 505–11); the claims of his opening speech are no more than a novel version of the self-satisfied pretension typical of these characters.

A character whose function in comedy has something in common with that of the soldier is the *leno*, a combination of brothel-keeper and dealer in slave-girls. If the soldier's main failing is his absurd pretension, that of the *leno* is greed. The 'religion' of these characters is neatly summed up by Cappadox in the *Curculio*:

> quoi homini di sunt propitii, lucrum ei profecto obiciunt.
>
> (*Curc.* 531)[23]
>
> Whom the gods favour, they bless with profit.

Like the comic soldier, the *leno* with his greed stands in the way of the triumph of young love, since he owns the young girl in question and the young men of comedy are usually short of ready cash. The defeat of the *leno* thus means victory for the 'heroes' and the end of the play. The *Persa* concludes with the words *spectatores, bene ualete. leno periit. plaudite* ('Spectators, farewell! The brothel-keeper is done for! Give us your applause'), and the *Poenulus* as follows:

> multum ualete. multa uerba fecimus:
> malum postremo omne ad lenonem reccidit.
> nunc, quod postremum est condimentum fabulae,
> si placuit, plausum postulat comoedia.   (*Poen.* 1368–71)

> Farewell. We have said much; but all the trouble has finally
> descended on the brothel-keeper. Now, for the final seasoning of the
> play – if you enjoyed it, the play asks for your applause.

The wickedness of these characters ranges from the pathetic and ailing Cappadox of the *Curculio* to that triumph of evil, Ballio in the *Pseudolus*, but their discomfiture is always a matter for rejoicing. The brothel-keeper in the *Rudens* states this baldly:

> nam lenones ex Gaudio credo esse procreatos,
> ita omnes mortales, si quid est mali lenoni, gaudent.   (*Rudens* 1284–5)

> I think that we brothel-keepers are the sons of Joy, because if one of
> us meets with a misfortune, everyone rejoices.

71

Scenes in which these characters are abused are a commonplace in Roman comedy, and Ballio himself comments upon this:

SIMO   quid ait? quid narrat? quaeso, quid dicit tibi?
BALLIO nugas theatri, uerba quae in comoediis
       solent lenoni dici, quae pueri sciunt:
       malum et scelestum et peiiurum aibat esse me.

(Pseud. 1080–3)

SIMO   What did he say? What was his story? Tell me, what did he say to you?
BALLIO The usual jokes in drama, the sort of things that people do say to brothel-keepers in comedy; the little boys have heard them all before. He said that I was evil and wicked and a breaker of oaths.

The fact that these characters do have such standard features may be used to interpret a passage in Terence's *Adelphoe* in which the young man Aeschinus steals his brother's beloved from the brothel-keeper Sannio (*Ad.* 155–287). Some critics have put down Aeschinus' forcible removal of the girl as a black mark against him, but this is both inherently unlikely (even though we do not at first know that Aeschinus is taking the girl not for himself but for his brother) and disproved by the character of Sannio himself. This obscenely named slave-dealer[24] behaves like an upright citizen who has been wronged (cf. vv. 155–6, 182–3), but he is in fact well aware that, like all the members of his profession, he has few claims to our sympathy (cf. vv. 160–1, 188–9, 265); it is amusing when a *leno*, who is almost proverbially *inpurus* (cf. 281), applies that term to someone else, as Sannio does to Aeschinus at v. 183. The humour of these scenes lies in the ironic contrast between Sannio's pretensions and the truth of his situation.[25] As for Aeschinus, we can only applaud the sternness and wit (cf. vv. 193–6)[26] with which he handles the ridiculous brothel-keeper.

Far from seeking to conceal the fact that comedy relied heavily upon stock situations and stock characters, poets emphasised and exploited this for a number of purposes. For Terence this feature of his genre was particularly useful as he sought to excuse the fact that he had used in his *Eunuchus* characters from Menander's *Colax* which had already been transferred to the Roman stage:

quod si personis isdem huic uti non licet,
qui mage licet currentem seruom scribere,
bonas matronas facere, meretrices malas,
parasitum edacem, gloriosum militem,
puerum supponi, falli per seruom senem,
amare odisse suspicari? denique
nullumst iam dictum quod non dictum sit prius.　　　(*Eun.* 35–41)

But if the poet is not allowed to use the same characters, why is it
more permissible to have the running slave, worthy matrons, evil
courtesans, greedy parasites, boastful soldiers, changelings, scenes of
slaves deceiving their old masters, of love, hate and suspicion? Let's
face it – nothing's ever been said which hasn't been said before.

The argument of this passage is highly specious but effective. If
comedy is based on stock characters, what then is the difference
between using precisely the same character as another poet and using
another specimen from the same assembly-line? The prologue of the
Eunuchus is long finished and the play well under way before we have
time to formulate some of the more obvious objections to this
argument. Secondly, the repetitiveness of comedy allowed poets to
play with the dramatic illusion by equating what is normal on the
comic stage with what is normal in 'real life'. I do not refer here to
the blatant shattering of the dramatic illusion[27] which is so common
in Plautine comedy, as in the following example from the *Mercator*,

ACANTHIO quid id est igitur quod uis? CHARINVS dicam. AC. dice.
　　　　　CH. at enim placide uolo.
AC.　　　dormientis spectatores metuis ne ex somno excites?
CH.　　　uae tibi.　　　　　　　　　　　　　　　(*Merc.* 159–61)

ACANTHIO What is it you want?
CHARINUS I'll tell you.
AC.　　　Get on with it.
CH.　　　I want to do it quietly.
AC.　　　Are you worried about waking up the audience?
CH.　　　Damn you!

or from the *Persa*,

TOXILVS　　　　　　　　　　et tu gnatam tuam
　　　　　ornatam adduce lepide in peregrinum modum.
SATVRIO πόθεν ornamenta? TOX. abs chorago sumito;
　　　　　dare debet: praebenda aediles locauerunt.　　(*Persa* 157–60)

73

TOXILUS Bring your daughter, all dressed up as a foreigner.
SATURIO Where shall I get the clothes?
TOX. From the stage-manager: he'll give them, as the aediles
have given him a contract to supply them.

Nor are we here concerned with the more subtle examples of this type
of humour, such as Alexis fr. 116 in which a parasite differentiates two
types of parasites, the 'ordinary' type and the ones 'you see in
comedies'; in such an example the speaker hovers somewhere between
being the character he is impersonating and being an actor *pretending
to be* that character. There are, however, other situations where the
dramatic context of the action is neither made explicit nor (as in Alexis
fr. 116) hinted at, but where we nevertheless clearly feel that we are
moving in the self-referential world of the theatre.

Although the characters of New Comedy engage in activities which,
to some extent at least, reproduce the activities of real life, the range
of these activities in drama is so restricted that the total experience
of comic characters may be limited to a group of commonly occurring
dramatic situations. 'Everyday experience' for some comic characters
is only that which is sanctioned by repeated appearance on the comic
stage. A few examples will help to illustrate this feature of comedy.
In the following fragment of the comic poet Phoenicides a courtesan
reviews her unhappy career:

εὐθὺς ἐπιχειρήσασα φίλον ἔσχον τινὰ
στρατιωτικόν· διαπαντὸς οὗτος τὰς μάχας
ἔλεγεν, ἐδείκνυ ⟨δ'⟩ ἅμα λέγων τὰ τραύματα,
εἰσέφερε δ' οὐδέν. δωρεὰν ἔφη τινὰ
παρὰ τοῦ βασιλέως λαμβάνειν, καὶ ταῦτ' ἀεὶ
ἔλεγεν· διὰ ταύτην ἣν λέγει τὴν δωρεὰν
ἐνιαυτὸν ἔσχε μ' ὁ κακοδαίμων δωρεάν.
ἀφῆκα τοῦτον, λαμβάνω δ' ἄλλον τινά,
ἰατρόν. οὗτος εἰσάγων πολλούς τινας
ἔτεμν', ἔκαε· πτωχὸς ἦν καὶ δήμιος.
δεινότερος οὗτος θατέρου μοι κατεφάνη·
ὁ μὲν διήγημ' ἔλεγεν, ὁ δ' ἐποίει νεκρούς.
τρίτωι συνέζευξ' ἡ τύχη με φιλοσόφωι
πώγων' ἔχοντι καὶ τρίβωνα καὶ λόγον·
εἰς προῦπτον ἦλθον ἐμπεσοῦσα δὴ κακόν.
οὐδὲν ἐδίδου γάρ· †ταῦτ' ἀλλ' ἂν αἰτῶντι† ἔφη
οὐκ ἀγαθὸν εἶναι τἀργύριον. ἔστω κακόν,
διὰ τοῦτο δός μοι, ῥῖψον· οὐκ ἐπείθετο.   (Phoenicides fr. 4.4–21)

When I first started I had a soldier as lover. All he ever talked about was battles, showing me his wounds as he babbled on, giving me nothing. He said – and kept on saying – that he was getting a retainer from the king; because of that retainer, the wretched man retained me for a whole year and it cost him nothing. I gave him up and started up with a doctor. He had lots of patients whom he cut and burnt, but he was a public quack without money. Worse than the first! The soldier only told stories, the doctor really killed people. Thirdly, Fortune joined me to a philosopher complete with beard, cloak and twaddle. I might have known what was coming to me: precisely nothing. If I asked for something, he'd tell me that money was not a good. Okay then, give it to me, throw it away! I couldn't persuade him.

What is interesting about this passage is that the courtesan's three clients, a soldier, a doctor and a philosopher, are all regular butts of comic humour. This speech is thus both very vivid, as we can readily visualise these theatrical characters whom the courtesan describes, and also illustrates the enclosed world of New Comedy. The very productivity of the genre encouraged this habit of not going outside the comic repertoire for illustrative material. From a large number of possible examples, I choose two further cases.[28] In Terence's *Phormio*, Demipho returns from an overseas trip to find that his son has made an unwelcome (for Demipho) marriage. He reflects upon the situation:

> quam ob rem omnis, quom secundae res sunt maxume, tum maxume
> meditari secum oportet quo pacto aduorsam aerumnam ferant,
> pericla damna exsilia; peregre rediens semper cogitet
> aut fili peccatum aut uxoris mortem aut morbum filiae
> communia esse haec, fieri posse, ut ne quid animo sit nouom;
> quidquid praeter spem eueniat, omne id deputare esse in lucro.
>
> (*Phormio* 241–6)

Therefore, whenever things are going really well, that's the time when each of us ought to rehearse how to bear misfortunes – legal dangers, financial loss, exile. Whenever we return from abroad we must always bear in mind the possibility that our son has been up to no good, our wife has died, our daughter's sick. These things happen to everybody and can happen to each of us. Nothing should take us by surprise. Anything which turns out better than expectation, we should count a gain.

Here Demipho's list of the possible calamities which await a returning father contains common comic motifs; such passages do not, however, shatter the dramatic illusion, as they obviously have a meaning with reference to the world outside, as well as inside, the theatre. Sons misbehave in the real world as well as in comedy, but in drama this has become a standard pattern of behaviour. Finally, there is the unfortunate cook in Menander's *Aspis*, whose hopes of a lucrative contract are wrecked by the false news of Chairestratos' death:

> ἂν καὶ λάβω ποτ' ἔργον, ἢ τέθνηκέ τις,
> εἶτ' ἀποτρέχειν δεῖ μισθὸν οὐκ ἔχοντά με,
> ἢ τέτοκε τῶν ἔνδον κυοῦσά τις λάθραι,
> εἶτ' οὐκέτι θύουσ' ἐξαπίνης, ἀλλ' οἴχομαι
> ἀπιὼν ἐγώ. τῆς δυσποτμίας.   (*Aspis* 216–20)

> If ever I do get a job, there's a death in the family and I have to make myself scarce without pay, or one of the daughters gives birth after a secret pregnancy and suddenly the sacrifice is off and I'm done for. What wretched luck!

The suggestion[29] that behind these words of the cook lie other comic scenes which brought misfortune to a cook is surely correct. The character and habits of comic cooks were, no doubt, based upon those of real cooks, but the Greek audience were so familiar with the theatrical specimen that they may have come to give him a separate identity, as though the actor *was* a 'comic cook' rather than *pretending to be* a 'real cook'.

In considering passages such as these from the *Phormio* and the *Aspis*, we must always ask (even if we can expect an answer only rarely) whether the reference is not simply to commonly occurring situations but rather to one particular play, perhaps a play still fresh in the minds of the audience. A particularly intriguing example occurs in the *Asinaria* in which the ridiculous *senex* Demaenetus announces his desire to do his son a favour:

> uolo me patris mei similem, qui causa mea
> nauclerico ipse ornatu per fallaciam
> quam amabam abduxit ab lenone mulierem;
> neque puduit eum id aetatis sycophantias
> struere et beneficiis me emere gnatum suom sibi.
> eos me decretumst persequi mores patris.   (*Asin.* 68–73)

76

I want to be like my father who for my sake dressed up as the master of a ship and tricked a slave-dealer out of the girl I loved. He was not ashamed to indulge in such foolery at his age and to buy the affection of his son by acts of kindness. I have decided to follow his example.

The situation which Demaenetus describes is clearly similar to the end of the *Miles Gloriosus*, in which the lover disguises himself as a sailor in order to get his girl away from the soldier. The differences between the two plots, however, make it unlikely that the *Asinaria* passage actually refers to the *Miles Gloriosus*. What this passage does tell us is that the trick which we find at the end of the *Miles* was of a sort common in drama,[30] although we cannot tell whether Demaenetus here refers to a particular play (perhaps by the same poet as the original of the *Asinaria*) or simply to a wide tradition. Apart from giving the audience the pleasure of remembering a scene which they had enjoyed in the past, the comic point of this passage is that Demaenetus' brand of 'madness', which consists in wanting to further his son's love affairs even at great financial cost and in a manner quite foreign to most comic fathers, runs in his family. Just as Euclio in the *Aulularia* inherited his miserliness, Saturio his vocation as a parasite (Plaut. *Persa* 53–61) and Aristophanes' sycophant his wretched trade (*Birds* 1451–2), so too Demaenetus is a 'chip off the old block'.

I wish now to consider in greater detail two plays in which 'playing with the conventions' is an important constituent element of the drama. The first is Terence's *Andria*. Twice in this play the suspicious *senex* Simo calls the audience's attention to the improbability of the happenings on-stage. In III.1 Simo overhears for the first time that the poor girl whom his son loves is pregnant and he assumes that this story is a trick devised by the slave Davus to hinder the marriage which he is planning for his son. At v. 473 we hear the girl's cries of pain behind the stage as she gives birth:

GLYCERIVM	Iuno Lucina, fer opem, serua me, obsecro.
SIMO	hui tam cito? ridiculum: postquam ante ostium
	me audiuit stare, adproperat. non sat commode
	diuisa sunt temporibus tibi, Daue, haec. DAVVS mihin?
SIMO	num inmemores discipuli? DAVVS ego quid narres nescio.

(Andria 473–7)

GLYCERIUM	Goddess of childbirth, help me, save me. I beg you!
SIMO	What? So quickly? Ridiculous. She certainly got a move on when she heard that I was in front of the door! You haven't worked out your timing very well, Davus.
DAVUS	I beg your pardon?
SIMO	You're not going to tell me that your actors have got their cues wrong?
DAVUS	I haven't the faintest idea what you're talking about.

Here Simo fools himself by mistaking the truth for a deliberate deception. In so doing, he calls attention to the fact that the action of a comedy frequently takes place on the day of a birth and that a young girl's labour, with its attendant pain and screams, often commences at a crucial moment of the on-stage events. Such fortuitous timing, regular in the world of the theatre, is simply too good to be true in Simo's view. Rather similar is III.2, in which the midwife, Lesbia, emerges from the young girl's house and speaks back into the house; this common comic convention allowed the audience to discover what was going on behind the stage and to learn where an entering character was going. Like most dramatic conventions, this one seems to have its origins in a habit of real life. Simo is, however, not convinced:

SIMO	uel hoc quis credat, qui te norit, abs te esse ortum? DAVVS quidnam id est?
SIMO	non imperabat coram quid opus facto esset puerperae, sed postquam egressast, illis quae sunt intus clamat de uia. o Daue, itan contemnor abs te? aut itane tandem idoneus tibi uideor esse quem tam aperte fallere incipias dolis? saltem accurate, ut metui uidear certe, si resciuerim.
DAVVS	certe hercle nunc hic se ipsum fallit, haud ego.

(Andria 489–95)

SIMO	Of course, no one who knew you would believe that you had anything to do with this.
DAVUS	With what?
SIMO	She gave her instructions about what should be done for the new mother not inside the house, but she screamed them back inside from out in the street? Davus, do you think me so stupid? Do I really look so gullible that I would fall for those obvious tricks? You might at least show that you were afraid of my finding out.
DAVUS	One thing's sure – it's him, not me, who's deceiving him.

78

For Simo, the midwife's behaviour is a sure sign that the whole story of the birth is a charade put on for his benefit, and the audience will have enjoyed this fun at the expense of the 'unrealistic' conventions of drama.[31] These two scenes are an integral part of a play whose plot is very largely concerned with deception – a marriage which is not really a marriage is met by a deceitful willingness to go through with the marriage; this in turn is then taken at face value and so deception becomes truth; what is believed to be lying fable is in fact the truth (vv. 217–24); the ultimate deception (in terms of releasing Pamphilus from the threat of an unwanted marriage) is carried out by openly presenting the truth (IV.4). It is a pleasing irony that Simo is deceived because he refuses to take dramatic conventions at their face value; nothing but trouble can come from mixing the real world with the world of the theatre.

The second play which deserves particular notice in this context is the *Amphitruo* of Plautus. This is another play which concerns pretence – Jupiter and Mercury pretend to be Amphitruo and Sosia, and this offers a situation rich in comic possibilities. The prologue is delivered by Mercury who, as a prologue god who also has a part in the action, stands both inside and outside the play proper. Divine prologists were not shackled by any necessity to preserve 'dramatic illusion' (nor indeed were human ones),[32] but Mercury goes much further than is usual in inviting the audience to watch 'a play' rather than to watch 'an imitation of reality'. In vv. 26–31 he jokes about the fact that both he and Jupiter are really actors afraid of a beating, in vv. 39–44 he refers to other divine prologists of drama and in vv. 50–63 he discusses whether the play should properly be called a tragedy or a comedy and decides for *tragicomoedia*.[33] The stress on pretence is continued in the long discussion of acting and of audience behaviour in the theatre in vv. 64–96, which concludes with the fact that Jupiter himself is going to *facere histrioniam* ('to engage in some acting') and it is to this idea that Mercury recurs at the end of his speech:

> erit operae pretium spectantibus
> Iouem et Mercurium facere hic histrioniam.   (*Amph.* 151–2)

> It will be worth the spectators' while to watch Jupiter and Mercury acting here.

The themes of this long and witty prologue are picked up most clearly in the role that Mercury himself plays. Mercury throws himself into the part of comic slave with gusto. In 1.3 we see him trying to be a helpful *parasitus* (cf. 515, 521) like Chaireas in Menander's *Dyscolos*, but his attempt is decidedly unsuccessful. Then in III.4 we see him imitating one of the most familiar figures of Roman comedy, the *seruus currens* or 'running slave':[34]

> concedite atque abscedite omnes, de uia decedite,
> nec quisquam tam auidax fuat homo qui obuiam obsistat mihi.
> nam mihi quidem hercle qui minus liceat deo minitarier
> populo, ni decedat mihi, quam seruolo in comoediis?
> ille nauem saluam nuntiat aut irati aduentum senis:
> ego sum Ioui dicto audiens, eius iussu nunc huc me adfero.
> quam ob rem mihi magis par est uia decedere et concedere.
>
> (*Amph.* 984–90)

> Out of the way, stand aside, make way everyone! Let no man be so bold as to stand in my way. Surely I've got as much right to threaten those who stand in my way as do paltry slaves in comedy – after all, I'm a god. The slave brings news that a ship has arrived safely or that the old man is coming and he's angry. I, on the other hand, am working for Jupiter, and I am coming here on his instructions. Therefore it's more just to stand aside and get out of my way.

The 'running slave' was so common in Roman drama that 'play with the conventions' is almost a regular feature of scenes in which he appears. In *Captivi* the parasite announces his intentions:

> nunc certa res est, eodem pacto ut comici serui solent,
> coniciam in collum pallium, primo ex med hanc rem ut audiat;
> speroque me ob hunc nuntium aeternum adepturum cibum.
>
> (*Capt.* 778–80)

> Just like slaves in comedy, I'll bundle my cloak around my neck and run so that I shall be the first to bring him this news. I hope that my reward will be eternal nourishment.

In the *Epidicus* a slave pretends, like Mercury in the *Amphitruo*, to be a *seruus currens*:

> age nunciam orna te, Epidice, et palliolum in collum conice
> itaque adsimulato quasi per urbem totam hominem quaesiueris.
>
> (*Epid.* 194–5)

> Come now, Epidicus, bundle your cloak around your neck and pretend that you've been looking for the man all over town.

In Terence's *Phormio*, the *seruus currens* Geta comments on a common feature of such scenes, the fact that the running slave is normally hailed by someone behind his back:

> GETA   ad lenonem hinc ire pergam: ibi nunc sunt. ANTIPHO heus
>   Geta. GETA em tibi:
>   num mirum aut nouumst reuocari, cursum quom institeris?
>   (*Phormio* 847–8)

> GETA   I shall go on to the brothel-keeper's house. That's where
>   they are.
> ANTIPHO Hey Geta!
> GETA   There you are: it's nothing new or surprising, is it, to be
>   called back when you've set off?

Rather different in point is *Phormio* 177–8 where a *seruus currens* is seen to approach:

> sed quid hoc est? uideon ego Getam currentem huc aduenire?
> is est ipsus. ei, timeo miser quam hic mihi nunc nuntiet rem.
>   (*Phormio* 177–8)

> But what's this? Do I see Geta approaching at the run? Yes, it's
> him! Ah, I tremble at the news he might bring.

The joke here is that the audience will have no doubts at all as to what message Geta bears: the whole of the early part of the play has looked forward to the father's arrival (cf. *Amph.* 988 cited above), and nothing could be more certain than that this will be the substance of Geta's news. Antipho's melodramatic exclamation thus acknowledges the formulaic nature of the slave's hurried entrance. It is clear that Roman poets, building upon a Greek foundation,[35] elaborated the 'running slave' into a cherished part of the comic apparatus. To play this part was a challenge which Mercury in the *Amphitruo* could not resist, even though he had no message to bring.

The *Amphitruo* thus toys openly with standard comic conventions and with the very idea of dressing-up and imitation. New Comedy as a whole is very rich in such effects partly because of the obvious similarity between play-acting and the kind of intrigue (often involving impersonation) with which New Comedy abounds. The equation of intrigue and trickery with dramatic pretence is indeed a commonplace in the extant plays.[36] This feature of New Comedy is, however, also a result of an awareness by poets, actors and audience that the genre stood at the culmination of a long tradition with its own practices and conventions. The preservation and nourishment of those conventions came to be more important than the attempt to reproduce faithfully the pattern of life outside the theatre.

4

Themes and conflicts

Men and women

The relationship between the sexes is central to the plot of many plays of the New Comedy, which thus forms a significant body of evidence for the position of women in antiquity.[1] Nevertheless, this evidence cannot simply be accepted at face value; a number of factors suggest that the picture which comedy presents is a very partial one, and it is worth setting out the most important of these.

The first fact of obvious significance is that all ancient comic poets were male and the audiences for whom they wrote, in both Athens and Rome, were predominantly (in Athens perhaps exclusively) male.[2] Comedy may thus be more valuable as a source for public (male) attitudes to women than for privately held sentiments, and the women of comedy can only speak for their sex to the extent that a male dramatist is able to create a convincing character. It is, however, with a male audience that this character must carry conviction, and so we might expect that the verses which male poets give female characters will be phrased so as to accord with male assumptions and avoid giving offence to male prejudices. Two examples will, I hope, give sufficient illustration of this. The first one comes from a play of which neither title nor author is known. A father wishes to take his daughter away from her husband who has somehow become impoverished, and in a surviving speech the daughter defends her husband; the following verses come from the opening section of her speech:

ἐκεῖνος εἰ μὲν μεῖζον ἠδίκηκέ τι,
οὐκ ἐμὲ προσήκει λαμβάνειν τούτων δίκην·
εἰ δ' εἰς ἔμ' ἡμάρτηκεν, αἰσθέσθαι μ' ἔδει.
ἀλλ' ἀγνοῶ δή, τυχὸν ἴσως ἄφρων ἐγὼ
οὖσ'· οὐκ ἂν ἀντείπαιμι· καίτοι γ', ὦ πάτερ,
εἰ τἄλλα κρίνειν ἐστὶν ἀνόητον γυνή,
περὶ τῶν γ' ἑαυτῆς πραγμάτων ἴσως φρονεῖ.
ἔστω δ' ὃ βούλει τοῦτο· τί μ' ἀδικεῖ λέγε.

83

ἔστ' ἀνδρὶ καὶ γυναικὶ κείμενος νόμος,
τῶι μὲν διὰ τέλους ἣν ἔχει στέργειν ἀεί,
τῆι δ' ὅσ' ἂν ἀρέσκηι τἀνδρί, ταῦτ' αὐτὴν ποεῖν.   (Pap. Didot 1.6–16)

If my husband has committed a serious crime, it is not my business
to exact retribution for this. If, however, he has committed a wrong
towards me, I ought to know about it. But I know of no offence.
Perhaps this is because I am not intelligent: I won't deny this.
Nevertheless, Father, even if a woman is silly about most other
things, she may have some sense about her own affairs. Let us
assume that your account is correct; tell me how he wrongs me. The
rule for a husband and wife is that he should always cherish her until
the end, and she should do whatever he decides.

The daughter's references to female foolishness in this passage clearly
tell us more about male attitudes than female ones,[3] and the view of
marriage set out in vv. 14–16 is one calculated to win the approval of
her father and the audience. It is thus clear that the rhetorical context
of any speech by a female character must be carefully evaluated. A
similar lesson emerges from the speech in Aristophanes' *Lysistrata* in
which the heroine seeks to reconcile the warring Athenians and
Spartans. In this speech Lysistrata's rhetorical strategy is much the
same as that of the wife on the Didot papyrus:

ἐγὼ γυνὴ μέν εἰμι, νοῦς δ' ἔνεστί μοι.
αὐτὴ δ' ἐμαυτῆς οὐ κακῶς γνώμης ἔχω,
τοὺς δ' ἐκ πατρός τε καὶ γεραιτέρων λόγους
πολλοὺς ἀκούσασ' οὐ μεμούσωμαι κακῶς.   (*Lys.* 1124–7)

I am a woman, but I have sense. By myself I have reasonable
intelligence, but I have also often listened to my father and the old
men, so I have been well educated.

Lysistrata's speech is much more comic and robust than that of the
New Comedy wife,[4] but both reveal a careful assessment of the
audience at which they are aimed.

Just as the speeches of female characters are subject to special
constraints, so too must the context of speeches by male characters be
carefully considered. In particular, the very large number of comic
fragments in which women and the institution of marriage are attacked
is not necessarily good evidence for a misogynist tone in comedy as
a whole. Just as we would be badly mistaken if we interpreted the

scathing attack upon women which Hippolytos launches in Euripides'
tragedy (vv. 616–68) without reference to the dramatic situation and
to Hippolytos' very unusual character, so too the speeches of comedy
must never be considered apart from their dramatic context. In the
Hecyra of Terence, for example, the husband Laches falsely believes
that his wife's behaviour to their daughter-in-law during their son's
absence overseas has caused the young girl to return to her family. He
expresses his anger in forceful and generalised terms:

> pro deum atque hominum fidem, quod hoc genus est, quae haec est
>   coniuratio.
> utin omnes mulieres eadem aeque studeant nolintque omnia
> neque declinatam quicquam ab aliarum ingenio ullam reperias.
>   itaque adeo uno animo omnes socrus oderunt nurus.
> uiris esse aduorsas aeque studiumst, similis pertinaciast,
> in eodemque omnes mihi uidentur ludo doctae ad malitiam; et
> ei ludo, si ullus est, magistram hanc esse satis certo scio.
>
> (Hec. 198–204)

> Good God! What a gang they are, how they stick together! How is
> it that all women have the same likes and dislikes, and you can't find
> one who's any different from the rest? It is a universal principle that
> mothers-in-law hate daughters-in-law. So too all women are equally
> obstinate in opposing their husbands, and they've all attended the
> same school for mischief-making; if there is such a school, I'm quite
> certain my wife is head-teacher.

The truth, however, is that the girl has left in order to conceal the fact
that she is about to give birth to a child she believes is not her
husband's, and Sostrata turns out to be a mother-in-law of quite
unusual kindness. It is amusing that Laches immediately interprets
the situation in terms of the stereotyped male view of women, and is
completely wrong; we too would probably have gone badly astray in
our interpretation of these verses if they had been preserved only as
an isolated fragment torn from its dramatic context.

With these various limitations upon our evidence constantly in
mind, I wish now to survey the picture of women and the relationship
between the sexes which New Comedy presents.

We may begin with a very striking treatment of this theme in the
Epitrepontes of Menander. In this play Charisios has left his wife
because he believed her to be the mother of a child fathered by another

man before their marriage; in the course of the play he is reminded that before his marriage he himself raped a young girl and thus fathered a child, although he does not at first learn that the two incidents are one and the same and that his wife's child is also his. In two highly emotional speeches, one reported and one delivered before the audience (vv. 878–932), he reflects that his wife has treated him far better than he has treated her and that his wife was the helpless and innocent victim of an attack, whereas in the other case he was the brutal aggressor. Charisios does not, however, need to point out that the social and legal consequences of the situation, as he imagines it to be, are immeasurably more serious for his wife than they are for him; the audience will supply this knowledge for themselves and use it in interpreting, and perhaps learning from, the dramatic situation as it unfolds. Comedy's concern with the unequal position of women is visible already in the fifth century, most notably in a powerful passage of the *Lysistrata* in which Lysistrata laments the wretched fate of young girls whose husbands are killed in war (*Lys.* 591–7); where Aristophanes speaks in general terms about widespread phenomena, Menander deals in specific cases and does not normally allow his characters to draw general lessons from the action for the instruction of the spectators. In Plautus, however, we do find a generalised plea for equal treatment for both sexes. In the *Mercator*, the *matrona* Dorippa returns from the countryside to be confronted with apparent evidence that her husband Lysimachus has been enjoying himself with a music-girl; this situation leads her maid, Syra, to address the audience with a proposal for social and legal reform:

> ecastor lege dura uiuont mulieres
> multoque iniquiore miserae quam uiri.
> nam si uir scortum duxit clam uxorem suam,
> id si resciuit uxor, inpunest uiro;
> uxor uirum si clam domo egressa est foras,
> uiro fit causa, exigitur matrumonio.
> utinam lex esset eadem quae uxori est uiro;
> nam uxor contenta est quae bona est uno uiro:
> qui minus uir una uxore contentus siet?
> ecastor faxim, si itidem plectantur uiri,
> si quis clam uxorem duxerit scortum suam,
> ut illae exiguntur quae in se culpam commerent,
> plures uiri sint uidui quam nunc mulieres.

(*Merc.* 817–29)

Life is hard for women, and much more unfair for them, poor
things, than for men. If a wife finds out that her husband's been
enjoying himself with some tart, the husband gets off scot-free; but
once a wife puts a foot outside the door without permission, the
husband's got a perfect right to divorce her. I wish that there were
the same rule for both. A good wife is content with one husband;
why shouldn't a husband be content with one wife? If husbands who
have some fun behind their wife's back got the same punishment as
wives who misbehave, I'm sure there would be more ex-husbands
than there are now ex-wives.

The earnestness of Syra's speech must be seen in the context both of
her character and of the dramatic situation: Lysimachus has in fact
landed in trouble simply by trying to help a friend. It may also be
thought that Syra's proposal is so outrageous in terms of conventional
morality that no member of the Roman audience would have even
considered the possibility that it was to be taken seriously. The
situation of Charisios and Pamphile in the *Epitrepontes* is far removed
from Plautus' warring married couple. They are still young and
idealistic: Pamphile describes herself as 'a partner in Charisios' life'
(v. 920), a concept of marriage which we find both in surviving ancient
discussions of this institution and in actual marriage contracts from
the time of the Roman Empire.[5] These scenes in the *Epitrepontes*,
therefore, recall rather wistfully an innocence which many of the
audience will have long since lost.

Many of the female characters of New Comedy are, unlike Pamphile,
either slaves or women whose parentage and status is obscure. We
meet also women who are free and of independent means but who have
come to Athens from elsewhere in the Greek world, and we see clearly
reflected in comedy the precarious legal and social position in which
such women found themselves. The central female character of the
Samia, for example, is Chrysis, a woman from Samos who came to
Athens and worked as a free courtesan (vv. 21, 25), but who then
formed a stable relationship with Demeas, an Athenian citizen.
Chrysis retains some of the characteristics of her profession, such as
a cool assessment of how to control men:

ΜΟΣΧΙΩΝ ὁ πατὴρ χαλεπανεῖ ⟨σοι⟩. ΧΡΥΣΙΣ πεπαύσεται πάλιν.
ἐρᾶι γάρ, ὦ βέλτιστε, κἀκεῖνος κακῶς,
οὐχ ἧττον ἢ σύ· τοῦτο δ' εἰς διαλλαγὰς
ἄγει τάχιστα καὶ τὸν ὀργιλώτατον.   (*Samia* 80–3)

MOSCHION   Father will be angry with you.
CHRYSIS   He'll calm down again. He too, you see, is very much in
           love, like you. Even the most bad-tempered man is soon
           reconciled when he's in that state.

In the course of the play Demeas comes to believe falsely that Chrysis
has seduced his son, and we understand that he is readier to believe
this fantasy and to throw Chrysis out because she is only his παλλακή
('concubine'), not his citizen wife, and because of her past. In his
anger, he sees her no longer as a ἑταίρα ('courtesan', lit. 'companion')
but as a χαμαιτύπη ('whore', v. 348). He savagely casts in her face
a description of the lifestyle from which he saved her and to which
he now consigns her:

> ἐν τῆι πόλει
> ὄψει σεαυτὴν νῦν ἀκριβῶς ἥτις εἶ.
> οὐ κατά σε, Χρυσί, πραττόμεναι δραχμὰς δέκα
> μόνας ἕτεραι τρέχουσιν ἐπὶ τὰ δεῖπνα καὶ
> πίνουσ' ἄκρατον ἄχρι ἂν ἀποθάνωσιν, ἢ
> πεινῶσιν ἂν μὴ τοῦθ' ἑτοίμως καὶ ταχὺ
> ποῶσιν.   (*Samia* 390–6)

When you're on the streets, you'll realise what you're really worth.
They're not like you, Chrysis, those other women who, for ten
drachmas, run to dinner-parties and drink themselves to death on
unmixed wine, or starve if they're not prepared to do this at the drop
of a hat.

Demeas' cruelty is a product of the despair he feels,[6] but it is unlikely
that the picture he paints is greatly exaggerated.[7] As citizen girls were
strictly segregated from male contact until marriage, non-citizen
hetairai performed useful social and physical services for young men
before they were ready to marry and beget new citizens, which was
the central purpose of Athenian marriage. Nevertheless, these women
had no legal standing and thus needed to acquire the protection of a
male citizen who was willing to represent their interests (cf. Ter.
Andria 286–96). There is an interesting example of this in Terence's
Eunuchus where the courtesan Thais puts herself under the protection
(*clientela et fides*, vv. 1039–40) of the father of Chaerea, the young man
who had infiltrated Thais' house disguised as a eunuch and raped the
young girl in her charge. Thais' action has been foreshadowed earlier

in the play when Chaerea begs her forgiveness and asks to marry the poor girl:

> nunc ego te in hac re mi oro ut adiutrix sies,
> ego me tuae commendo et committo fide,
> te mihi patronam capio, Thais, te obsecro:
> emoriar si non hanc uxorem duxero.　　　　　　*(Eun.* 885–8)

> In this matter, Thais, I beg you to help me; I entrust and commit
> myself to your protection, I take you as my patron, I beseech you.
> I shall die if I do not marry this girl.

Here the reversal of roles as a non-citizen courtesan assumes the position of *patrona* is a very striking dramatic effect, and one which emphasises to what extent all the male characters of the *Eunuchus* are dependent upon her favours (cf. below p. 93).

A particularly memorable comic slave-girl is Habrotonon in the *Epitrepontes*. Habrotonon is the music-girl with whom Charisios seeks solace when he leaves home in the mistaken belief that his wife has borne a child by another man. She is characterised by a very lively style of speech,[8] well illustrated by the verses with which she enters in the third act. It seems that, in his despondency, Charisios will not allow her to approach him, although he is paying for her company:

> ἐμαυτήν, ὡς ἔοικεν, ἀθλία
> λέληθα χλευάζουσ'· ἐρᾶσθ[αι προσεδόκων,
> θεῖον δὲ μισεῖ μῖσος ἄνθρωπός με τι.
> οὐκέτι μ' ἐᾶι γὰρ οὐδὲ κατακεῖσθαι, τάλαν,
> παρ' αὑτόν, ἀλλὰ χωρίς....
> 　　　　　　　　　　　...τάλας
> οὗτος. τί τοσοῦτον ἀργύριον ἀπολλύει;
> ἐπεὶ τό γ' ἐπὶ τούτωι τὸ τῆς θεοῦ φέρειν
> κανοῦν ἔμοιγ' οἷόν τε νῦν ἐστ', ὦ τάλαν·
> ἁγνὴ γάμων γάρ, φασίν, ἡμέραν τρίτην
> ἤδη κάθημαι.　　　　　　　　　*(Epitr.* 431–41)

> It looks as though I've been making a fool of myself and I didn't
> know it. How silly! I expected some loving, but the fellow's
> conceived a strange distaste for me. He doesn't even allow me to sit
> beside him, but I'm kept well away...Poor chap! Why is he wasting
> so much money? For all he's done about it, I'm qualified to carry
> the basket in Athena's procession. I've been idle and celibate for two
> days now.

Habrotonon's puzzlement at her client's peculiar behaviour and her joke about her own 'ritual purity' are wittily expressed. She has a professional's interest in physical beauty and fine clothes (vv. 484, 489), and a pleasing horror at the thought of being saddled with a child (vv. 546–7). It is she who master-minds the scheme by which the identity of the exposed child is established, and she acts out of kindness towards Charisios and a wish that the foundling child should not be brought up as a slave if it is really free-born (vv. 468–70), a wish made particularly piquant by her own servile status. It is the slave Onesimos, not Habrotonon herself, who first makes explicit the possibility that, if her scheme is successful, she may be rewarded with her freedom (vv. 538–40), and Onesimos' consistently low opinion of her motives (cf. vv. 557–60) is a good illustration of how the misrepresentation by male characters of the sentiments and actions of female characters is often shown up by what the audience itself sees. So too when Pamphile's father, in seeking to persuade his daughter to give up Charisios for good, refers to Habrotonon as a πόρνη ('whore', fr. 7), the audience has already seen enough to know that this harsh term does not do her justice. Unfortunately, not enough of the play is preserved for us to know whether Habrotonon received any reward for services rendered at the end of the play.

With a few exceptions, such as Cnemon's daughter in the *Dyscolos*, whose appearance on stage emphasises the loneliness of her life, the only women with recognised citizen status who appear on the stage are either married or widowed; as young, unmarried citizen girls appeared in public only at festivals, dramatic realism denied them a major role in comedies whose action was imagined to take place in public. Perhaps the most memorable comic marriages are those which Plautus presents in a number of plays (*Asin.*, *Casina*, *Men.*, *Merc.* and *Most.*). In these plays the marital home is a battleground, and we recognise a classic situation of comic drama, versions of which fill many hours each day on modern television. The constant complaint of Plautus' errant and henpecked husbands is that they sold their freedom when they took a wife with a large dowry. In order fully to understand this stereotyped situation it is necessary to be aware of the legal background of marriage in Athens and Rome.[9]

In Athens a wife was under her husband's control in virtually all matters, and the husband also controlled any monetary dowry which the wife brought with her into the marriage; this dowry was intended, however, as a guarantee that the woman would be well cared for in her new home and it was repayable, if the marriage was dissolved, to the man who had bestowed the wife in marriage, her κύριος before the marriage, who was usually the girl's father. This was an obvious limitation on the husband's freedom of action.[10] In Greek comedy we find not only girls whose marriages have been arranged by their fathers but also παρθένοι ἐπίκληροι, a phrase which is usually translated as 'heiresses' although this term is rather misleading. 'Heiresses' were women without surviving father or brother (either natural or by adoption) who could be claimed in marriage by the nearest male relative. They brought with them into such a marriage the whole of their father's estate which was then kept in trust during the marriage for the children which the 'heiress' was expected to produce. If the estate was a large one, marriage with an 'heiress' was clearly an attractive proposition, as such an estate could be made to yield a healthy profit; this is the situation which, for example, forms the basis of Daos' scheme in the *Aspis* to outwit the greedy Smicrines by tempting him to renounce his claim to one 'heiress' in favour of a financially more advantageous marriage with another. In some fragments of Greek comedy we find men complaining of their 'servitude to a dowry',[11] and it is likely that some of the wives concerned were 'heiresses'; the large estate which the wife brought with her gave her (or could be imagined by a comic poet to give her) an unusually powerful position in the marriage. Thus we find Aristotle too noting that, although in most marriages men rule the home, 'sometimes women rule, because they are heiresses; so their rule is not in virtue of excellence but due to wealth and power, as in oligarchies' (*EN* 8.1161 a1–3, trans. W. D. Ross).

In Plautus, we find the complaints by husbands about their wife's dowry have greatly increased, and the *uxor dotata* ('dowered wife') has been elaborated into a stock character-type.[12] In broad terms, there were two forms of marriage in Rome: marriage *cum manu* where the wife and her dowry became the property of the husband, and marriage *sine manu* where the wife and her property remained under *patria potestas*, i.e. in the control of her own family. There has been much discussion of whether Plautine comedy presents Greek forms or one or other of the Roman forms,[13] but for some plays the evidence is insufficient to allow a decision and in other cases the legal status of the marriage is irrelevant to the dramatic situation. The important thing in these marriages is the dowry, and an *uxor dotata* ('a wife with a (large) dowry') is portrayed by comedy as a peril for her husband, *cum* or *sine manu*. This is particularly clear in the *Aulularia*, where the rich bachelor Megadorus chooses to marry the poor daughter of Euclio because he likes her (v. 174) and because he does not want a richly dowered wife who will make extravagant demands upon him. It is likely that the Roman comic dramatists here built upon a Greek foundation by emphasising the farcical elements in these marriages of convenience, and the differences between a Greek 'heiress' and a Roman 'dowered wife' were small enough to allow the Roman poets on occasions to transform one into the other with very little difficulty.[14] Roman dowries were, on the whole, larger than Attic ones,[15] and this helped to emphasise the discomfort of comic husbands locked in a private, married hell.

Another class of female characters whom the Roman poets elaborated and made almost larger than life are the courtesans who dominate the *Bacchides*, *Menaechmi* and *Truculentus* of Plautus and the *Eunuchus* of Terence. These free women played a significant role in Attic Middle Comedy and were a conspicuous feature of the social life of the well-to-do classes in the major Hellenistic cities; their houses sometimes provided not only physical relief but also a place of social and cultural entertainment for men both before and after marriage. In Greek New Comedy, or at least in Menander, these women seem to have less prominence, although the discovery of more plays might quickly alter this impression; the character who gave her name to Menander's play *Thais*, for example, became a by-word for her power to attract numerous admirers. To the Roman *populus* such women might well seem interesting and exotic, and the comic poets readily satisfied this interest. In this connection it may be noted that Roman comic poets did not always bother to preserve Greek distinctions between different classes of 'professional women';[16] in the *Pseudolus*, for example, the girl whose freedom the young lover of the play wishes to secure is represented as working in a seething brothel of a kind that certainly did not appear in the Greek original of the play.[17]

Plautus' courtesans are confident, greedy and dominating. Thais in the *Eunuchus* of Terence, however, is placed in a plot where she becomes herself to some extent weak and dependent. I wish thus to complete the present survey of female characters in comedy by considering the *Eunuchus* in somewhat greater detail. For the modern reader this play, more than any other, raises serious questions about the status of ancient women and comedy's treatment of them.

The *Eunuchus* concerns the efforts of the courtesan Thais to restore a young girl, who had been stolen from Attica when she was very small, to her brother Chremes. This girl was brought up with Thais' family on Rhodes and has now fallen into the possession of a soldier who is in love with Thais. In order to secure the girl from the soldier, Thais asks her lover Phaedria to leave her alone for a few days so that the soldier will believe that he has no rival and will be happy to give the young girl to her as a gift. This plan succeeds but, before Thais can hand over the girl to Chremes, Phaedria's younger brother Chaerea sees the girl, is struck by her beauty and, having infiltrated Thais' house in the disguise of a eunuch, rapes her. All ends happily, however: Chaerea marries the young girl whom he loves (and had raped) and Phaedria accepts the soldier as a rival for Thais' favours so that there will be someone on hand to pay the dinner bills.

Although Thais is the epicentre of the play, it is the three main male characters who show us the different aspects and varieties of *eros*. The soldier Thraso is a complete *miles gloriosus*: boastful, stupid, cowardly and proud of his (believed) sexual attractiveness; for Thraso the physical side of love is outwardly everything (cf. 479), but inwardly he is insecure and craves affection (cf. 434–5, 446, 1053). By way of contrast, Phaedria's love for Thais is sentimental and emotional, indeed comic in its exaggerated emotion (cf. 191–6 and the whole of I.1–2). Phaedria's expressions of anger and love seem to look forward to the self-conscious and emotional love poetry of Propertius and Tibullus.[18] Looking back rather than forward in time, we can see that Phaedria has much in common also with other Menandrian lovers like Sostratos in the *Dyscolos* and Moschion in the *Samia*: these characters are earnest, virtuous and indecisive. Nevertheless, it is clear that Thais' affection for Phaedria is quite genuine, and this sets her apart from the Plautine courtesans whose affection is largely reserved for the gifts which their admirers can bestow. It is for this reason too that many critics have considered the conclusion of the play, in which Phaedria accepts the absurd Thraso as a rival for the favours of Thais,

93

to be seriously misjudged; moreover, Thais does not seem to be the sort of lady to be bargained away behind her back and, as she has accepted the protection of Phaedria's father (cf. above pp. 88–9), it seems improbable that there should be any further role for Thraso. It is, in fact, not unlikely that in fashioning this conclusion Terence was influenced by the end of Menander's *Colax*[19] from where, as he states in the prologue, he has taken the soldier and the parasite, but we should, even so, be slow to label this ending incoherent. The continued presence of the wealthy and stupid Thraso has obvious advantages for both Phaedria and Thais and, most importantly, we applaud the successful stratagem of the parasite, who manages to remain on the right side of everybody; the parasite has, after all, been at the heart of the purely farcical aspects of the play, and it is farce which Terence chooses to emphasise at the end (cf. below pp. 108–9 on the end of the *Adelphoe*).

The third variety of *eros* which we see in this play is the sudden, overmastering 'love at first sight' which sweeps Chaerea off his feet when he catches sight of the young Pamphila. When Chaerea discovers that Parmeno knows who and where the girl is, he begs him to find a way that he can get his hands on her (vv. 319–20). Rather jokingly, Parmeno suggests that he swap clothes with the eunuch whom Phaedria is sending to Thais as a gift; the result of this suggestion is the rape of Pamphile, and it is hardly possible for a modern reader to find the subsequent delight which Chaerea expresses in his achievement (vv. 549ff.) anything but repulsive. It is clear that Donatus too was worried by Chaerea's action; a number of notes in his commentary seek to explain or mitigate this deed.[20] It can be argued that Parmeno did not know, or forgot that he had heard Thais saying, that the girl was probably a citizen (cf. vv. 952–3); here we may wish to point to supposed Terentian changes to the Greek original, or to note that Parmeno is a sceptical slave who is likely to have dismissed from his mind Thais' obviously (to him) fictional tale and that such inconsistencies of knowledge are not uncommon throughout ancient drama.[21] Donatus' second argument in Chaerea's defence is from the hot-bloodedness of youth and the power of love; this is an argument which even Thais will accept (vv. 877–81). Chaerea's deed was, moreover, performed in the house of a courtesan where such actions are not always out of place (cf. Parmeno's remarks at vv. 923–33); it is indeed one of the ironies of the play that a lady of Thais' profession attempts, but fails, to preserve a young girl's virginity. Nevertheless, the *Eunuchus* is the only surviving ancient comedy in which a rape occurs during the course of the play rather than merely being one of the incidents which gives rise to a plot set months or even years later.[22] As such it leaves upon the modern reader a very stark impression of the gulf which separated free and not free, man and woman.

Fathers and sons

Although the clash of the generations is most familiar to us as a theme of the New Comedy, it has very strong roots in Old Comedy also. The plot of the *Wasps*, for example, revolves around the attempts of Bdelycleon first to prevent his father from exercising the malicious power of an Athenian juror and then to introduce him to the ways of 'polite society', a scheme which badly misfires when strong drink goes to the old man's head and, having stolen a music-girl from a dinner-party, he staggers through the streets committing random violence on those unlucky enough to cross his path. Philocleon addresses the music-girl in a way indicative of the rejuvenation which alcohol and the abandonment of jury-service have effected:

> ἐὰν γένηι δὲ μὴ κακὴ νυνὶ γυνή,
> ἐγώ σ', ἐπειδὰν οὑμὸς υἱὸς ἀποθάνηι,
> λυσάμενος ἔξω παλλακήν, ὦ χοιρίον.
> νῦν δ' οὐ κρατῶ 'γὼ τῶν ἐμαυτοῦ χρημάτων·
> νέος γάρ εἰμι. καὶ φυλάττομαι σφόδρα·
> τὸ γὰρ ὑίδιον τηρεῖ με, κἄστι δύσκολον
> κἄλλως κυμινοπριστοκαρδαμογλύφον.
> ταῦτ' οὖν περί μου δέδοικε μὴ διαφθαρῶ·
> πατὴρ γὰρ οὐδείς ἐστιν αὐτῶι πλὴν ἐμοῦ.   (*Wasps* 1351–9)

If you're nice to me, I'll set you free and have you as my concubine when my son dies, my little pussy.[23] Just at the moment I'm not in charge of my own money, for I'm still under age. And I'm kept under very close guard: my son watches me and he's a spoil-sport and extraordinarily tight with money. He's afraid I'll be corrupted, and I'm the only father he's got.

Just as Philocleon's escapade itself seems to look forward to the scene in Terence's *Adelphoe* in which Aeschinus steals a girl from a brothel-keeper, so too we are reminded of the young men of New Comedy, whose love affairs are hindered by tight parental control of finance,[24] when Philocleon claims that he is not yet 'of age' and that when his son dies he will buy the girl. Philocleon's outing brings financial loss for his son (vv. 1419–20), as also does the lifestyle of New Comedy sons for their fathers. The reversal of roles in the *Wasps* is an example of a favourite Aristophanic device, seen also in the *Clouds*, in which it is the father, Strepsiades, who goes to school in place of the son. It is likely that in the *Wasps* Aristophanes is inverting an already familiar comic situation of the rivalry of father and son.[25] In the fragments of a play of Pherecrates, the *Corianno* (the name of a courtesan), we see a contrast between two characters one of whom is past the age for love (fr. 71) and in another fragment a son has been abusing his father (fr. 73); it is a reasonable, though not certain, guess that this play too foreshadowed the amatory rivalry of father and son which recurs in the *Asinaria*, *Casina* and *Mercator* of Plautus.

The *Clouds* of Aristophanes also foreshadows important themes of New Comedy. In particular this play has elements in common with Plautus' *Bacchides*. In both plays a 'conservative' figure describes and praises the education offered in schools in what he believes to have been 'the good old days' (*Clouds* 961–1023, *Bacch.* 419–48),[26] and in both plays this older view of life is completely disregarded. In the first scene of the *Bacchides* to have been preserved we see a comically virtuous and priggish young man called Pistoclerus (cf. 56, 66–73) cross the barrier between subdued adolescence and the dissipation of young adulthood. Having crossed this barrier, with the help of two sexy courtesans, Pistoclerus shows all the enthusiasm of the newly converted. It is amusing when he describes his new 'duties' with the moral language more at home in his former upright way of life:

> ego opsonabo, nam id flagitium meum sit, mea te gratia
> et operam dare mi et ad eam operam facere sumptum de tuo.
>
> (*Bacch.* 97–8)
>
> I'll do the shopping, as it would be a disgrace if I allowed you to show me kindness and spend your own money doing so.

In the following scene he instructs his former tutor Lydus in 'the facts of life'. Lydus has asked him who lives in the house where he is going:

> PISTOCLERVS Amor, Voluptas, Venus, Venustas, Gaudium,
> Iocus, Ludus, Sermo, Suauisauiatio.
> LYDVS   quid tibi commercist cum dis damnosissumis?

P.	mali sunt homines qui bonis dicunt male;
	tu dis nec recte dicis: non aequom facis.
L.	an deus est ullus Suauisauiatio?
P.	an non putasti esse umquam? o Lyde, es barbarus;
	quem ego sapere nimio censui plus quam Thalem,
	is stultior es barbaro †poticio,
	qui tantus natu deorum nescis nomina. (*Bacch.* 115–24)

PISTOCLERUS Love, Pleasure, Charm, Grace, Joy, Jest, Playfulness, Wit, Voluptuous Kisses.

LYDUS What business have you with gods which bring nothing but loss?

P. Only evil people abuse the good. You're blaspheming the gods. That's naughty.

L. Is there a god called Voluptuous Kisses?

P. Didn't you know? O Lydus, you are a barbarian! I thought you were so much wiser than Thales, but not to know the names of the gods at your age! You must be pretty stupid.

Here again we may be reminded of the *Clouds*, in this instance of vv. 814–55 and 1232–1302, in which Strepsiades shows off the new things which he has learned in Socrates' school. Strepsiades is from the countryside and very tight with money, whereas his son runs up large debts through his addiction to the aristocratic pursuit of horse-racing; these interests Pheidippides has inherited from his mother, a grand lady from a grand family. Strepsiades therefore looks forward to the grim countryman Demea in Terence's *Adelphoe*, whereas Pheidippides' maternal uncle who, the lad assures his father, will not leave him 'horseless' (v. 125) foreshadows the indulgent Micio of Terence's play (cf. below pp. 105–9). It is Strepsiades' misfortune to have married a lady from a different social group, and if the *Clouds* as a whole has any one 'message' it might be that one should stick to what one knows.[27]

The relationship between a father and his son[28] stands at the centre of a number of plays of the New Comedy and, in particular, comedy is interested in young men in the period just before marriage, which marks the cooling-off of youth and the adoption of the responsibilities of adulthood. The idea is often expressed in comedy that older men should remember that they too were once young and that youth is marked by 'extravagance, pugnacity, thoughtlessness, drunkenness and sexual excess'[29] (cf. Plaut. *Bacch.* 408–10, *Epid.* 382–93, *Pseud.* 436–42, Ter. *Ad.* 101–10).[30] The problems which these characteristics cause in the relations between fathers and sons lie at the heart of four plays of Menander which survive either in Greek or in adaptation into Latin, the *Samia*, the *Adelphoe*, the *Andria* and the *Heauton Timorumenos* ('The Self-Punisher'). Before examining each of these plays in turn, it may be useful to glance at an extant account of how fathers should treat their sons which, although from the period of the Roman empire, probably contains material from the age of Menander or at least which would have been familiar to an educated contemporary of Menander.[31] This is the treatise περὶ παίδων ἀγωγῆς ('On the Upbringing of Children') which is transmitted with the works of Plutarch. In the final section of the treatise the author turns to the education of young men, rather than children, and notes (12b) that young men are given to 'gluttony, stealing their father's money, gambling, revels, drinking-bouts and affairs with both maidens and married women'. Fathers must, therefore, use both instruction and threats to quieten their sons and should point to examples of virtue rewarded and vice punished. Fathers should make sure that their sons do not associate with wicked men, particularly flatterers, but should also remember (13d) that they too were once young and should be prepared to temper their firmness with a little licence and occasionally to turn a blind eye or a deaf ear to misdeeds of various kinds. It is, moreover, better for fathers to express their anger and then cool off again quickly than to remain hostile and suspicious. Young men who are, however, resistant to this approach should be made to marry as a means of sobering them up ('for marriage is the most secure bond (δεσμός) for young men'), but they should not marry women above their station as then they will merely become slaves of their wife's dowry. Most important of all, fathers should in their own lifestyle set an example for their sons so that the latter 'may look at their fathers' lives as at a mirror and so turn away from wicked deeds and words' (14a). It is clear, even from this short summary, that there are many points of contact between this treatise and the plays of New Comedy, and it is reasonable to suppose that both reflect a fairly wide ancient consensus about the duties of the older generation towards the younger. The difference between the two is that whereas the author of the treatise is forced to generalise about the characteristics of young men, comedy is able to investigate individual cases. The best poets used the audience's familiarity with the stereotyped characteristics of each age-group (a stereotyping reinforced by comedy itself) to explore specific relationships in which generalised rules are often of little use.

The *Heauton Timorumenos* concerns two fathers.[32] The 'self-punisher' of the title is Menedemus, whose constant criticisms put an end to his son's love affair with a poor girl. When he himself was young, Menedemus used to tell his son, he had gone off to win glory and property as a mercenary soldier instead of wasting his time on affairs of the heart. In the end, the young man, Clinia, did as his father urged and went off to serve as a soldier. When the play opens, Menedemus is wracked with remorse and works himself extremely hard in the fields so that he can suffer as he imagines his son to suffer. Menedemus is very conscious of the fact that he has acted in the way in which conventionally grim stage-fathers act, *ui et uia peruolgata patrum* 'in the violent way usual with fathers' (v. 101) as he puts it, and later he exclaims *satis iam, satis pater durus fui*, 'for long enough I have been the tough father' (v. 439). By thus assimilating his behaviour to a familiar pattern of stage action, Menedemus allows us to understand much about the history of the relationship between himself and Clinia which need not be expressly stated. As an audience we use our knowledge of other comic fathers to visualise what happened in this particular case. A close parallel does in fact survive in Plautus' *Mercator* (= Philemon's *Emporos*) in which a father's constant criticism forced his son to abandon an affair with a courtesan and take up overseas trade. The robust Plautine father is, however, in other respects a quite different character from Terence's gentle spirit. Menedemus tells his story in the opening scene to Chremes, one of the most memorable characters of the New Comedy. Chremes is Menedemus' neighbour in the area where the latter has bought a farm; he is a man with an insatiable interest in other people's affairs, and a little influence in the small, provincial world he inhabits (cf. vv. 498–501) has given him a completely inflated view of his own importance. His opening speech reveals that he has spent far more time than is healthy in observing the habits of his new neighbour. When Menedemus asks him sharply but fairly whether he has so much time on his hands that he can concern himself with what is no business of his, Chremes does not have the social tact to withdraw gracefully. He continues to urge Menedemus to tell his story, absurdly promising before he knows anything about it:

> aut consolando aut consilio aut re iuuero   (*HT* 86)

> I shall help you by consolation or advice or material assistance.

Here the careful rhetoric of Chremes' language (cf. also vv. 67–9, 200–10) clearly indicates just how seriously he takes himself. His first reaction to Menedemus' narrative is to pass judgement on the rights and wrongs of the situation (vv. 119–20, 151–7) and, like so many of comedy's most splendid fools, he will be shown in the course of the play not to have followed his own banal advice:

>   hoc
> scitumst: periclum ex aliis fac tibi quod ex usu siet   (*HT* 209–10)

> The wise man learns valuable lessons from the experience of others.

Throughout the play Chremes remains very free both with advice and with Menedemus' money (cf. vv. 469ff.). He is a man who preaches the virtues of openness in social relationships (v. 154) and who pompously informs a slave *non meast simulatio* 'pretence is not in my nature' (v. 782), but who does not hesitate to urge the same slave to use falsehood, despite the latter's protest.[33] Chremes in fact is as much concerned with appearances as with truth (vv. 469–89, 572–8), even to the extent of forcing an elaborate and ridiculous charade on the unhappy Menedemus (vv. 940ff.). It is thus particularly appropriate that Chremes himself is fooled simply because he refuses to believe what is in fact the truth about the love affairs of the two young men (cf. vv. 709–12). He is, moreover, much given to platitudes on the subject of education, many of which are, by themselves, sound and laudable (cf. vv. 151–7, 200–10, 469–89) but which take on a new colour in the mouth of this silly man. The gulf between theory and practice, a gulf which has resulted in his son according him scant respect (vv. 213–29), here casts suspicion on the very process of reasoning and suggests that the relationshp between father and son is not something which can be reduced to a simple formula. When Chremes learns the truth of how he has been fooled his rage is understandable, but we feel for him none of the sympathy which we shall feel for Demea when he finds himself in a similar situation in the *Adelphoe*; Chremes' major concerns are the financial implications of the situation and the fact that he has been made to look foolish (vv. 928ff.). Our sense of poetic justice is not, however, outraged by the fact that his fortunes end on a higher note when his son is forced to agree to an unwanted marriage, because his son has always been a rather poor specimen with whom it is difficult to sympathise. Each father thus has the son he deserves.

The best commentary on Chremes' behaviour is the behaviour of another Terentian father, Simo in the *Andria*. In the opening scene of this play Simo tells his freedman about his son Pamphilus:

> SIMO quod plerique omnes faciunt adulescentuli,
> ut animum ad aliquod studium adiungant, aut equos
> alere aut canes ad uenandum aut ad philosophos,
> horum ille nil egregie praeter cetera
> studebat et tamen omnia haec mediocriter.
> gaudebam. SOSIA non iniuria; nam id arbitror
> adprime in uita esse utile, ut nequid nimis.
>
> SIMO sic uita erat: facile omnis perferre ac pati;
> cum quibus erat quomque una eis sese dedere,
> eorum obsequi studiis, aduersus nemini,
> numquam praeponens se illis; ita ut facillume
> sine inuidia laudem inuenias et amicos pares.   (*Andria* 55–66)

> SIMO Most young men pursue some interest with
> enthusiasm – horses, hunting dogs, philosophy; Pamphilus,
> however, didn't give himself to any one of these more than the
> others and yet he took a moderate interest in all of them. I
> was pleased.
> SOSIA Quite rightly so; for in my view the first rule in life is
> 'nothing in excess'.
> SIMO This is how he was: he put up with the habits of all his
> friends, devoted himself to whomever he happened to be with,
> followed their pursuits, made no enemies, never pushed
> himself forward. This is the best way to avoid envy and win
> both praise and friends.

Simo explains how by careful observation of his son he discovered that he was having an affair with the younger sister of a courtesan who had come to Athens from Andros. Simo wants to put an end to this affair because his friend Chremes has asked for Pamphilus as husband for his daughter and has offered a splendid dowry as well. Simo's problem is that Pamphilus has so far done nothing for which he could be rebuked, and so he has devised a charade to see whether his son really will refuse a sensible marriage. During this long narrative in the first scene Simo is presented as an observer of his son's development rather than as an educator. His son has turned out well and so he is pleased, but he claims no personal credit for this success; Simo is no educational theorist. Unlike Chremes in *Heauton Timorumenos* and Demea in the *Adelphoe*, Simo has a realistic view of how far a father can influence his son's development. In the final scenes of the play Simo does lose his temper with Pamphilus who he believes is trying every possible trick to avoid marriage, but the provocation has been very great and, as we laugh, we also feel for him. Simo has worked very hard to save what would be a very advantageous match for his son (cf. vv. 533–74), and when an old man turns up unexpectedly and claims that Pamphilus' beloved, Glycerium, is an Athenian citizen, Simo quite naturally recalls the story which Davus said the lovers would concoct to delay Pamphilus' marriage (vv. 220–4, cf. above pp. 77–9 on the role of deception in this play). Simo has suffered at the slave's hands before and is thus not unreasonably suspicious. When Simo's anger does finally explode, he is not concerned with how he looks to the outside world, or with money, but rather with social morality (vv. 879–81), and whereas Chremes in *Heauton Timorumenos* went through the elaborate charade of disowning his son, Simo merely washes his hands of the whole business. We can understand that he is tired of it. Pamphilus' response to his father's outburst is moving, if rather melodramatic:

> ego me amare hanc fateor; si id peccarest, fateor id quoque.
> tibi, pater, me dedo: quiduis oneris inpone, impera.
> uis me uxorem ducere? hanc uis mittere? ut potero feram.
>
> *(Andria* 896–8)

> I confess that I love her; if this is a sin, I confess that I have sinned. Father, I place myself in your power: impose whatever task you wish. Simply give your instructions. You want me to marry? You want me to give Glycerium up? I shall bear this as best I can.

These final scenes do credit to the relationship between Simo and Pamphilus, just as Pamphilus' treatment of Glycerium also reflects credit upon him. Chremes and Clitipho in *Heauton Timorumenos* never treated each other like this.

Menander's *Samia* resembles the *Andria* in that it too deals with misunderstandings and conflicts caused by pretence, but in the *Samia* we approach the relationship of father and son from the point of view of the younger man. The prologue is here delivered by Moschion, who tells us that he is the adopted son of Demeas, who has given him all the educational and material advantages of the well-to-do Athenian. Moschion is suitably grateful to his adopted father, but also apparently a little pleased with himself. His claim to have behaved properly in his youth (ἦν κόσμιος, v. 18) is later confirmed by Demeas (v. 273), but it may cause us to reflect that such a judgement about one's actions is usually best left to others. He is also pleased that he was able to help secure for his father the Samian courtesan with whom Demeas was in love; he tells us that his father had tried to conceal this love from him out of shame, and this foreshadows the real affection for his son which Demeas is to reveal as the play proceeds. Shame is something which Moschion too feels,[34] when he recalls how he raped the daughter of a neighbour at a festival which the women of the two households were celebrating;[35] Moschion has promised to marry this girl as soon as the respective fathers return from a trip abroad together and he thus looks to the future with some trepidation. The girl has given birth to a child which Demeas' concubine Chrysis has offered to pretend is hers; it is this pretence which is to cause all the trouble.

Our suspicion that Moschion is not to be taken too seriously is only hardened by the scenes which follow the prologue. Like the young lover Sostratos in the *Dyscolos*, Moschion relies heavily on the help of others, the slave Parmenon and Demeas' concubine Chrysis. He wanders off to an empty spot to rehearse what he will say to his father (v. 94), but on his return he tells the audience that all he could do was fantasise about the wedding. On finding that his father is very angry because Chrysis has had a child (which Moschion and we know is really the child of Moschion and the neighbour's daughter), he preaches to his father a sermon on the supremacy of character over social status. We know nothing about Moschion's real parentage, but it is tempting to believe that there is real irony in his appeal to the unimportance of status at birth:

οὐθὲν γένος γένους γὰρ οἶμαι διαφέρειν,
ἀλλ' εἰ δικαίως ἐξετάσαι τις, γνήσιος
ὁ χρηστός ἐστιν, ὁ δὲ πονηρὸς καὶ νόθος
καὶ δοῦλος...   (*Samia* 140–3)

In my view, it's not birth which makes one man better than another, but if you look at it justly, it is the good man who is legitimate and the bad who is a bastard and a slave...

Moschion next appears in the fourth act, where his interventions on Chrysis' behalf only increase poor Demeas' confusion until the young man finally gets a chance to explain the whole truth. The most surprising part of Moschion's role is, however, the fifth act in which he tells the audience that he wants to punish and frighten his father by pretending to go off on military service overseas; his father's crime, we learn, is having suspected that Moschion had fathered a child on Chrysis. One critic has written of this final act: 'Moschion's discontent is natural for someone who values his relationship with his father so highly.'[36] Perhaps, but his behaviour is in fact quite absurd, as is made clear by his sudden doubts about whether the charade might backfire (vv. 682–6); γελοῖος ἔσομαι, νὴ Δί', ἀνακάμπτων πάλιν ('if I turn around and come back, I'll look foolish') he says, little realising how foolish he already looks. The measure of how seriously we are to take this young man emerges in vv. 630–2:

νῦν δ' οὐ ποήσω διὰ σέ, Πλαγγὼν φιλτάτη,
ἀνδρεῖον οὐθέν· οὐ γὰρ ἔξεστ' οὐδ' ἐᾶι
ὁ τῆς ἐμῆς νῦν κύριος γνώμης Ἔρως.   (*Samia* 630–2)

Because of you, dearest Plangon, I shall do nothing bold. I cannot, nor does Love which controls my mind allow me.

Something bold (lit. 'manly') is the very last thing we would have expected from Moschion. We should not examine too closely the 'psychology' of Moschion which binds the final act to the rest of the play. The *Samia* is not the only play in which the action is given a new impulse at the start of the fifth act (cf. above p. 41), and we enjoy the humour of Moschion's charade and Menander's reversal of a traditional motif – Moschion who is lucky in love pretends to go overseas, thus aping comic lovers who use this as a remedy for unhappiness in love – and we will not worry too much about whether Moschion's behaviour is consistent throughout the play. This last act does, however, tell us something important about Demeas.

In the face of Moschion's charade, Demeas offers his adopted son far more kindness and sympathy than he had any right to expect. He urges Moschion to set off his one mistake against all his acts of kindness and not to expose him to ridicule when he had done everything in his power to conceal what he believed to be Moschion's shameful act (vv. 694–712). Demeas' speech is a mark of his devotion, and we recall that for a long period Demeas had raised Moschion single-handed and that even Chrysis, to whom Demeas is very attached (cf. vv. 80–3, 376–80), does not really constitute a proper family for him. Demeas is almost a bachelor father, like Micio in the *Adelphoe*, and his love for his adopted son is such that he refused to believe the very plain testimony of his eyes and ears. In the final act of the *Samia*, therefore, we are presented with a delicate blend of the serious and the farcical, and it is this mixture which seems to have been characteristic of Menander at his best.

The *Adelphoe*,[37] like the *Heauton Timorumenos*, concerns two fathers. In this, his last surviving play, Terence has laid great emphasis on the extent to which the two fathers, Micio and Demea, are 'types', Micio the urban bachelor who indulges his adopted son and Demea the hard-working rustic, well suited to the role of *pater durus* (cf. vv. 42–6, 863–7). Menander's interest, already visible in the *Samia*, in the relationship between a man and his adopted son is given full play in the *Adelphoe*. Micio indulges Aeschinus' whims and appetites, not merely to win his affection,[38] but out of a belief, which some would consider mistaken, that such an approach is educationally valuable:

> nimium ipsest durus praeter aequomque et bonum,
> et errat longe mea quidem sententia
> qui imperium credat grauius esse aut stabilius
> ui quod fit quam illud quod amicitia adiungitur.[39]
> mea sic est ratio et sic animum induco meum:
> malo coactus qui suom officium facit,
> dum id rescitum iri credit, tantisper cauet;
> si sperat fore clam, rursum ad ingenium redit.
> ille quem beneficio adiungas ex animo facit,
> studet par referre, praesens absensque idem erit.
> hoc patriumst, potius consuefacere filium
> sua sponte recte facere quam alieno metu:
> hoc pater ac dominus interest. hoc qui nequit,
> fateatur nescire imperare liberis.   (*Ad.* 64–77)

The man who believes that the authority which is based on force is weightier or more stable than that which exercises influence through friendship is tough beyond all reasonableness and fairness and, in my view, quite mistaken. My view and outlook are as follows: the man who does his duty under the constraint of punishment takes care as long as he thinks his actions will be known; if he has hopes of escaping detection, he goes straight back to his natural inclinations. The man whom you bind to you by kindness wants to give back like for like and will always be the same, whether you are there or not. The real father accustoms his son to do the right thing because he wants to, not because he is afraid. This is the difference between a father and a master. The man who can't do this should admit that he doesn't know how to control children.

In many respects Micio resembles Philoxenus in the *Bacchides*, who is also prepared to give his son his head (vv. 408–18), provided that things do not go too far and that the young man does not become incurably idle (vv. 1076–86). The apparently sensible and moderate policy which these two characters advocate must not, however, be mistaken for an educational 'doctrine' which the poet wishes to preach. We can applaud Micio without necessarily wanting to pattern our behaviour in the real world outside the theatre on him: in this he is the true heir of Dicaiopolis and Philocleon.

For most of the *Adelphoe* Demea is made to look silly. Even before the audience knows the truth about what Aeschinus has done they may well guess that Demea's opening speech is wildly exaggerated and suggests that we should not take this character completely seriously:

> fores effregit atque in aedis inruit
> alienas; ipsum dominum atque omnem familiam
> mulcauit usque ad mortem; eripuit mulierem
> quam amabat. clamant omnes indignissume
> factum esse. hoc aduenienti quot mihi, Micio,
> dixere. in orest omni populo. (*Ad.* 88–93)

He's smashed a door and broken into someone else's house; beaten the owner and all the household within an inch of their lives; carried off the girl he loves. The whole town is screaming that this is an outrageous scandal. Micio, how many people met me on my way here and told me about it! It's on everyone's lips.

So too in IV.2 Syrus sends Demea off on a wild-goose chase around town, and in an earlier confrontation Demea's pompous and banal[40] moralising is savagely mocked by the slave who turns Demea's words into a lecture on the cooking of fish (vv. 412–34). In vv. 413–14, *fit sedulo:* | *nil praetermitto; consuefacio* ('I work hard at it; I overlook nothing; I train him'), Demea echoes Micio's account of his own educational practice in the prologue (vv. 49–54). Does this echo mean that 'Terence...wishes us to take Micio's principles, as well as Demea's, with a pinch of salt' (Martin on v. 413)? Perhaps, but what is important in the relationship between father and son is not principles but actions. The behaviour of Micio's son, Aeschinus, towards the girl whom he has raped and the sentiments which he expresses when Micio finally confronts him with the truth are to his (and Micio's) credit. Demea, on the other hand, is just fooling himself when he says 'I overlook nothing', and his son Ctesipho is a poor figure who is entirely dependent upon Aeschinus' assistance and whose utterances hardly rise above the level of a sigh or a melodramatic exaggeration. It may not be Demea's fault that his son cuts such a poor figure, but Terence goes out of his way to make Demea look foolish by having him announce at every possible opportunity how wonderful this son is, when the audience knows that this is far from the truth. By way of contrast, Aeschinus conceals his misdeed from Micio not out of fear but out of shame (vv. 643, 690); such shame may not make him virtuous, but it certainly reveals a proper sense of values. Aeschinus' actions towards his brother are praiseworthy and, in dealing with the *leno*, he shows a firm authority which we applaud (cf. above p. 72). In short, both the older and the younger 'brothers' are firmly differentiated, and Terence could hardly have done more to guide our response to his characters.

The passage around which most controversy has centred is vv. 787ff. When Demea has finally learned that Micio has been harbouring Ctesipho and his girl-friend, he rebukes Micio for having broken the agreement made in the first act (vv. 129–40) that each would only concern himself with his own son. Micio's reply to the charge is to quote the old proverb *communia esse amicorum inter se omnia* ('the possessions of friends are common goods'), an answer with which critics as early as Donatus have expressed dissatisfaction. In his following speech Micio addresses himself largely to financial questions and he urges Demea to let the boys do as they wish as he himself will foot the bills. Micio does not, however, really answer Demea's charges. It has been argued that Micio could do little else but offer

Ctesipho hospitality and the 'agreement' between the older pair of brothers can hardly have been intended to prevent common courtesies between uncle and nephew.[41] Against such considerations must, however, be set the scene in which the audience has seen Micio taking considerable delight in the fooling of his brother (vv. 719–62); whatever the exact terms of the agreement between the brothers, the audience will sense that Demea has been treated unfairly, much as it has enjoyed seeing him done down. Terence has thus carefully prepared the surprise which the final scenes have in store for us.

In a long speech to the audience after he has discovered the truth (vv. 855–81), Demea claims that he is tired of being hated; Micio, in his view, has bought love and affection 'through bribery and compliance', and now he too will try this method. This speech is riddled with bitterness and jealousy, and as these are emotions which cannot stay concealed for long, we are not surprised when, at the end of the play, Demea reveals that his new amiability was simply a sham designed to show Micio that his success with the boys was the result of weakness and foolish indulgence. That Demea is merely playing a role in the final scenes is clear too from the language he uses.[42] More surprising perhaps is the active assistance which Demea receives from Micio's son, and the helplessness to which Micio himself is reduced in the final scene: we are not disturbed so much by the acts of generosity which Demea forces upon him as by the language in which his reactions are couched. Micio has, for example, never unambiguously expressed an aversion to marriage and when this course is suggested to him his reply may not seem wholly consistent with the character of the rest of the play:

> ego nouus maritus anno demum quinto et sexagensumo
> fiam atque anum decrepitam ducam?   (*Ad.* 938–9)

> I'm sixty-four, and you want me to marry some broken-down old woman?

Donatus informs us that in the Greek original of the *Adelphoe* Micio raised no objection to this marriage, but Terence has preferred to play the scene strictly for its farcical possibilities.[43] In doing so he has managed to offend the sensibilities of generations of critics, but in fact he is merely following a traditional preference, which flourishes at all periods of ancient comedy, for humour over dramatic coherence. It would be attractive to interpret the reversals at the end of the *Adelphoe* as a victory for stern Roman morality over Greek laxness, but the very ambiguity of the ending should warn against any attempt to associate this play with a very specific social and historical context.[44] If no very clear moral pattern emerges from the *Adelphoe*, we should not be surprised: Terence's interest is focused on the comic characters themselves, not the principles of action which underlie their behaviour.

Town and country

The description of a simple and innocent life in the countryside is a familiar feature of Hellenistic and Roman literature. The vision of an uncorrupted bucolic existence was used by poets to create complex effects by playing off the *naïveté* of this bucolic world against the sophistication of their poetry and its readers, and by moralists to denounce the evils of contemporary urban society. Juvenal's third satire, for example, consists largely of a denunciation by one Umbricius of the ills of life in modern Rome; Umbricius has decided to leave Rome for the quieter and more virtuous surroundings of provincial Cumae. In Rome corruption, dishonesty and inequality are rife. Umbricius stands in the same tradition as Cnemon in Menander's *Dyscolos*, whose miserable, solitary life is not the result of poverty (cf. vv. 327–8),[45] but of a dislike of human contact fostered by experience of the dishonesty of mankind. Already in the fifth century we see the heroes of Aristophanes' *Birds* fleeing the litigiousness of Athens in order to found a new city in the wild, and it seems that plots of this type were not uncommon in Old Comedy.[46] The special circumstances of the Peloponnesian War, in which the Athenians defended themselves behind their city walls and allowed the Spartans to ravage the countryside, clearly accelerated the process by which an opposition between 'town' and 'country' became an increasingly common structuring device in drama and literature. In the *Acharnians* and the *Peace* of Aristophanes the countryside is associated with peace, prosperity and a healthy 'normal' sexuality, the city with war and perversion. The town–country contrast is also basic to Strepsiades' problems in the *Clouds*: not only did this silly countryman marry a sophisticated girl from the city (vv. 43–8), but he brings disaster upon himself by meddling with quintessentially urban, intellectual pursuits;

in this play we meet for the first time[47] the word ἄγροικος ('belonging to the countryside') carrying the clear implication of 'stupid' and 'boorish' (vv. 628, 646, both in the mouth of that committed city-dweller Socrates).

New Comedy is essentially an urban genre; it concerns the amatory and commercial affairs of well-to-do citizens which, for the most part, take place in cities and towns where the opportunities for such business were obviously centred. In this matter comedy reproduces life with reasonable accuracy. The wealthier classes of Menander's day tended to invest their wealth in a wide diversity of activities and few were solely dependent upon agriculture.[48] Residence in the city away from one's landholdings seems to have become more and more regular in the fourth century;[49] this is reflected in a large number of plays, both Greek and Roman (*Dysc.*, *Casina*, *Merc.*, *Asin.*, *Eun.*, etc.), although it is to be noted that we do not yet have a Greek exemplar for the contrast of town-slave and country-slave familiar from the *Casina* and the *Mostellaria* nor a Greek comic equivalent of the *uilicus* or 'bailiff' who plays important roles in the *Casina* and the *Poenulus* (and cf. *Merc.* 277).[50] This may very well be the result of chance, but it is possible also that we should see in Plautus the influence of Atellan farce, which presented a comic picture of Italian rustic life (cf. above pp. 20–1). In both Greek and Roman comedy, however, the countryside can represent the antithesis of normal 'comic' life. In the *Eunuchus* of Terence, for example, the separation of the lover Phaedria from the courtesan Thais takes the form of a trip to the countryside (v. 187), and in the *Heauton Timorumenos* it is to the countryside that Mene-demus moves to punish himself for the way he has treated his son.

The most common form of the city–country contrast in comedy is between the frivolity and luxury of the city and the virtue and stern morality of the country. This contrast is most vivid for us in the matched pairs of the slaves Grumio and Tranio in the *Mostellaria* and of Demea and Micio in the *Adelphoe*, but we know that it has a very long history on the comic stage. In his earliest play, the *Banqueters*, Aristophanes portrayed a very conservative father with two quite different sons whom the poet elsewhere (*Clouds* 529) describes as ὁ σώφρων τε χὠ καταπύγων ('the sober and the debauched one'). The former lived in the countryside, whereas the latter was a 'victim' of modern education, like Pheidippides in the *Clouds*, and probably led a riotous life in the city. So too Menander's lost *Hypobolimaios* ('The Supposititious Child') concerned a father who had one son who lived in the country and another in the city, and a fragment of Alexis' *Kouris* makes it very probable that that play also presented a similar contrast between two sons.[51] A related contrast is that between Sostratos and the young rustic, Gorgias, in Menander's *Dyscolos*. Sostratos is a well-to-do young man with nothing better to do than fall in love on a hunting trip. For him a trip to the country is nothing more than an entertainment. The rustic girl he falls in love with, however, is pious and virtuous (vv. 34–9, 384–9) and is protected by the stern morality of Cnemon and Gorgias (vv. 218–29, 271–98). It is noteworthy, however, that in the *Dyscolos* Menander does not draw any rigid equations between virtue and need, moral laxness and wealth. Sostratos' father is a very wealthy man (vv. 39–41), but is acknowledged by Gorgias to be a γεωργὸς ἄμαχος ('an indomitable farmer'). Sostratos himself acts honourably throughout the play, even if he falls short of his father's worldly common sense (cf. below pp. 143–4). The equation of virtue with rusticity is certainly exploited in other plays. The ancient comedy which is most explicitly set in a moral frame where virtue is rewarded and vice castigated, the *Rudens*, takes place on a lonely seashore to which Daemones has retreated after losing his fortune in the city through generosity to unworthy men. A particularly interesting example is Menander's *Georgos*. This play presents rich and poor neighbours; the rich son has raped the poor daughter, who is now about to give birth. We see the rich son caught out by his father's plans to marry him off to his half-sister; he declares his resolution not to desert his poor beloved but, like so many rich lovers of comedy, resolution is one characteristic he does not really possess (vv. 17–21). By contrast, the son of the poor family has been working hard in the countryside as a hired labourer and by his devotion to his employer has won the latter's land for his sister, a prospective marriage which will obviously come to nothing as the rich son will, in the inevitable way of comedy, eventually marry the poor girl. This situation presents again the contrast of well-to-do weakness and struggling virtue, and of particular interest is the following advice

from Daos, a slave from the wealthy house, to the poor girl's mother
after he has told her of the marriage which has been arranged:

ἥξουσιν ἤδη δεῦρ', ἄπεισιν εἰς ἀγρὸν
αὐτὴ]ν λαβών. παύσεσθε πενίαι μαχόμενοι,
δυσνουθετήτωι θηρί[ωι καὶ δυσκόλωι
καὶ ταῦτ' ἐν ἄστει· δεῖ γὰρ ἢ πλουτεῖν ἴσως
ἢ ζῆν ὅπως μὴ μάρτυρας τοῦ δυστυχεῖν
πολλούς τις ἕξει τοὺς ὁρῶντας· ἔστι δὲ
ἀγρὸς εἰς τὸ τοιοῦτ' εὐκτὸν ἥ τ' ἐρημία.   (*Georgos* 76–82)

They'll soon be here and he'll take her off to his farm. You will stop
your battle with poverty, a difficult, moody beast, and that in the
city, too. One should either be rich or live where there aren't many
witnesses of one's misfortune looking on. A lonely farm's the perfect
answer for this.

That the countryside is a mask for πενία, that state where one has
to work hard for a living, fits well with the general ethos of
comedy; πενία is not a common affliction among the characters of New
Comedy, and both such need and a hard life in the countryside are
foreign to the normal comic situation. The pomposity of the slave's
advice here also indicates the self-satisfaction which riches and a life
of ease can bring.[52]

Well represented in comedy also is what may be considered as the
reverse side of 'the rustic coin'. If the countryside was a place of
honesty and upright morality, it was also a place of bad smells, dirt
and lack of sophistication. It may serve not only as a moral exemplar,
but also as a foil to highlight the pleasures of urban life. In the *Casina*
of Plautus, the opening scene is an exchange of abuse between the
bailiff Olympio and the town-slave Chalinus,[53] and this establishes the
contest for the hand of Casina as a clash between these two spheres
(or *prouinciae*, as Chalinus calls them, v. 103). It is in this light that
we should view the homosexual jokes which characterise the meetings
of Olympio and his master Lysidamus (vv. 451–66, 810–13). This
feature gives concrete expression to the fact that their designs on
Casina are offensive to the bourgeois decency of comedy, as well as
foreshadowing the homosexual 'marriage' which awaits them at the
end of the play. Their lewd behaviour is linked to their status as rustic
bumpkins, just as the herdsmen of Theocritus' *Fifth Idyll* are

similarly characterised. This pattern in the play is neatly expressed
in the closing admonition to the audience:

> nunc uos aequomst manibus meritis meritam mercedem dare.
> qui faxit, clam uxorem ducet semper scortum quod uolet;
> uerum qui non manibus clare quantum poterit plauserit,
> ei pro scorto supponetur hircus unctus nautea.   (*Casina* 1015–18)

> Now, spectators, it is right that you give us deserved applause. He
> who does so shall always have the girl he wants and his wife won't
> know about it; but the man who does not clap loudly with all his
> strength, he'll not get a girl, but a he-goat perfumed with
> bilge-water.

The *scortum* ('tart') symbolises the happy, urban world of New
Comedy, the he-goat the rude, uncultured world that we have just seen
defeated in the *Casina*. In the *Mercator* also, 'he-goat' is used to
describe the *senex* who seeks to interfere with his son's love-life, and
who thus brands himself as rustic and randy (vv. 272–6). In that play,
the *senex* who represented himself to his son as a hard-working man
who, in his youth, kept well clear of the decadent lure of the city (vv.
61–72) falls in love with his son's newly-acquired girl-friend; the old
man's friend takes the girl to his house where she is found by his wife
and marital trouble ensues. It is typical of the patterns of thought that
I have outlined in these pages that it is from the countryside that the
wife returns to catch her husband's urban and scandalous behaviour
(vv. 667–9, 714–17).

Comedy and tragedy

The exploitation of tragic poetry for a wide variety of humorous effects is one of the most striking and memorable features of Aristophanic drama. New Comedy too made use of language and motifs borrowed from tragedy. As, however, virtually all the Greek tragedy which was written during the fourth and third centuries B.C. has perished and only fragments remain of the Latin adaptations of Greek tragedies with which the audiences of Plautus and Terence were familiar,[1] we must resign ourselves to the fact that there is probably a great deal of 'tragic exploitation' in the extant comedies which we are unable fully to appreciate. Nevertheless, two important facts assist us in assessing this aspect of comic technique. The first is that, as part of the firm separation between the two genres in the Greek world, the linguistic and metrical practice of Greek tragedy is sharply distinguished from that of comedy, and so passages of elevated style in comedy can usually be identified even where the text does not specifically call attention to this feature in a character's speech. In Latin, unfortunately, identification of specifically tragic style is much less easy as neither the language (particularly in the time of Plautus) nor the metrical practice of comedy were differentiated from tragedy in the sharp Greek manner.[2] It is reasonable to suppose that this difference is a result of the fact that, unlike their Greek counterparts, the earliest Latin adapters of Greek drama (Livius Andronicus, Gnaeus Naevius) wrote both tragedies and comedies. Nevertheless, by studying the extant fragments of Roman tragedy and the style of other grand genres such as epic, we can identify many passages where the comic poets seem to have exploited the audience's knowledge of the style of tragedy. The second favourable factor is that during the period of the New Comedy tragedies of Aeschylus, Sophocles, and Euripides were produced in public performances alongside new tragedies and were thus firmly established as 'classics' to which allusion could freely be made. The result of this is that we find in our texts of New Comedy references to extant classical tragedies, and in such cases we are in a very good position to evaluate the effect for which the comic poet was striving. We must, however, always remember that we possess only a small fraction of the total output of the classical tragedians and we must not try to force those passages of New Comedy in which tragic poetry is exploited into a direct relationship with the few tragedies which have survived.

For many elements of New Comedy, as ancient scholars were well aware,[3] we may postulate an ancestry in the older genre of tragedy. Sometimes there is no reason to think that the comic poet wished the audience to recall this ancestry, and knowledge of the particular piece of literary history involved adds nothing to our appreciation of the comic scene as a piece of practical drama. Examples of this are the scenes in the *Perinthia* of Menander and the *Mostellaria* of Plautus in which a slave takes refuge from his master's fury at the altar on the stage and the master threatens to burn the slave out of his sanctuary. The earliest extant scene in comedy in which someone takes sanctuary at an altar is the parody of Euripides' *Telephos* in the *Thesmophoriazousai* of Aristophanes, and it is not improbable that such scenes entered the comic repertoire first in parody and then in non-parodic assimilation to the comic milieu. We shall see below (cf. pp. 130–4) how, in the case of recognition scenes, a motif which has been completely assimilated to the comic stage may nevertheless retain clear signs of its origins in tragic drama.

The identification of parody or exploitation of Greek tragedy in the Greek models of our extant Latin dramatic scripts is particularly difficult, as the linguistic features of Greek parody are necessarily absent from our texts. Very often we can merely note a parallelism of thought or structure between a passage of Greek tragedy and one of Latin comedy and must leave open the precise nature of the relationship between them. A few examples will help to illustrate the range of situations with which we are confronted.

The attempt of the *leno* to seize Palaestra and Ampelisca in the central scenes of the *Rudens* bears a strong resemblance to the scene in the *Oedipus at Colonus* of Sophocles in which Creon attempts to seize Antigone and Ismene from the altar where they have sought protection. The language of this scene in Diphilos' Greek comedy may have made a debt to tragedy obvious, but we have no right to assume that this was so. As for the Latin scene, there are no clear indications of tragic style and no reason to assume that the exploitation of tragedy was a significant element in the appreciation of this scene by Plautus' Roman audience. A second example is the similarity between the opening of Plautus' *Pseudolus* and the prologue of Euripides' *Iphigenia at Aulis*.[4] Both plays begin with a request by a loyal servant that his master reveal the contents of a letter which he has been carrying around with him, and there are also clear similarities in the conduct of the dialogue. The case for the direct influence of the tragedy upon the comedy might be strengthened by the observation that the opening scene of the *Pseudolus* is characterised by elevated and melodramatic language,[5] although this may also simply be a function of the comical 'emotion' in this scene (cf. below, pp. 123–4). The parallels between the two plays are not exact, as in Euripides the master has written the letter and in Plautus he has received it. Perhaps, therefore, the comic poets were here drawing upon a much wider stage tradition than is available to us, and so we should reserve judgement as to whether the comic scene was directly inspired by the *Iphigenia at Aulis*. Euripidean drama is often concerned with relationships which may be found as easily in the real world of 'ordinary people' as in the heroic world; both the *Hippolytos* and Menander's *Samia*, for example, concern the consequences of a misunderstanding between a father and his son over the woman with whom the former lives. The tragedy concerns mythological figures, the comedy ordinary Athenians. As with the *Iphigenia–Pseudolus* similarity, we must not hurriedly assume that New Comedy borrows directly from classical tragedy.

A final illustration may be sought in the *Captivi* of Plautus. In this play Philocrates and his slave Tyndarus have been captured in war and subsequently purchased by Hegio who is, unbeknown to all the characters, Tyndarus' father. Hegio plans to send Tyndarus home to arrange an exchange between Philocrates and Hegio's other son, who is a prisoner-of-war on the other side; in order to fool Hegio, the two captives swap clothes so that Philocrates will be set free. Tyndarus lays great stress upon his own spirit of generosity and self-sacrifice. There is here a strong similarity to the situation of Orestes and Pylades in the *Iphigenia at Tauris* of Euripides. The tragic characters are captured by Orestes' sister, the priestess of Artemis, who does not recognise them and who plans to put one of them to death. Pylades nobly offers to be the victim in order to secure Orestes' safety.

Whether or not there is any direct relationship between the plays we cannot tell. What is clear, however, is that the tone of the two dramas is quite different. Pylades' high-minded sentiments of self-sacrifice in the tragedy (vv. 674–86) have become in the comedy a very amusing melodrama. In place of Iphigenia with her divided loyalties and ultimate gentleness, the *Captivi* offers us the bumbling Hegio,[6] whose love for his son is real enough, but whose simple-mindedness is no match for the real world and whose expressions of joy at the end of the play weary even the son who has been restored to him (v. 929). The *Captivi* has often been seen as a near-tragedy,[7] but the emotional sentiments and declarations of friendship of Philocrates and Tyndarus must be seen in the context of the situation in which these characters find themselves; they draw out their charade to ridiculous lengths in order to fool poor Hegio. Tyndarus the slave is given the sentiments and upbringing appropriate to the free-born man he will turn out to be – he is the male equivalent of the young slave-girl who has remained chaste so that the play can have a happy ending when she is found to be free-born and can make a splendid marriage – but in the bold front which he presents after Hegio has discovered the trick which has been played upon him, the slave glories in his goodness (*qui per uirtutem periit, at non interit*, 'he who is killed by his virtue does not perish utterly'), much to the amusement of the audience who know that all will turn out well in the end. The poet extracts considerable dramatic advantage from the audience's superior knowledge (cf. vv. 444,[8] 577 etc.), and it is clear that it is comedy and farce which predominate in this play and not the serious sentiments which many critics have found.

Tragic and comic poets faced many similar problems of structure and organisation, and so it is hardly surprising that we find many scenic patterns common to the two genres. Often, as in the cases I have already considered, there may be reasons for postulating the influence of one genre upon the other but, just as commonly, there is no reason to see any direct relationship; rather we can see two dramatists finding similar solutions to similar problems. I choose one illustration. In the opening scene of Sophocles' *Oedipus the King* Oedipus tells the suffering citizens that he has already dispatched Creon to Delphi to learn Apollo's advice as to how to rescue the city from plague; he expresses his surprise at the length of Creon's absence and immediately thereafter Creon's arrival is announced, followed eight verses later by the man himself. A very similar arrangement is found in the scene of Menander's *Dyscolos* which follows immediately after Pan's prologue. Sostratos tells his parasite that he has sent his slave Pyrrhias to find the male relatives of the girl with whom he has fallen in love and he expresses his surprise at the length of time which the slave has been away. At that moment Pyrrhias bursts in as he seeks to escape from the pursuing Cnemon (*Dysc.* 70–81). Here Sophocles and Menander have used the same structural device to direct the audience's attention to the importance of the immediately following entry, but there is no reason to posit any historical link between the two scenes.[9]

A starting-point for a consideration of comedy's use of tragedy will be to examine the ways in which comedy uses the words τραγωιδία, *tragicus* and so on. I begin with a very interesting passage from a lost play of Menander:[10]

εἰ γὰρ ἐγένου σύ, τρόφιμε, τῶν ἄλλων μόνος,
ὅτ' ἔτικτεν ἡ μήτηρ σ', ἐφ' ὧι τε διατελεῖς
πράσσων ἃ βούλει καὶ διευτυχῶν ἀεί,
καὶ τοῦτο τῶν θεῶν τις ὡμολόγηκέ σοι,
ὀρθῶς ἀγανακτεῖς· ἔστι γάρ σ' ἐψευσμένος
ἄτοπόν τε πεπόηκ'· εἰ δ' ἐπὶ τοῖς αὐτοῖς νόμοις
ἐφ' οἷσπερ ἡμεῖς ἔσπασας τὸν ἀέρα
τὸν κοινόν, ἵνα σοι ⟨καὶ⟩ τραγικώτερον λαλῶ,
οἰστέον ἄμεινον ταῦτα καὶ λογιστέον.
τὸ δὲ κεφάλαιον τῶν λόγων· ἄνθρωπος εἶ,
οὗ μεταβολὴν θᾶττον πρὸς ὄγκον καὶ πάλιν
ταπεινότητα ζῶιον οὐδὲν λαμβάνει.
καὶ μάλα δικαίως· ἀσθενέστατον γὰρ ὂν
φύσει μεγίστοις οἰκονομεῖται πράγμασιν·
ὅταν πέσηι δέ, πλεῖστα συντρίβει καλά.
σὺ δ' οὔθ' ὑπερβάλλοντα, τρόφιμ', ἀπώλεσας
ἀγαθά, τὰ νυνί τ' ἐστι μέτριά σοι κακά.
ὥστ' ἀνὰ μέσον που καὶ τὸ λυπηρὸν φέρε.   (Menander fr. 740 K–T)

Master, if when your mother brought you into the world, you were born the only man who could always do as you like and always be prosperous, if some god made this agreement with you, then you are right to be upset. For the god has cheated and injured you. But if on the same terms as the rest of us you draw in the common air of heaven – if I can be a bit tragic for a moment – you must put up with these things philosophically. The essence of the matter is that you're a man and no animal changes more quickly between high and low than man. Rightly so too: for although man is by nature a very weak creature, he has control over (?) matters of the greatest importance and whenever he slips up he brings down with him very many fine things. But, master, the things you've lost were not blessings quite out of the ordinary and your present misfortunes are not too bad. Put up, then, with a grief of a moderate kind.

τραγικώτερον ('rather tragic') in v. 8, appearing in a striking phrase with the very unpoetical verb λαλεῖν,[11] points specifically to the style of the grand phrase ἔσπασας τὸν ἀέρα | τὸν κοινόν ('you draw in the common air of heaven') but more generally also to the quasi-philosophical tone of the slave's speech.[12] Here we see comedy using tragedy as an authority for gnomic wisdom, a repository of sound sense about the laws which govern human life. In a similar vein is a fragment (Philippides fr. 18) in which a slave tells his master that if ever he is unlucky in anything he should remember the wise words of Euripides, 'no man is fortunate in everything'. We find a more obviously comic application of the same attitude in Plautus' *Curculio*:

> antiquom poetam audiui scripsisse in tragoedia
> mulieres duas peiores esse quam unam. res itast. (*Curc.* 591–2)

> I've heard that an old tragedian wrote that two women are worse
> than one. Too true!

Here too tragedy is invoked as an authority which lends validity to the speaker's generalising observation.[13] Rather different in its implications is Menander, *Sicyonios* 260–3 where it is reported that Moschion described the soldier's attempt to claim Athenian citizenship and to assert his rights over the disputed maiden as a κενὴ τραγωιδία ('an empty tragedy'). By this phrase Moschion wishes to imply that the soldier's plea was full of melodramatic exaggeration and absurdly emotional rhetoric; it seems likely that Moschion also treats the soldier's story of separated families and fortuitously appearing recognition-tokens as a nonsense suitable only for use in tragic drama. So too at *Epitrepontes* 1125 τραγικὴ ῥῆσις ('a tragic speech') means both 'a speech taken from a tragedy' and 'a pathetic, melodramatic story'. That Menander was fond of exploiting this double sense of τραγικός is suggested by a sequence of action in the *Aspis*. In order

to fool Smicrines into abandoning his claim to Cleostratos' sister, the
slave Daos thinks of the plan of pretending that Chairestratos has died
so that Smicrines will turn his attention to the greater financial
attractions of the latter's daughter. Daos tells the plotters δεῖ
τραγωιδῆσαι πάθος | ἀλλοῖον ὑμᾶς ('you must stage a tragic and
unpleasant misfortune'). That the melodrama which Daos has in mind
is specifically connected with tragedy becomes clear when the plan is
put into operation. In the opening scene of the third act Daos recites
for the benefit of Smicrines, whom he knows to be within earshot,
many exclamations of despair taken from tragedy:

ΔΑΟΣ   "οὐκ ἔστιν ὅστις π[άντ' ἀνὴρ εὐδαιμονεῖ."
       πάλιν εὖ διαφόρως. ὦ πολ[υτίμητοι θεοί,
       ἀπροσδοκήτου πράγματος καὶ ἀ[
ΣΜΙΚΡΙΝΗΣ   Δᾶε κακόδαιμον, ποῖ τρέχεις; ΔΑΟΣ καὶ τοῦτό που
       "τύχη τὰ θνητῶν πράγματ' οὐκ εὐβουλία."
       ὑπέρευγε. "θεὸς μὲν αἰτίαν φύει βροτοῖς,
       ὅταν κακῶσαι δῶμα παμπήδην θέληι."
       Αἰσχύλος ὁ σεμνά – ΣΜΙΚ. γνωμολογεῖς, τρισάθλιε;
ΔΑΟΣ   "ἄπιστον, ἄλογον, δεινόν." ΣΜΙΚ. οὐδὲ παύσεται;
ΔΑΟΣ   "τί δ' ἐστ' ἄπιστον τῶν ἐν ἀνθρώποις κακῶν; "
       ὁ Καρκίνος φήσ'. "ἐν μιᾶι γὰρ ἡμέραι
       τὸν εὐτυχῆ τίθησι δυστυχῆ θεός."
       εὖ πάντα ταῦτα, Σμικρίνη. ΣΜΙΚ. λέγεις δὲ τί;
ΔΑΟΣ   ἀδελφός – ὦ Ζεῦ, πῶς φράσω; – σχεδόν τι σου
       τέθνηκεν. ΣΜΙΚ. ὁ λαλῶν ἀρτίως ἐνταῦθ' ἐμοί;
       τί παθών; ΔΑΟΣ χολή, λύπη τις, ἔκστασις φρενῶν,
       πνιγμός. ΣΜΙΚ. Πόσειδον καὶ θεοί, δεινοῦ πάθους.
ΔΑΟΣ   "οὐκ ἔστιν οὐδὲν δεινὸν ὧδ' εἰπεῖν ἔπος
       οὐδὲ πάθος –" ΣΜΙΚ. ἀποκναίεις σύ. ΔΑΟΣ "τὰς γὰρ
       συμφορὰς
       ἀπροσδοκήτους δαίμον[ες δι]ώρισαν."
       Εὐριπίδου τοῦτ' ἐστί, τὸ δὲ Χαιρήμονος,
       οὐ τῶν τυχόντων.   (*Aspis* 407–28)

DAOS   'No man is fortunate in everything.' That too is a
         beauty. O reverend gods, what an unexpected grief!
SMICRINES   Daos, damn you, where are you running to?
D.   This too is perhaps appropriate: 'The affairs of men not
         prudence but luck controls.' Very good indeed. 'When
         god wishes utterly to destroy a house, he plants the guilt
         in men.' Aeschylus, a noble poet...
S.   Are you reciting maxims, you idiot?

DAOS	'Beyond belief, beyond reason, terrible.'
SMICRINES	Will he not stop?
D.	'What of mortal ills surpasses belief?' that's Carcinos.
	'In one day gods make the happy man unhappy.' These
	are all splendid observations, Smicrines.
S.	What are you on about?
D.	Your brother – O Zeus, how shall I say it? – is all but
	dead.
S.	The one who was here talking to me a moment ago?
	What happened?
D.	Bile, grief, an attack of madness, choking!
S.	Poseidon and the gods! How terrible!
D.	'There is no tale so terrible to tell, no disaster...'
S.	You'll kill me.
D.	'For the gods ordained that misfortunes strike without
	warning.' That's Euripides, the other's Chairemon; no
	second-raters.

This string of tragic tags would be funny enough on its own, but it is Daos' remarks between the various quotations and his identification of their sources, both of which clearly indicate that Daos is in complete control of himself, which anchor this scene firmly in farce; Smicrines' increasing frustration is very amusing. Whether Daos' elaborate scheme is modelled on the plot of any particular tragedy is uncertain,[14] but it is clearly legitimate to speak of 'parody' in this scene. In watching Daos as he rants we do not simply regard the quotations from tragedy as part of a skilful plan: we are also made to see how banal and pretentious the quotations themselves are.

The link between the use of tragic language and emotional or melodramatic situations is a very close one. Feigned emotion (as in Daos' plot in the *Aspis*) is often, both in drama and real life, expressed in a much more exaggerated form than real feeling, and examples of this in comedy are not hard to find. In the *Casina*, the maid Pardalisca bursts out of the house in a charade designed to terrify the old lecher Lysidamus:

nulla sum, nulla sum, tota tota occidi,
cor metu mortuomst, membra miserae tremunt,
nescio unde auxili, praesidi, perfugi
mi aut opum copiam comparem aut expetam:
tanta factu modo mira miris modis
intus uidi, nouam atque integram audaciam.   (*Casina* 621–6)

I am nothing! I am nothing! Dead, completely dead. My heart has
stopped from fear, my limbs tremble. Woe is me! Where shall I find
help, protection, refuge, aid? Where shall I look? So amazing are the
amazing things I have just seen inside: a new, unheard-of outrage.

This song draws upon the audience's familiarity with similar outbursts
in tragedy, and a close parallel (in both language and metre) is in fact
preserved in a lament by Andromache from a tragedy of Ennius:[15]

> quid petam praesidi aut exequar? quoue nunc
> auxilio exili aut fugae freta sim?
> arce et urbe orba sum. quo accedam? quo applicem?
>
> (Ennius scaen. 81–3 Jocelyn)

What protection can I seek or follow? What help in exile or flight
can I find? No more do I have citadel or city. Where shall I go? To
whom shall I turn?

Another example of feigned emotion occurs in the scene in the *Miles
Gloriosus* where the courtesan Acroteleutium pretends to be madly in
love with the ludicrous soldier:

> si pol me nolet ducere uxorem, genua amplectar
> atque opsecrabo; alio modo, si non quibo impetrare,
> consciscam letum: uiuere sine illo scio me non posse.   (*MG* 1239–41)

If he will not marry me, I shall embrace his knees and beg. If all else
fails, I shall do away with myself. I know that I cannot live without
him.

Here a melodramatic and emotional utterance is clothed in suitably
elevated language (*consciscam letum*).[16] Not all emotion in comedy is,
however, feigned. Our text of the *Aspis* of Menander begins with a
lament by the slave Daos for his master who, so Daos believes, has
perished on a military campaign:

>] ἡμέραν ἄγω
> ὦ τρόφιμε, τὴν νῦν, οὐδὲ διαλογίζομαι
> παραπλήσι᾽ ὡς τότ᾽ ἤλπισ᾽ ἐξορμώμεν[ος.
> ὤιμην γὰρ εὐδο[ξο]ῦντα καὶ σωθέντα σε
> ἀπὸ στρατείας ἐν βίωι τ᾽ εὐσχήμονι
> ἤδη τὸ λοιπὸν καταβιώσεσθαί τινι,
> στρατηγὸν ἢ σύμβουλον ὠνομασμένον,

καὶ τὴν ἀδελφήν, ἧσπερ ἐξώρμας τότε
ἕνεκα, σεαυτοῦ νυμφίωι καταξίωι
συνοικιεῖν ποθεινὸν ἥκοντ᾽ οἴκαδε,
ἐμοί τ᾽ ἔσεσθαι τῶν μακρῶν πόνων τινὰ
ἀνάπαυσιν εἰς τὸ γῆρας εὐνοίας χάριν.
νῦν δὲ σὺ μὲν οἴχει παραλόγως τ᾽ ἀνήρπασαι,
ἐγὼ δ᾽ ὁ παιδαγωγός, ⟨ὦ⟩ Κλεόστρατε,
τὴν οὐχὶ σώσασάν σε τήνδ᾽ ἐλήλυθα
ἀσπίδα κομίζων ὑπὸ δὲ σοῦ σεσωμένην
πολλάκις· ἀνὴρ γὰρ ἦσθα τὴν ψυχὴν μέγας,
εἰ καί τις ἄλλος.   (*Aspis* 1–18)

This is [a sad] day, master, and things have not turned out as I
hoped when I set out. I thought that you would come back safe and
covered in glory from the expedition and that you would live the rest
of your life in proper style with the title of General or Adviser. I
thought that after your happy return you would marry your sister,
for whose sake you set out, to a man worthy of you, and that as a
reward for my kindly services I would enjoy a rest from these long
toils in my old age. But now, contrary to my expectations, you are
gone and snatched away, and I your tutor (*paidagōgos*), O
Cleostratos, have brought back this shield which did not save you
though you often saved it. For you were a man of spirit, if anyone was.

Here the language is elevated, the metre closer to the norms of tragedy
than to those of comedy and the passage replete with echoes of extant
laments, both real and literary.[17] The sombre sound of tragedy suits
Daos' sombre mood, and the elevated, rhetorical style suits a slave
who, in earlier years, had been responsible for his young master's
education.

Sincere emotion also can, of course, be funny if it is expressed in
a ludicrous or exaggerated way, and I now select a few examples of
the use of tragic language in these contexts. In the *Mercator*, the
hapless young lover Charinus greets the news that his father has seen
his new girl-friend with the following exclamation:

nequiquam, mare, supterfugi a tuis tempestatibus:
equidem me iam censebam esse in terra atque in tuto loco,
uerum uideo med ad saxa ferri saeuis fluctibus.   (*Merc.* 195–7)

O sea, in vain have I escaped from your storms! I thought that I was
now on the safety of dry land; I see, however, that terrible waves are
driving me onto the rocks.

Here the address to the sea is melodramatic and paratragic,[18] and this is in keeping with much of Charinus' subsequent absurd behaviour (cf. below pp. 128–9). In Menander's *Samia* the reaction of the intellectually humble Niceratos to the discovery of Chrysis' 'promiscuity' is similarly expressed in paratragic language:

> ἀλλ' ἐγὼ πρὸς τοῖσιν ἄλλοις τὴν τὰ δείν' εἰργασμένην
> εἰσεδεξάμην μελάθροις τοῖς ἐμοῖς.   (*Samia* 516–17)

On top of everything else I received this criminal into my abode.

μελάθροις ('abode') is a word not normally used in comedy, and its unusual prosody (⌣−−) also betrays a debt to the style of tragedy. So too, in the same play, Demeas' initially violent reaction to what he believes he has discovered is expressed in tragic quotation:

> ὦ πόλισμα Κεκροπίας χθονός,
> ὦ ταναὸς αἰθήρ, ὦ – τί, Δημέα, βοᾶις;   (*Samia* 325–6)

O city of the land of Cecrops, O o'erstretching ether, O – why do you scream, Demeas?

So also in the *Epitrepontes* Charisios expresses his self-disgust with an echo of Euripides' *Orestes* (cf. E. *Or.* 922):

> ἐγώ τις ἀναμάρτητος εἰς δόξαν βλέπων
> καὶ τὸ καλὸν ὅ τι πότ' ἐστὶ καὶ ταἰσχρὸν σκοπῶν,
> ἀκέραιος, ἀνεπίπληκτος αὐτὸς τῶι βίωι...   (*Epitr.* 908–10)

I, the blameless one, with my eyes fixed on reputation and my mind concerned with discerning what is honourable and what shameful, pure and beyond reproach in my own life...

Charisios' highly excited state almost naturally expresses itself in the language of tragedy, and we are prepared for this elevated tone by the reference in vv. 908–9 to moral philosophy of a kind in which comic characters rarely indulge.

A type of scene related to the charade of the *Aspis* is the grandiose behaviour of Plautine slaves who celebrate their 'achievements' in language borrowed from the higher genres of poetry and from Roman political, military and religious life. I choose two examples where the

124

exploitation of tragic style is particularly clear. In the *Pseudolus* the scheming slave glories in his trickery:

PSEUDOLVS io te, te, turanne, te, te ego, qui imperitas Pseudolo,
quaero quoi ter trina triplicia, tribus modis tria gaudia,
artibus tribus tris demeritas dem laetitias, de tribus
fraude partas per malitiam, per dolum et fallacias;
in libello hoc opsignato ad te attuli pauxillulo.
CALIDORVS illic homost. CHARINVS ut paratragoedat carnufex.

(*Pseud.* 703–7)

PSEUDOLUS Io! You, you king, you, you, who give orders to
Pseudolus, you I seek, that I may thrice give you joys,
threefold and triple, three delights in three ways, won by
three arts, by cunning and guile and deceit from three
men won. This is what I bring you sealed up in this tiny
little document.
CALIDORUS That's the man.
CHARINUS How the rascal plays the tragedian!

The second example comes from the great song in the *Bacchides* in which the slave Chrysalus compares his achievement in fooling his old master to the conquest of Troy by the Greeks:

nunc prius quam huc senex uenit, lubet lamentari dum exeat.
o Tróia, o patria, o Pergamum, o Priame periisti senex,
qui misere male mulcabere quadrigentis Philippis aureis.
nam ego has tabellas opsignatas, consignatas quas fero
non sunt tabellae, sed equos quem misere Achiui ligneum.

(*Bacch.* 932–6)

Now before the old man comes out here, I'll take the chance to sing a dirge for him. O Troy, O fatherland, O Pergamum, O aged Priam, you have perished. Wretchedly, in misery will you be stripped of 400 gold coins. For these tablets, signed and sealed, are not tablets but a wooden horse which the Greeks have sent.

The tragic colour of this passage is best appreciated by comparing another verse from the song of the Ennian Andromache to which I have already referred:[19]

o pater, o patria, o Priami domus   (Ennius *scaen.* 87 Jocelyn)

O Father, O fatherland, O house of Priam

In the *Pseudolus* and the *Bacchides* the paratragedy is part of the
amusing pretension of a scheming slave; he sees his own role as
important enough to be expressed in the grand language of comedy's
nobler sister. It may be convenient at this point to say a word about
this aspect of the Roman *cantica* in general. Whether or not those
scholars are correct who posit an origin for the *cantica* in a borrowing
from tragedy (cf. above p. 21), it is clear that the style of these comic
songs has much in common with tragedy, and in broad terms,
therefore, parody may be detected through a combination of situation
and language and not through language alone. Thus, both Pardalisca
in the *Casina* (vv. 621ff.) and the young girls of the *Rudens* (vv. 185ff.)
express their fears in elevated and grand language, but the effect is
quite different in the two plays because of the difference in situation:
Pardalisca is staging a charade, whereas Palaestra and Ampelisca are
really scared. Plautus' use of the higher registers of poetic language
is thus by no means simple or always open to interpretation of only
one kind.

Certain characters in Plautus are noteworthy for a consistently
elevated style of speech. The parasite's daughter in the *Persa* speaks
in a high-minded and serious fashion, and some of her utterances find
their closest parallels in Greek tragedy.[20] The point of this device
seems clear: it is amusing that the parasite, who would do anything,
however base, to get a good meal, has a daughter whose standards of
morality rise a long way above the usual comic level. That the girl also
takes part (and a leading part) in the deception of the *leno* may be put
down to comedy's traditional lack of concern with coherent characterisation, particularly when such a virtue would get in the way of the
humour,[21] and to the fact that everything is justified when dealing with
a *leno*. A second character whose high moral tone is matched by an
elevated diction is Alcumena in the *Amphitruo*. She is the only
adulteress in extant New Comedy, but as she herself is entirely
innocent, Plautus has emphasised her uprightness by turning her into
the epitome of the respected Roman *matrona*.[22] Many critics have
wished to see a heroine of Greek or Roman tragedy behind this
memorable character, and such a view may be helpful in terms of the
development of ancient drama over a long period of time. Nevertheless, we do not have to assume any direct inspiration from tragedy.
Greek comedy too reveals some very high-minded ladies with firm

views about the sanctity of marriage,[23] and it would indeed be surprising, in view of the generally high moral tone of New Comedy (cf. above pp. 12–13), if the free-born married women who appear as characters in such plays did not defend the sternest moral standards.

From the use of paratragic language in comedy we may turn now to scenes and larger units in which the exploitation of tragedy is part of the comic texture. I hope that this survey will make clear that comic poets sought a wide range of different effects with this device and that no single formula can be used to explain every case. First, the appearance of the wretched Cnemon after his rescue from the well at Menander, *Dyscolos* 690ff.

How precisely the stricken Cnemon is brought onto the stage is unclear, but εἰσκυ]κλεῖτ' εἴσω με ('wheel me in') in v. 758 makes it very likely that he appeared on the ἐκκύκλημα or wheeled trolley, so familiar from Aristophanes' parodies of classical tragedy in the *Acharnians* and *Thesmophoriazousai*.[24] This device enabled events taking place inside a stage-house to be represented by temporarily bringing an interior scene into the sight of the spectators; Aristophanes treated the *ekkyklema* as a specifically tragic device which was a fair target for parody. So too in the *Dyscolos*, Cnemon's appearance on the trolley must have immediately evoked a tragic atmosphere for the audience, and the impression was reinforced by the tragic tone of his exchange with Gorgias (θάρρει.::τεθάρρηκα, 'Be of good cheer.' 'I am of good cheer')[25] and perhaps also Sostratos' exclamation, ὦ Ζεῦ Σῶτερ, ἐκτόπου θέας ('Zeus the saviour! What a strange (lit. 'out of place') sight'), where the adjective seems to hint that Cnemon's appearance was unusual on the comic stage, i.e. a borrowing from tragedy.[26] The precise effect of Cnemon's appearance is difficult to assess, but it is clear that a wry humour pervades the whole scene. To fall down a well is so unheroic a fate that it is amusing when the victim of such an accident is made to resemble the stricken Heracles or Hippolytos of tragedy. Cnemon's melodramatic use of his own name, [οὐκέτι] | ὑμῖν ἐνοχλήσει τὸν ἐπίλοιπον γὰρ [χρόνον] | Κνήμων, ('Cnemon will not trouble you in future') finds a parallel in the emotional outburst of the soldier at *Misoumenos* 262–3, εἰ μὴ γὰρ οὗτος δοκιμάσει με, κυρίως | δώσει τε ταύτην, οἴχεται Θρασωνίδης ('if he doesn't approve of me and give her to me as my wife, it's all over with Thrasonides') and of the ridiculous fisherman Gripus at *Rudens*

1288–9, *numquam edepol hodie ad uesperum Gripum inspicietis uiuom* | *nisi uidulus mihi redditur* ('if the box is not returned to me, you'll find Gripus dead by sunset'). In these three instances the emotion is real enough, but our pity is tempered by an important element of amusement. So too Cnemon's speech of self-defence is marked by a very fine balance of seriousness and amusing irony (cf. below pp. 144–5).

Easier to assess than Cnemon's appearance in the *Dyscolos* is *Menaechmi* 831ff., where the travelling brother pretends to be mad in order to scare away his brother's wife and father-in-law. Scenes of madness had a long history in Greek and Roman tragedy,[27] where Orestes and Heracles are the most familiar characters who are afflicted in this way, and also in comedy. Comedies entitled 'The Mad One' were written by Anaxandrides, Diodoros and Diphilos, and in a fragment of Alexis (fr. 3) a character parodies the two verses with which the onset of a fit of madness is marked in Euripides' *Orestes*. Unfortunately the context of that fragment is completely unknown. In the verses of Menander's *Theophoroumene* ('The Girl Possessed') which have survived, it is clear that the girl referred to in the title is suspected of feigning an attack of madness, but not enough survives for us to judge whether this suspicion was correct. Nevertheless it is clear that the mad scene of the *Menaechmi* is an interesting mixture of tragic and comic traditions. At 840ff. Menaechmus pretends to receive orders from Apollo to attack his tormentors, and 'divine voices' were doubtless a stock element in the tragic version of such scenes. We can, however, also trace this sort of joke in comedy as early as the end of Aristophanes' *Clouds*, where the enraged Strepsiades is 'told' by the herm in front of his house to burn down Socrates' school (vv. 1481–5); just as Strepsiades pretends to talk to the statue of Hermes, so too Menaechmus' 'orders' presumably come from the altar of Apollo which was a regular feature of the stage of the *comoedia palliata*.[28] Closely related to this scene is *Mercator* v.2, in which the young lover Charinus pretends to travel around the Aegean in search of his lost girl-friend. Again we have parody of a tragic scene of madness, and a close parallel for such a journey in the mind survives in the account of Heracles' madness in Euripides' *Heracles*.[29] Charinus' trip, unlike the madness of Menaechmus, is however not an isolated incident, but rather the culmination of a series of speeches which have shown him to be a young man of very exaggerated emotions, much given to melodrama (cf. vv. 335ff., 483, 588ff., 613). With hindsight we can see that it was appropriate for Charinus to begin his prologue with a reference to the standard practice of dramatic lovers: he is a character who positively revels in his suffering, who likes to strike a pose for the outside world, whose unhappiness must be seen in order to be real.

The messenger-speech is a type of scene which we particularly associate with tragedy. In comedy also, however, there is a need to report matters that have taken place off-stage, and there are very many such speeches in both Old and New Comedy where no hint of tragic exploitation or of a debt to the older genre can be detected. There are, however, also a number of cases in Aristophanes where messengers employ a tragic style[30] and, although this may sometimes be simply a sign of the excitement which attends the entry of such characters, it probably also indicates that such speeches could be seen as a piece of tragic machinery. Of such scenes we have one certain example in Greek New Comedy, the messenger-speech at Menander, *Sicyonios* 169ff. The messenger begins with a verse whose elevated style is completely at variance with its surrounding linguistic context, ὦ γεραιέ, μεῖνον ἐν παραστά[σιν] δόμων ('Reverend sire, halt in the porch of the abode') and he is answered in like fashion, μένω. τίνος δὲ τοῦτο θωύσ[σεις] χάριν; ('I halt. For what purpose do you cry this request?'). The effect of this very peculiar exchange has been well described as follows: '...the tragic language...must be regarded as a signal of what is afoot. "Here is a messenger such as you know in tragedy."'[31] The long narrative which follows begins and ends with allusions to the two messenger-scenes of Euripides' *Orestes* and recounts how a soldier convinced a public gathering at Eleusis that a young girl and a slave should be entrusted to the care of the priestess until he could prove that the girl was a citizen and that they should not allow them to fall into the hands of a young man of suspicious appearance. The meeting which the first messenger in Euripides' *Orestes* describes is one where the fate of the matricide Orestes and his sister is decided – they are both condemned to death – and so the parallel between the fate of the couple in the *Sicyonios* and of Orestes and Electra is at best a weak one, but the link was enough to give Menander a platform from which to exploit for the pleasure of his audience a famous tragedy with which they were probably very familiar. In the context of the comedy the events at Eleusis are serious and important, but they are related by the messenger in a very lively and colloquial way, and it would be wrong to see the tragic allusions which frame the speech as deepening the emotional level of this report. We may perhaps compare Dicaiopolis' famous account of the origins of the Peloponnesian War in Aristophanes' *Acharnians* (vv. 496–556); the framework of this speech is borrowed from the *Telephos* of Euripides, but the verbal echoes of the tragedy cluster at the beginning and the end of the comic verses.[32] There is of course a world of difference in tone and purpose between the speeches of Dicaiopolis and of Menander's messenger, but the technique for using the audience's knowledge of tragedy is basically the same.

Another motif which comic poets clearly regarded as a borrowing from the tragic repertoire was the 'recognition' (ἀναγνώρισις). Ancient theory traced such scenes in New Comedy back to the influence of classical tragedy (particularly Euripides), and indeed the first full-scale comic recognition-scene which survives is the burlesque of Euripides' *Helen* in the *Thesmophoriazousai*;[33] in the parabasis of the *Clouds* Aristophanes refers to the famous recognition-scene of Aeschylus' *Choephoroi*, and it seems that this link between tragedy and the recognition was never lost. In many comic scenes of recognition and reunion tragic language is used both to emphasise the emotional excitement and perhaps also to acknowledge comedy's debt to tragedy in this matter. A survey of such scenes may begin with the return of Cleostratos, who had been believed dead, in the fourth act of Menander's *Aspis*:

ΚΛΕΟΣΤΡΑΤΟΣ παιητέα δ' ἐσθ' ἡ θύρ[α.
ΔΑΟΣ   [τίς τὴν θύραν;
ΚΛΕΟ.   ἐγώ.
ΔΑΟΣ   τίνα ζητεῖς; ὁ μ[ὲν γὰρ δεσπότης
            τῆς οἰκίας τέθνηκ[ε
ΚΛΕΟ.   τέθνηκεν; οἴμοι δυ[σ
ΔΑΟΣ

            καὶ μὴ 'νόχλει πενθ[οῦσι
ΚΛΕΟ.   οἴμοι τάλας· ὦ θεῖ'. ἀν[
            ἄνθρωπέ μοι κακόδ[αιμον

ΔΑΟΣ

μειράκιον. ὦ Ζεῦ,[

ΚΛΕΟ.   Δᾶε, τί λέγεις;

ΔΑΟΣ   .[

ἔχω σε.   (*Aspis* 499–507)

CLEOSTRATOS	I must knock at the door.
DAOS	[Who's there?]
C.	It's me.
D.	Who do you want? The [master] of the house has died...
C.	Died? Alas!
D.	...Don't disturb us in our grief.
C.	Alas! Alas! O uncle! [Open up], damn you.
D.	...young man. O Zeus...
C.	Daos, what are you saying?
D.	...I hold you.

The very broken state of the text at this point cannot entirely obscure the effect of these verses. Cleostratos here greets the news of his uncle's 'death' (which the audience knows to be feigned) with an emotional exclamation. His repetition of Daos' τέθνηκε ('he has died') recalls the parody of Euripides' *Helen* in the *Thesmophoriazousai*:

ΚΡΙΤΥΛΛΑ οὐκ ἔσθ' ὅπως οὐ ναυτιᾷς ἔτ' ὦ ξένε,

ὅστις ⟨γ'⟩ ἀκούσας ὅτι τέθνηκε Πρωτέας

ἔπειτ' ἐρωτᾷς· "ἔνδον ἐστ' ἢ 'ξώπιος; "

ΕΥΡΙΠΙΔΗΣ αἰαῖ τέθνηκε. ποῦ δ' ἐτυμβεύθη τάφωι;   (Ar. *Thesm.* 882–5)

CRITYLLA	There's no doubt you're still feeling the effects of your voyage, stranger, or else you wouldn't ask whether Proteas is in or out when you've already been told that he's dead.
EURIPIDES	Alas! Dead! In what grave is he entombed?

In the *Aspis* Cleostratos' emotional language does not so much parody the tragic manner as underline the familial affection which all the characters in this play, except Smicrines, reveal. So too ἔχω σε ('I hold you') in v. 508 is in the style normally associated with recognition and reunion. What is particularly noteworthy about this scene (even in its present state of preservation) is Menander's restraint and fine touch in hinting at believable human emotions with a very few words. Rather

Comedy and tragedy

different is the scene in Terence's *Heauton Timorumenos* where the
lovers Antiphila and Clinia are reunited after a long separation:

BACCHIS   quisnam hic adulescens est qui intuitur nos? ANTIPHILA
          ah retine me, obsecro.
B.   amabo quid tibist? A. disperii, perii misera. B. quid
          stupes,
          Antiphila? A. uideon Cliniam an non? B. quem uides?
CLINIA   salue, anime mi. A. o mi Clinia, salue. C. ut uales?
A.   saluom uenisse gaudeo. C. teneone te,
          Antiphila, maxume animo exspectatam meo?
SYRVS   ite intro; nam uos iamdudum exspectat senex.
                                                       (*HT* 403–9)

BACCHIS   Who is that young man looking at us?
ANTIPHILA Ah, hold me, I beg you!
B.   What's wrong, my dear?
A.   Ah me! I'm gone, sinking.
B.   Why are you staring, Antiphila?
A.   Is it Clinia or not?
B.   Who is this?
CLINIA   Welcome, my darling!
A.   O Clinia, welcome!
C.   How are you?
A.   I rejoice that you have arrived safely.
C.   Do I hold you, Antiphila, for whom my soul has so
          longed?
SYRUS   Go inside. The old man has been waiting for you for a
          long time.

Here we cannot speak of 'recognition' as the couple were in fact
expecting to see each other at this point in the play, but the language
and the conventions of the recognition-scene amusingly emphasise the
exaggerated force of their love. A 'recognition' proper occurs in the
Misoumenos when Crateia and her father find each other:

ΔΗΜΕΑΣ ὦ Ζεῦ, τίν' ὄψιν οὐδὲ προσδοκωμένην
        ὁρῶ; ΚΡΑΤΕΙΑ τί βούλει, τηθία; τί μοι λαλεῖς;
        πατὴρ ἐμός; ποῦ; ΔΗΜ. παιδίον Κράτεια. ΚΡΑΤ. τίς
        καλεῖ με; πάππα· χαῖρε πολλά, φίλτατε.
ΔΗΜ.   ἔχω σε, τέκνον. ΚΡΑΤ. ὦ ποθούμενος φανείς,
        ὁρῶ σ' ὃν οὐκ ἂν ᾠόμην ἰδεῖν ἔτι.   (*Mis.* 210–15)

132

DEMEAS O Zeus, what unhoped for sight do I see?
CRATEIA What do you want, nurse? What are you saying? My
         father? Where?
D.   Crateia, my child!
C.   Who calls me? Daddy! Welcome, dearest one!
D.   I hold you, my child!
C.   Oh, how I have longed for you to appear! I thought I
         would never see you again and now I do.

The language of this scene has many parallels in tragedy, and τέκνον
('my child') in v. 214 is scanned in a way common in tragedy but
foreign to comedy;[34] these features stress the joy of the characters and
there seems to be no element of parody in this exchange. Noteworthy
again is the brevity of this scene, which is cut off sharply by the purely
comic entry and speech of the slave Getas, who misunderstands the
reasons for the embrace which he discovers (vv. 216–21), and we
should also observe that the grand language is restricted to Demeas
until his daughter has recognised him. It is almost as if Demeas briefly
infects Crateia with an elevation of language: vv. 214b–15 thus stand
in sharp linguistic contrast to the childish greeting which precedes.

In a quite different category is an exchange in Menander's *Periceiromene* which leads to the recognition by Pataicos of his daughter
Glycera and, in a neat twist, to the realisation by Moschion, who is
eavesdropping on Pataicos and Glycera, that Pataicos is his father also
and that the girl whom he has been pursuing amorously is his own
sister. The scene begins with an examination by father and daughter
of the tokens which were exposed with her at birth and then there
follows a lengthy conversation which imitates the style of tragic
stichomythia. The following excerpt gives some of the flavour of this
scene:

ΠΑΤ.   μόνη δ᾽ ἔκεισο; τοῦτο γὰρ σήμαινέ μοι.
ΓΛΥΚ. οὐ δῆτ᾽, ἀδελφὸν δ᾽ ἐξέθηκε κἀμέ τις.
ΜΟΣΧ. τουτὶ μὲν ἕν μοι τῶν [πάλ]αι ζητουμένων.
ΠΑΤ.   πῶς οὖν ἐχωρίσθητ᾽ ἀπ᾽ ἀλλήλων δίχα;
ΓΛΥΚ. ἔχοιμ᾽ ἂν εἰπεῖν πάντ᾽ ἀκηκουῖά σοι·
       τἀμὰ δέ μ᾽ ἐρώτα, ῥητὰ γὰρ ταῦτ᾽ ἐστί μοι·
       ἐκεῖνα δ᾽ αὐτῆι μὴ φράσειν ὀμώμοκα.
ΜΟΣΧ. καὶ τοῦτό μοι σύσσημον εἴρηκεν σαφές·
       ὀμώμοκεν τῆι μητρί. ποῦ πότ᾽ εἰμὶ γῆς;   (*Periceir.* 785–93)

PATAICOS	Were you exposed alone? Indicate this to me.
GLYCERA	No indeed. Someone exposed both myself and a brother.
MOSCHION	This is one of the things I have long been seeking.
P.	How then were the two of you sundered from each other?
G.	I have heard and thus can tell all. You must question me about my story and I must expound. The other things I swore to her not to reveal.
M.	This too is a clear sign. She swore to my mother. Where am I?

Some modern critics can find no trace of parody here, but at the very least v. 788 (cf. E. fr. 484.3, *HF* 104) and v. 809 (cf. E. *Tr.* 88) clearly point to an amusing pastiche of the tragic idiom; the presence of Moschion, moreover, adds an element of farce to this scene, which works like a fragment of tragedy torn out of its context and deposited in a comic setting. The audience knew well enough that Glycera and Pataicos would find each other before too long and so Menander has devoted most of his energies to entrancing them with the novelty and wit of the method by which the recognition is effected. This scene is a particularly good example of how a dramatist can demand a complex response from the audience: we are amused and concerned at the same time.

I conclude this survey with the play of Menander which, more than any other known to us, consciously exploits a debt to tragic drama. It has long been realised that in the *Epitrepontes* Menander probably had in mind the *Alope* of Euripides, in which a king arbitrated between two shepherds in a dispute about the recognition-tokens found with an exposed baby, who in fact turned out to be the king's grandchild. So too in the *Epitrepontes*, Smicrines acts as arbitrator between two slaves, a shepherd and a charcoal-burner, in a dispute about the trinkets found exposed with a baby, who is to turn out to be Smicrines' grandchild. We do not know whether Menander has included in his arbitration-scene any verbal reminiscences of the *Alope*, although the echoes of Euripides' *Orestes* in the messenger-speech in the *Sicyonios* (cf. above p. 129) make this a not unlikely guess. What is, however, clear is that vv. 326ff. of the *Epitrepontes* direct our attention away from the *Alope* to another tragedy, probably the *Tyro* of Sophocles, and thus it is most unlikely that the Menandrian scene follows its Euripidean model at all closely:

Comedy and tragedy

τεθέασαι τραγωιδούς, οἶδ᾽ ὅτι,
καὶ ταῦτα κατέχεις πάντα. Νηλέα τινὰ
Πελίαν τ᾽ ἐκείνους εὗρε πρεσβύτης ἀνὴρ
αἰπόλος, ἔχων οἵαν ἐγὼ νῦν διφθέραν,
ὡς δ᾽ ἤισθετ᾽ αὐτοὺς ὄντας αὐτοῦ κρείττονας,
λέγει τὸ πρᾶγμ᾽, ὡς εὗρεν, ὡς ἀνείλετο.
ἔδωκε δ᾽αὐτοῖς πηρίδιον γνωρισμάτων,
ἐξ οὗ μαθόντες πάντα τὰ καθ᾽ αὑτοὺς σαφῶς
ἐγένοντο βασιλεῖς οἱ τότ᾽ ὄντες αἰπόλοι.   (*Epitr.* 325–33)

You've seen tragedies, I know, and you understand all these things.
There was an old goatherd, wearing a skin just like me, who found
Neleus – was it? – and Pelias, and when he realised that they were
superior to him, he told them the whole story: how he found them,
picked them up. He gave them a wallet of recognition-tokens, and so
they learned who they were and those who had been goatherds
became kings.

There need not be any tension between real life and drama or any
suggestion of 'illusion-breaking' when tragedy is mentioned on the
comic stage, as it was presumably not unusual for citizens in real life
to discuss or refer to what they had seen in the theatre,[35] but in this
instance I believe that it is legitimate to see a significant element of
theatrical self-consciousness in the speech which Menander puts into
the charcoal-burner's mouth. The reference to tragedies within a
scene modelled on a tragic forerunner shows us Menander lightly
toying with the motifs of his plot. It is here a very pleasing effect, as
it acknowledges the dramatic debt without in fact parodying the tragic
model. That we are justified in such an interpretation is partly
confirmed by the last scene of our text of this play. The slave Onesimos
hints to Smicrines at what has happened by means of assigned
quotations from the *Auge* of Euripides (*Epitr.* 1123–5),[36] and this again
identifies the action of the comedy with a pattern familiar from
tragedy. Unfortunately, the plot of Euripides' *Auge* is obscure,[37] and
so we cannot tell just how near the plot of the *Epitrepontes* is to this
tragic pattern. Nevertheless, I would suggest that Menander is subtly
reminding his audience that they are watching a play and one with a
long and distinguished ancestry. This self-consciousness is clear in the
slave's words at vv. 1121–2, νυνὶ δ᾽ ἀναγνωρισμὸς αὐτοῖς γέγονε καὶ |
ἅπαντ᾽ ἀγαθά ('now they have recognised each other and everything

is fine'). It seems probable that ἀναγνωρισμός ('recognition') is here used as a semi-technical term of the theatre and of dramatic criticism.[38] So too in vv. 1108–9, καταλαμβάνεις | διαλλαγὰς λύσεις τ' ἐκείνων τῶν κακῶν ('you find reconciliation and an end (*lusis*) to those troubles'), there is language that we recognise from ancient discussions of drama.[39] λύσις is a favourite word of Aristotle (cf. LSJ s.v. II 4), and here we should remember that it is used in the *Poetics* to denote that part of a tragedy in which the problems are 'resolved' one way or another (1455 b24–31).[40] We are partly prepared for Onesimos' use of such terms by the immediately preceding passage (vv. 1084ff.) in which he uses quasi-philosophical puzzles to infuriate Smicrines. The total effect is rather as though Onesimos were to say to Smicrines (and to the audience) 'This is the Happy Ending'; the discomfiture of Smicrines has indeed something in common with the ritual discomfiture of the villain at the end of a melodrama. Menander's technique in the final scene of the *Epitrepontes* may well be thought to indicate a mature and experienced dramatist revelling in the opportunities that a very long theatrical tradition and a very experienced audience afforded him.

6

The didactic element

From its earliest beginnings Greek poetry was intimately bound to the social, moral and political life of the societies which gave birth to it. Poetry was not the plaything of a cloistered elite, but a powerful medium for the transmission of ideas. In the epics of Homer the element of moral teaching is as clear as in the more overtly didactic poetry of Hesiod. The poets of the following period, known as the Archaic Age, often speak directly to their fellow citizens on matters of social and political importance; in the case of men such as Archilochos, Alcaios, Solon and Theognis, we see poets taking a very active role in the public affairs of their societies. The drama of fifth-century Athens is the direct heir to this tradition. Classical tragedy, no less than Aristophanic comedy, is a product of the *polis* and reflects continually upon the life of the *polis*. Plays such as *The Persians* and *The Eumenides* of Aeschylus, the *Antigone* of Sophocles and *The Trojan Women* of Euripides are merely very striking instances of this general truth. On the comic stage, Aristophanes stresses again and again his role as a social and political reformer and, although we must not simply accept these claims at face value, there can be no doubt that drama was an accepted medium in which to air matters of general importance to the citizens. As we have already noted however (above p. 13), the situation appears to have altered completely by the time of Menander. Poets no longer preach to their audience directly, and what political (in a narrow sense) content there is in these plays is often of a general, and not a specifically Athenian, kind.[1] The comedies of Plautus are indeed full of references to contemporary Roman social and political institutions, but the Roman comic stage was never an arena for serious political discussion. What we do find in Plautus is a number of passages in which a character proposes legal reform. In the *Persa*, for example, the parasite Saturio introduces himself to the audience as a man who has inherited his vocation from his ancestors (vv. 53–61); he then proceeds to reject another possible way of earning a living:[2]

neque quadrupulari me uolo, neque enim decet
sine meo periclo ire aliena ereptum bona,
neque illi qui faciunt mihi placent. planen loquor?
nam publicae rei causa quicumque id facit
magis quam sui quaesti, animus induci potest,
eum esse ciuem et fidelem et bonum.
[*Lacuna of one verse*]
si legirupam qui damnet, det in publicum
dimidium; atque etiam in ea lege adscribier:
ubi quadrupulator quempiam iniexit manum,
tantidem ille illi rursus iniciat manum,
ut aequa parti prodeant ad trisuiros.
si id fiat, ne isti faxim nusquam appareant,
qui hic albo rete aliena oppugnant bona.   (*Persa* 62–74)

I don't want to live by the proceeds of prosecutions, and it's hardly
fitting for me to snatch other people's possessions without taking any
risks myself. I don't approve of people who do that. Do I make
myself clear? If someone does this for the public good rather than
for private profit, I may be prepared to accept that he is a loyal and
good citizen... If someone brings a lawbreaker to book, he should
give half the proceeds to the public purse. The following too should
be added to the law: if a professional informer summons a man to
court, the latter may in turn summon the informer for the same
amount, so that they may appear before the court on a basis of
parity. If this were to happen, I guarantee that we would see a lot
less of those men who attack other people's property with their white
nets [i.e. tablets of indictment].

The apparent earnestness of these remarks forms an amusing contrast
to the obviously farcical character of the parasite who delivers them.
This is a humorous technique which is very common in Plautus; we
may compare the purely humorous effect of the plea for the equality
of the sexes delivered by the old maid, Syra, in the *Mercator* (cf. above
pp. 86–7).

In passages such as these from the *Persa* and the *Mercator* we can
see one way in which New Comedy inherited and adapted the didactic
role of earlier comedy. Of greater importance, however, is the general
moral and ethical tone of New Comedy, and in this chapter I wish
to consider two aspects of these plays which may grouped under the
broad heading of 'the didactic element': the place of moralising in
comedy, and the links between comedy and contemporary philosophy.

Moralising in comedy

By the term 'moralising' I mean general reflection upon human behaviour and the laws which govern human relationships; this term is necessarily rather wide and imprecise, but the danger of misunderstanding seems small.

Before the papyrus discoveries of this century, by far the largest body of fragments of Greek New Comedy consisted of moralising excerpts quoted in later authors for their beauty or their utility. The ancients saw it as perfectly natural to seek moral comfort and guidance in the works of poets, and New Comedy was found to be particularly rich in passages of an improving kind. So too were the dramas of Euripides, and we can see clearly in plays such as the *Electra* and the *Orestes* just how extensive such passages could be and how Euripides seems to have foreshadowed New Comedy in this, as in so many features. If we are looking for uplifting sentiments in Euripides or Menander, then we can excerpt particular passages and apply them to our own situation without regard for the dramatic context in which they originally appeared; this is precisely what the anthologists, ethical philosophers and schoolmasters of later antiquity did. The dangers to the proper appreciation of a poet's art inherent in this technique may be amply illustrated. Two famous instances concern single verses. In Menander's *Dis Exapaton* (fr. 4) the beautiful verse ὃν οἱ θεοὶ φιλοῦσιν ἀποθνήισκει νέος ('whom the gods love dies young') is not part of a sad lament, but is spoken by an impudent slave to mock his stupid and aged master (cf. Plaut. *Bacch.* 816–17). So too in Terence's *Heauton Timorumenos* the memorable sentiment *homo sum: humani nil a me alienum puto* ('I'm a man; I consider nothing which concerns men no concern of mine', v. 77) is not an expression of serious social conscience but a ploy by a self-important busybody to defend his right to meddle in his neighbour's affairs.[3] Too often also anthologists did not preserve the reactions of others on stage to a piece of moralising, and these reactions are vital to our assessment of the use which the poet makes of general reflection. This is well illustrated by a sequence in Plautus' *Rudens*. After the casket of recognition-tokens has allowed Daemones to be reunited with his long-lost daughter, the hapless fisherman, Gripus, comes to ask him for the casket which Gripus still believes contains gold. Instead of the casket, however, he receives from Daemones a lecture on human greed:

> o Gripe, Gripe, in aetate hominum plurumae
> fiunt trasennae, ubi decipiuntur dolis.
> atque edepol in eas plerumque esca imponitur:
> quam si quis auidus poscit escam auariter,
> decipitur in trasenna auaritia sua.
> ille qui consulte, docte atque astute cauet,
> diutine uti bene licet partum bene.
> mihi istaec uidetur praeda praedatum irier,
> ut cum maiore dote abeat quam aduenerit.
> egone ut quod ad me adlatum esse alienum sciam
> celem? minime istuc faciet noster Daemones.   (*Rudens* 1235–45)

O Gripus, Gripus, life is full of traps wherein mankind is treacherously caught. Usually these traps are baited and if some greedy soul goes too eagerly for the bait, he's caught in the trap through his own greed. The man who takes sensible, wise and shrewd precautions may enjoy long use of what he has gained honourably. Plunder of the other kind will, I think, be plundered itself and, when it leaves, more will go than originally came. Am I to conceal property which I received and which I know to belong to another? The Daemones you know will never do that.

These noble sentiments are then completely undercut by the following speech of Gripus:

> spectaui ego pridem comicos ad istunc modum
> sapienter dicta dicere, atque eis plaudier,
> quom illos sapientis mores monstrabant poplo:
> sed quom inde suam quisque ibant diuorsi domum,
> nullus erat illo pacto ut illi iusserant.   (*Rudens* 1249–53)

Before now I've watched people in comedies mouthing wise sayings like this and winning applause for preaching these upright morals to the audience; but when everyone scattered homewards, not a single one acted as the actors had urged.

These verses, in which the reference to 'people in comedies' shows us the poet toying with the dramatic illusion, reveal Gripus as the suspicious servant with no time for the platitudes and rather ostentatious virtue of Daemones. Like Alfred Doolittle in George Bernard Shaw's *Pygmalion*, Gripus has seen through the self-perpetuating barrier of 'middle-class morality', and his realism prevents us from taking too serious a view of Daemones' moralising. Here we can see clearly the importance of the scenic context to an assessment of any moralising passage.

No subject for general reflection is more common in New Comedy than the role of Luck or Chance (Τύχη, Fortuna) in human affairs. The violent upheavals in the Greek world caused by the military successes of Alexander the Great must have given a new urgency to this old topic;[4] Τύχη in fact delivers the prologue of Menander's *Aspis*, which concerns a case of mistaken identity after a disastrous battle. The characters of New Comedy are much more exposed to the whims of Fortune than were the characters of Aristophanes; the latter tended to control, rather than be controlled by, changing circumstances. There is, however, an ambivalence inherent in the role of Luck in New Comedy, and this was exploited by the comic poets. In as much as comedy sought to represent 'the real world' under the cover of a reasonably continuous dramatic illusion, events on the stage could be ascribed to Luck or Chance just as they would be in everyday life. Nevertheless, both the audience and the actors knew that events do not happen on the stage 'by chance' but because a conscious intention, the dramatist's, and a positive force, dramatic necessity, make them happen. The tension between these two levels of causation can be a source of humour. In Aristophanes' *Knights*, for example, a sausage-seller enters the stage 'as if by divine providence' at the very moment when a sausage-seller is needed (vv. 144–7); no doubt a skilful actor could enunciate these words so as to gain the maximum effect. A rather similar, but much more extended, instance occurs in Plautus' *Pseudolus*. In this play the soldier to whom the *leno* is threatening to sell the young lover's girl sends his servant, Harpax ('Snatcher'), to the *leno* with a letter instructing him to hand over the girl to the bearer of the letter. Harpax is, however, intercepted by the lover's slave, who gives his name to the play, and the letter thus falls into the wrong hands. After Harpax has left the stage, Pseudolus reflects on how opportune his arrival was, and he then proceeds to some general reflections upon the role of Fortuna:

> centum doctum hominum consilia sola haec deuincit dea,
> Fortuna. atque hoc uerum est: proinde ut quisque Fortuna utitur
> ita praecellet atque exinde sapere eum omnes dicimus.

bene ubi quod scimus consilium accidisse, hominem catum
eum esse declaramus, stultum autem illum quoi uortit male.
stulti hau scimus frustra ut simus, quom quod cupienter dari
petimus nobis, quasi quid in rem sit possimus noscere.
certa mittimus dum incerta petimus; atque hoc euenit
in labore atque in dolore, ut mors obrepat interim.
sed iam satis est philosophatum. nimis diu et longum loquor.

(Pseud. 678–87)

The plans of one hundred clever men are outdone by this one
goddess, Fortune. The truth is that just as each man uses Fortune,
so he excels and we all call him wise. When we know that someone's
plan worked out well, we call him a clever man; foolish is the man
whose plan didn't work out. In our foolishness we do not know how
pointlessly we act, when we eagerly want something to be given to
us, as if we knew what was good for us. We lose what is ours in
seeking what we don't have. As we sweat and suffer, death creeps up
on us. But that's enough philosophy. I'm talking far too much.

These beautiful verses demand a complex response from the audience.
There is, on the one hand, a pleasant contrast between Pseudolus'
habitual self-confidence and the humility with which he acknowledges
the pre-eminent role of Fortuna. Nevertheless, the great stress which
Pseudolus lays upon this theme calls our attention to its unspoken
irony: coincidences such as Harpax's opportune arrival are a basic
element in the plots of New Comedy, and it is gently amusing that
this particular instance should lead a slave to reflect at length on the
futility of all human endeavour. The irony does not, of course, detract
from the power of the verses to move us as being a statement of an
acknowledged and unhappy truth.

The instability of Fortune is very often linked in New Comedy to
the themes of wealth and poverty, themes dear to the heart of the
characters who inhabit the stage-world which Menander and his
contemporaries created. In the *Dyscolos*, which contains much more
moralising than any other of Menander's plays which we possess, an
important role is given to these related themes of Fortune and wealth.
In the second act, the young countryman Gorgias accosts Sostratos,
the son of a wealthy family, whom he wrongly believes to be planning
an assault upon his sister. In a laboured and formal style[5] Gorgias
delivers a rather confused lecture on the proper behaviour of the rich

and the poor in the face of the instability of Fortune (vv. 271–87). Sostratos should not commit acts of injustice in the confidence of his wealth, as such acts will hasten the change in his fortunes; rather he should show himself deserving of his riches. Gorgias' ideas here are entirely conventional, but as a poor man struggling to overcome considerable problems (cf. vv. 23–9) we feel that he has some right to sermonise, even if his lack of rhetorical polish also amuses us. Quite different in its effect, however, is the matching lecture which Sostratos delivers to his father in the fifth act when the latter seems reluctant to welcome Gorgias as a son-in-law in addition to the poor daughter-in-law he has just acquired:

περὶ χρημάτων λαλεῖς, ἀβεβαίου πράγματος.
εἰ μὲν γὰρ οἶσθα ταῦτα παραμενοῦντά σοι
εἰς πάντα τὸν χρόνον, φύλαττε μηδενὶ
τοῦ σοῦ μεταδιδούς· ὧν δὲ μὴ σὺ κύριος
εἶ, μηδὲ σαυτοῦ τῆς τύχης δὲ πάντ' ἔχεις,
μή τι φθονοίης, ὦ πάτερ, τούτων τινί.
αὕτη γὰρ ἄλλωι, τυχὸν ἀναξίωι τινί,
παρελομένη σοῦ πάντα προσθήσει πάλιν.
διόπερ ἐγώ σε φημὶ δεῖν, ὅσον χρόνον
εἶ κύριος, χρῆσθαι σε γενναίως, πάτερ,
αὐτόν, ἐπικουρεῖν πᾶσιν, εὐπόρους ποεῖν
ὡς ἂν δύνηι πλείστους διὰ σαυτοῦ. τοῦτο γὰρ
ἀθάνατόν ἐστι, κἂν ποτε πταίσας τύχηις,
ἐκεῖθεν ἔσται ταὐτὸ τοῦτό σοι πάλιν.
πολλῶι δὲ κρεῖττόν ἐστιν ἐμφανὴς φίλος
ἢ πλοῦτος ἀφανής, ὃν σὺ κατορύξας ἔχεις.   (*Dysc.* 797–812)

It's money you're talking about, an unstable commodity. If you know that you're going to keep your money for all time, then guard it and don't give anyone a share. But, Father, don't begrudge someone a share in what's not really yours to control – all of your property belongs to Fortune, not to you. She might well take it all away from you and give it to someone else, perhaps someone who doesn't deserve it. Therefore, Father, I say that for as long as it is in your power, you yourself should use it generously, should help everyone and see that by your efforts as many people as possible have enough money. This does not perish, and if ever you should stumble yourself, you will receive like repayment back. For a friend you can see is far better than the hidden assets which you keep buried in the earth.

This extremely banal collection of commonplaces merely infuriates Sostratos' father, but he is won over in the end (as was Cnemon also) by Gorgias' honest virtue. It is amusing that Sostratos' purely conventional wisdom has been acquired in the course of the play, largely from Gorgias' own sermon in the second act. As recently as vv. 764–70 Gorgias had returned to the theme of riches and the mutability of Fortune; this teaching Sostratos can now turn on his father. Comedy often contrasts youthful idealism with the experienced realism of the older generation.[6] That it is idealism which triumphs is in keeping with the role of wish-fulfilment in comedy (cf. above p. 12).

The speeches of Gorgias and Sostratos frame the romantic plot of the *Dyscolos*; the crucial point in the other main strand of the play, the presentation of Cnemon's character, comes with Cnemon's great speech of self-defence in the fourth act. We have already seen how this speech is set off from the preceding context by a metrical change and the evocation of tragedy at Cnemon's entry (cf. above pp. 45, 127). His accident in the well and subsequent rescue by Gorgias have shown Cnemon that he cannot be completely independent of others as he had thought (vv. 713–17), and so he now reveals what led him to his life of almost complete isolation. He had observed that in their relations with each other men were motivated by considerations of profit (κέρδος) rather than genuine concern (εὔνοια) and so he had resolved to have nothing to do with human society.[7] Gorgias has proved himself an exception to the general rule and thus he is now entrusted with the management of Cnemon's affairs. There is, however, no sign of another such selfless soul, so that there is no reason for Cnemon to change his way of life; he asks only to live out his life in peace and quiet. It is a pleasing irony of the situation that the accident which has destroyed Cnemon's illusion of complete self-sufficiency also allows him to divest himself of his obligations towards his daughter by handing her over to the care of Gorgias. He has finally achieved total isolation. It is from this lonely position that he now offers his prescription for the ills of the world:

εἰ τοιοῦτ]οι πάντες ἦσαν, οὔτε τὰ δικαστήρια
ἦν ἄν, οὔθ' αὐτοὺς ἀπῆγον εἰς τὰ δεσμωτήρια,
οὔτε πόλεμος ἦν, ἔχων δ' ἂν μέτρι' ἕκαστος ἠγάπα.   (*Dysc.* 743–5)

If everyone was like me,[8] there would be no law-courts, men would not lead each other off to prison, there would be no war. Everyone would have enough to live on and be content.

These memorable verses have great appeal for modern sentiment, but we must not overlook their humour. If everyone was like Cnemon, there would not only be no social evils, there would not be any society, unless it were one which resembled Homer's Island of the Cyclopes.[9] Cnemon's speech thus treads a fine line between the serious and the farcical, the stirring and the absurdly maudlin. Ancient poetry abounds in both serious and ironic proposals for reforming the world,[10] but it is rare to find a speech with as many different resonances as Cnemon's. We may perhaps compare Propertius' desire to abolish war:

> qualem si cuncti cuperent decurrere uitam
>   et pressi multo membra iacere mero,
> non ferrum crudele neque esset bellica nauis,
>   nec nostra Actiacum uerteret ossa mare,
> nec totiens propriis circum oppugnata triumphis
>   lassa foret crinis soluere Roma suos.   (Prop. 2.15.41–6)

If everyone wanted to pass a life [of love] like mine, and stretch out, limbs heavy with deep drinking, there would be no grim iron nor ships of war, nor would the sea of Actium churn over the bones of our citizens and Rome, so often besieged on every side by victories over her own people, would not grow weary in letting down her hair in mourning.

The similarity lies not merely in the end desired, but also in the moral ambivalence of the means to be used.

It is broadly true that in New Comedy 'the good' are rewarded and 'the bad' punished,[11] and so we will not be surprised to find passages of general reflection extolling virtue or lamenting the decline of moral standards. Nevertheless, comedy also highlights the gap between words and deeds or between virtuous intentions and their results, and this forces us again to pay particular attention to the context surrounding passages of moralising. A group of Plautine passages concerned with 'the good slave' well illustrates this.[12] In the *Menaechmi*, Messenio, the slave of the wandering brother, is a very prim and virtuous servant (cf. vv. 258–72, 338–50, 375–445). At v. 966 he enters with a long song which contrasts the good slave (such as himself) who does his duty even in his master's absence and who has a healthy fear of punishment with the lazy servant who is merely storing up a beating for himself. Here is the opening passage:

> spectamen bono seruo id est, qui rem erilem
> procurat, uidet, conlocat cogitatque,
> ut absente ero rem eri diligenter
>   tutetur quam si ipse adsit aut rectius.
> tergum quam gulam, crura quam uentrem oportet
>   potiora esse quoi cor modeste situmst.
>   recordetur id, qui nihili sunt, quid eis preti
> detur ab suis eris, ignauis, improbis uiris:
>   uerbera, compedes,
> molae, lassitudo, fames, frigus durum,
>   haec pretia sunt ignauiae.   (*Men.* 966–76)

The test of a good servant who looks after his master's interests – sees to them, arranges things, gives careful thought – is that he protects his master's interests just as diligently when the master's not there as when he is, or even more carefully in fact. The servant with any sense will give more thought to his back than his gullet and to his legs than his stomach. He should remember what reward masters give to useless, lazy, worthless servants: whippings, fetters, a stint at the mill, exhaustion, hunger, bitter cold – these are the rewards of laziness.

Comedy only rarely makes heroes of the over-virtuous and it is very amusing when Messenio follows his song by saving, not his master, but his master's twin brother from an attack by the latter's father-in--law. This confusion reminds us that Messenio is a comic character, not a repository of sound moral advice. Like Messenio, Phaniscus ('Little Torch') in the *Mostellaria* sings of the contrast between good and bad slaves (vv. 858–84), but here there is a gentle humour in the combination of dutiful servitude and sexual attractiveness (cf. vv. 895, 947) in this slave-boy. The corresponding song in the *Pseudolus* (vv. 1103–20) is put into the mouth of the soldier's servant Harpax (cf. above p. 141). Harpax is indeed doing his best to serve his master, but the audience knows that he had been fooled at his last entry and he is destined to return home empty-handed; his master will certainly not be pleased with his day's work. In the final instance, *Aulularia* 587–607,[13] the slave himself undercuts his fine words by subsequently behaving like the usual comic slave for whom beatings and virtue are very secondary considerations.

There is no doubt that the poets of the New Comedy liked to moralise, and it is a reasonable inference that their audiences like to listen to such passages. There is also no doubt, however, that poets often took great care to link general reflection very closely to the scenic context and exploited moralising for a surprising variety of humorous effects.

Comedy and philosophy

Ancient writers on ethical subjects drew heavily upon New Comedy to illustrate the points they wished to make. This is in no way surprising. New Comedy, like Homer and classical tragedy, offered a large body of material, familiar to the educated classes, which illustrated a wide variety of possible situations in the field of human relationships; appeal to this material could be far more effective than creating wholly new and imaginary illustrations. Nevertheless, this habit of ancient writers must cause us to wonder about the possible links between comedy and philosophy, particularly as the high period of New Comedy coincided with very intense and productive work in the field of ethics by the Peripatetics and then by the Stoics and the Epicureans. It is easy enough to find in the fragments of Greek New Comedy slighting references to philosophers and their doctrines which are intended to raise a laugh;[14] in this, New Comedy stands directly in the tradition descending from Aristophanes' *Clouds*. The identification of unacknowledged links between a passage of comedy and specific philosophical doctrines is a far more difficult matter. In every possible case there are two basic questions to be asked: 'Has the comic poet been influenced by philosophical theory?', and 'Is it necessary to know this in order to appreciate fully the point of the comic passage?' In considering the latter question we must always remember that the same passage can suggest different associations to different members of the audience and that a particular word can have both a general and a technical or 'philosophical' meaning; for hearers familiar with both senses a passage will evoke a more complex response than for those only familiar with the word's non-specialised usage. It is, however, in the nature of the enquiry that general agreement on either of these two questions in any specific instance is probably more than can be realistically expected.

Late, and not necessarily trustworthy, ancient sources tell us that Menander was the friend or pupil of Theophrastos;[15] so too, we are told, was Demetrios of Phaleron, who governed Athens on behalf of the Macedonians from 317 to 307 and who also is said to have counted Menander among his friends. Demetrios was a voluminous writer on political, historical, ethical and literary subjects;[16] among his titles the following may remind us of the concerns of New Comedy, *On Love*, *On Fortune*, *On Marriage* and *On Old Age*. It is possible also that he wrote a monograph on Antiphanes, an important dramatist of the Middle Comedy period. Unfortunately, the remains of his works are so scanty that we can say nothing about his use of comedy or comedy's use of him. We may hope for better luck with Theophrastos.

Theophrastos succeeded Aristotle as head of the Peripatetic school in 322, but he had been an active teacher in Athens for many years before this. Even without the ancient notices which survive, it would have been reasonable to suppose that he and his work were known to Menander. Theophrastos' best known surviving work is not, however, in any real sense philosophical. *The Characters* is a series of sketches of the actions typical of a certain sort of individual; each action illustrates the characteristic which defines these people – suspiciousness, meanness, talkativeness and so on. Although the purpose and original position of this work are far from clear, there can be little doubt that Theophrastos drew some inspiration from the stereotyped characters of comedy; that he has in turn influenced comedy to any significant extent is most uncertain. Four of his characters also occur as titles of Menandrian comedies – the Rustic (ἄγροικος), the Suspicious Man (ἄπιστος), the Superstitious Man (δεισιδαίμων) and the Flatterer (κόλαξ) – but direct links between what survives of ancient comedy and these sketches are surprisingly rare. Like the Suspicious Man, Cnemon in the *Dyscolos* and Euclio in the (possibly Menandrian) *Aulularia* refuse to lend household equipment (*Char.* 18.7), but it is noteworthy that both Euclio and Cnemon have particular motives, in addition to their general suspiciousness, for this refusal. Theophrastos' rustic (ἄγροικος) bears only the most general resemblance to the rustics of New Comedy. There are indeed similarities between

Theophrastos' flatterer (κόλαξ) and characters such as Artotrogus in Plautus' *Miles Gloriosus* and Gnatho in Terence's *Eunuchus*,[17] but it would be absurd to suggest that Theophrastos has here taught the comic poets anything. Sostratos' mother in the *Dyscolos* is obviously superstitious (cf. esp. vv. 260–3) but no direct links with Theophrastos can be established. If we go outside these four sketches, we find traits of the mean (μικρολόγος) man in Euclio and of meanness and surliness (αὐθάδεια) in Cnemon.[18] In no case, however, is a specific debt by a comic poet to Theophrastos a necessary assumption.[19] Many have, however, supposed a more general indebtedness of the comic poets, especially Menander, to *The Characters*. According to this view, Theophrastos showed how to build up a typical character by illustrating how that character behaves in a series of isolated and unrelated situations; the common denominator in all of these situations will be the central characteristic involved. Comic characters are, however, portrayed in a quite different fashion.[20] Very few comic characters are as completely flat and one-sided as Theophrastos' specimens: Euclio is not simply suspicious or mean, Smicrines in the *Aspis* is not just a miser, Thraso in the *Eunuchus* is not just an absurd impostor (cf. above p. 93). Comic characters are by no means 'real human beings', but they usually have more than one dimension. Secondly, the plot of a comedy is a sequence of related actions portraying a single story; nothing could thus be further removed from the strategy which Theophrastos adopts in *The Characters*. This rejection of any dependence of comedy on *The Characters* does not mean, of course, that we should not see in both of them products of the same interest in human behaviour and the individual. Both too were heirs to the rich tradition of Old and Middle Comedy; the use that each made of the tradition was, however, widely different.[21]

In turning to consider the possible links between comedy and philosophy proper, we may begin with two passages of Menander's *Epitrepontes*. When we first see the young husband who left his wife because he wrongly believed that she had had a child by another man, he delivers a violent speech of self-denunciation because he has been reminded that he himself brutally raped a young girl before his marriage (cf. above p. 86). At the beginning of his speech (quoted on p. 124 above) he says that he was too wrapped up in moral philosophy to understand the real situation (vv. 908ff.); implied in his words is a rejection of moral theorising as remote from the real experiences of human life.[22] So too at the end of the play philosophical speculation is set in an ambivalent light. After everything has been sorted out and husband and wife reconciled, the wife's irate father turns up to protect his financial interests, ignorant of what has taken place. The slave Onesimos engages him in a rather confused discussion of the possibility of divine concern for mankind (vv. 1084–99). The language Onesimos uses is clearly intended to sound 'philosophical', but philosophical instruction for either Smicrines or the audience is not among Menander's aims here. Philosophy is used as a weapon to infuriate Smicrines and delay him on his mission. If anything, the scene depicts such intellectual puzzles as idle time-wasting. It would, of course, be absurd to use these passages in the *Epitrepontes* as evidence for Menander's own view of the value of philosophy, but it is not in fact uncommon for isolated fragments of Menander which seem serious or 'philosophical' to be taken as genuine expressions of the poet's view and to be linked to specific philosophical ideas or works. No case seems to me important enough to warrant discussion here.[23] In any event, it is hardly surprising that a comic poet should be familiar with certain philosophical ideas current in his day; what is important is how he uses those ideas, and this is something which fragments without a context can rarely tell us.

During Menander's lifetime, Aristotle and his followers worked intensively in the field of ethics and human behaviour; the results of their labours have come down to us primarily in the treatises known as *Nicomachean Ethics*, *Eudemian Ethics* and *Magna Moralia*. As the basis of the relevant sections of these works is a systematisation of ideas long current in Greek popular morality, it will not surprise us that many of the ethical situations which arise in New Comedy can (and should) be illustrated from these works. The *Periceiromene*, for example, concerns an obviously wrong action done in ignorance and a fit of misplaced jealousy; such actions and where the responsiblity for them lies are much discussed in the Aristotelian treatises.[24] Are we then to see a direct link between comedy and philosophy here? That Menander was familiar with such discussions and that they were in his mind when constructing the plot of his play is not unlikely, but there is nothing to suggest that a full appreciation of the play requires a knowledge of Peripatetic ethics or that Menander directs our attention to any 'philosophical' framework. The role of ignorance and the distinction between voluntary and involuntary errors had long been openly discussed in the Athenian courts and it is to the audience's legal, rather than philosophical, interests that Menander makes particular appeal (cf. vv. 500–3). A rather stronger argument can perhaps be made out in the case of Terence's *Adelphoe*, which is based on a play of Menander (cf. above pp. 105–9). Here we find many themes in common between Aristotle and Menander: the respective roles of shame and fear in education, whether young men should be given their head or not, the rejection of unbending dogmatism and the advocacy of a flexible and open approach to human relationships. In the light of Demea's interpretation of Micio's educational methods as nothing but 'complaisance, indulgence and wastefulness' (v. 988), it is easy enough to see how the Aristotelian view of virtue as a mean between two extremes may be applied to the conflicts of the play. Nevertheless, we have already seen (above pp. 95–109) how the main features of this play are firmly rooted in a long comic tradition whose influence is far more potent than that of contemporary philosophy. A similar conclusion is perhaps suggested by the considerable scholarly disagreement over where precisely the play stands on the ethical issues it seems to raise.[25] It may indeed be helpful for an individual reader or spectator to analyse the play in Aristotelian terms, but this cannot be said to be necessary.[26]

New Comedy and Peripatetic ethics both arose at the same time, in the same place and in the hands of educated men who were probably well known to each other. Both are concerned with how man functions within his society, and both shed valuable light on the society out of which they grew. If the one often reminds us of the other, this need not necessarily be taken as a sign that one is dependent on the other, but rather we may be comforted that this similarity confirms the reality of the social and moral patterns which both assume.

Notes

1 Introduction

1. It is not unlikely that Diphilos' career began before Alexander's death, but it cannot be proved from the extant fragments, cf. Webster [1970] 152–3; *pace* Webster, the relationship between Diphilos and a courtesan called Gnathaina about which Machon jokes (vv. 258–84 Gow) does not necessarily raise Diphilos into the generation before Menander, cf. A. S. F. Gow, *Machon* (Cambridge 1965) 7–10.
2. Cf. Jocelyn [1967] 3 n. 4.
3. Horace (*Sat.* 1.10.40–2) praises the comedies of one Gaius Fundanius, but these were probably literary exercises not intended for public performance. In his note on Hor. *Epist.* 1.10.1 Porphyrio calls M. Aristius Fuscus *scriptor comoediarum*, but there is no confirmation of this in Horace's poetry itself; elsewhere Fuscus is designated *scriptor tragoediarum* and *grammaticus*, cf. Klebs, *RE* 2.906, R. G. M. Nisbet and M. Hubbard, *A Commentary on Horace: Odes Book I* (Oxford 1970) 261–2.
4. Cf. C. F. L. Austin, *Comicorum Graecorum fragmenta in papyris reperta* (Berlin/New York 1973).
5. The majority of the extant texts seem to have been readers' or scholars' copies; this is certainly suggested by the prefatory material attached to our texts of the *Dyscolos* and the *Heros*, and note also the marginal glosses at *Dysc.* 113, 946 and *Samia* 656, the explanatory notes on the main papyrus of the *Colax* and the identification of a tragic source which is written into the margin of the Bodmer papyrus at *Samia* 325. On the other hand, it is probable, though not certain, that a text such as Adesp. 255 Austin in which the characters are designated A, B, Γ, Δ (i.e. first, second, third, fourth) is connected with a living theatrical tradition, cf. Andrieu [1954] 248–57, J. C. B. Lowe, *BICS* 9 (1962) 27–42, E. J. Jory, *BICS* 10 (1963) 65–78.
6. There are useful surveys of the survival of Menander at different periods of the ancient world by A. Dain, 'La survie de Ménandre' *Maia* 15 (1963) 278–309, and C. Corbato, *Studi Menandrei* (Trieste 1965) 7–60.
7. The blanket scepticism about our information concerning Menander in M. Lefkowitz, *The Lives of the Greek Poets* (London 1981) 113–14 ignores the channels of information open to ancient scholarship; a contemporary of Menander, Lynceus of Samos, wrote a work about the dramatist. For

the testimonia concerning Menander's life see Körte's edition Vol. II; there is a good discussion in Arnott's Loeb edition, Vol. I, pp. xiii–xix.

8. Cf. W. G. Arnott, 'The author of the Greek original of the Poenulus' *RhM* 102 (1959) 252–62, *id.*, *Dioniso* 43 (1969) 355–60, and pp. 58–61 of G. Maurach's edition of the *Poenulus*.

9. Cf. Philemon frr. 58 and 59; Alciphron (*Epist.* 4.18.5, 17) represents Philemon as having been invited by Ptolemy and perhaps implies that he accepted, but by itself this evidence is far from conclusive.

10. The most obvious title for the Greek original is *Phasma* and we know of three Greek plays with that title; as neither the extant fragments and plot summary of Menander's play nor the alternative title of Theognetos' play ('The Ghost or the Miser') fit Plautus' play, Philemon's *Phasma* is the most plausible candidate. Whether Plautus or the Greek poet is responsible for vv. 1149–51, *si amicus Diphilo aut Philemoni es,* | *dicito eis quo pacto tuos te seruos ludificauerit:* | *optimas frustrationes dederis in comoedias* [Kassel: *comoediis*] ('If you're a friend of Diphilos or Philemon, tell them how your slave fooled you; you'll give them splendid tricks for their comedies') is an interesting question, but hardly decisive for the authorship of the Greek original, cf. Bain [1977] 212 n. 1 and (most recently) G. W. Williams, *ICS* 8 (1983) 215.

11. The damaged prologue has been doubtfully deciphered as giving the title of the Greek play as *Schedia* ('The Raft'), a known title of Diphilos; the obvious likeness of this play to the *Rudens* seems also to strengthen Diphilos' claim to it. For some links between the *Vidularia* and the comedy of Menander cf. Hunter [1981] 42.

12. Cf. A. S. Gratwick, 'Titus Maccius Plautus' *CQ* N.S. 23 (1973) 78–84.

13. For the subsequent editing of these plays see Leo [1912] 19.

14. A. S. Gratwick *op. cit.* (n. 12) 84, (cf. *id.* [1982] 95), claims that single authorship for all twenty-one plays is proved by 'certain aspects of the deep-level style of the plays – e.g. Plautus' treatment of final -*s* after a short vowel'; as far as I know, Gratwick has never elaborated or substantiated this interesting claim.

15. Cf. Wright [1974] *passim*. It is also noteworthy that the *Commorientes*, a play which Terence explicitly assigns to Plautus (*Ad.* 7), did not qualify for inclusion in the Varronian canon.

16. I cannot suppress the observation that this detail reminds me of the exchange between Simo and Sosia at the opening of Terence's first play, the *Andria* (cf. especially vv. 35–9).

17. The text in fact gives the number of new plays Terence had with him as 108; this may be explained by the fact that 108 was one of the standard ancient figures for Menander's total output.

18. There are some interesting remarks on this subject by E. Segal in an article entitled 'The φύσις of comedy' *HSCP* 77 (1973) 129–36.

19. The most striking example here is the transvestite humour found in Aristophanes' *Thesmophoriazousai* and Plautus' *Casina*.

20. For the chorus in Middle Comedy see Hunter [1979].
21. Arist. *Pol.* 3.1276 b6 perhaps implies that the comic and tragic choruses could be the same size in Aristotle's day, and our evidence (cf. Pickard-Cambridge [1968] 234–5) suggests 12 or 15 as the number for a tragic chorus (at least in the fifth century). Aristotle's remark is, however, not to be pushed too hard; the chorus of *Periceiromene* consisted of μειράκια πάμπολλα ('very many young men', vv. 261–2). Professor Sandbach observes that the travelling troupes of actors (cf. above p. 19) may have recruited locals for non-speaking parts and to fill out their choruses.
22. There is a very useful (though now out-of-date as far as Menander is concerned) survey by K. J. Maidment, 'The later comic chorus' *CQ* 29 (1935) 1–24; further bibliography in Hunter [1979] 23 n. 1, to which add the interesting observations of M. S. Silk in *Yale Classical Studies* 26 (1980) 147–51.
23. Cf. L. Casson, 'The Athenian upper class and New Comedy' *TAPA* 106 (1976) 29–59, who, however, perhaps overstates the relative wealth of the average Menandrian character and underestimates the element of falsehood (and wish-fulfilment) in drama.
24. Cf. W. G. Arnott, 'Moral values in Menander' *Phil.* 125 (1981) 215–27. About the cessation of state subsidies from the so-called theoric fund we have no firm evidence; most scholars would point to 322/1 when the oligarchs introduced a property qualification of 2000 dr. for participation in the political life of the city, cf. W. S. Ferguson, *Hellenistic Athens* (London 1911) 23, J. J. Buchanan, *Theorika* (New York 1962) 81–2.
25. Cf. F. E. Winter, 'The stage of New Comedy' *Phoenix* 37 (1983) 38–47.
26. Cf. in particular Handley's edition of the *Dyscolos*, pp. 30–9; further details and rich illustration may be found in L. Bernabò Brea, *Menandro e il teatro greco nelle terracotte liparesi* (Genoa 1981).
27. Cf., e.g., C. Préaux, 'Ménandre et la société Athénienne' *Chronique d'Égypte* 32 (1957) 84–100 and 'Les fonctions du droit dans la comédie nouvelle' *Chronique d'Égypte* 35 (1960) 222–39, J. K. Davies, *Classical Journal* 73 (1977/8) 113–14.
28. Cf. Men. *Dysc.* 462, 892, *Periceir.* 482–5, fr. 397.11 K–T, J. N. Adams, *The Latin Sexual Vocabulary* (London 1982) 218. προσπέρδομαι ('I fart at') appears in the mouth of cooks at Damoxenos fr. 2.39 and Sosipater fr. 1.12. βινεῖν ('to screw') occurs at Adesp. 138.8 and 254.1 Austin; in the latter case the character seems not to come from the lower classes.
29. Cf. K. J. Dover, *Greek Homosexuality* (London 1978) 151–3.
30. For Demetrios' interests cf. Ath. 12.542d–3a; homosexuality is rare in the fragments of poets other than Menander, but cf. Diphilos fr. 50, Damoxenos fr. 3 and Baton fr. 7 K–A. Most scholars would ascribe to Plautus rather than to his Greek models the many jokes on this topic which occur in his plays (cf. S. Lilja, 'Homosexuality in Plautus' plays' *Arctos* 16 (1982) 57–64), and Plutarch explicitly says that there is no paederasty in Menander (*Mor.* 712c).

31. Of the few cases in the extant corpus, the most notable is Philippides' attack on Stratocles, the henchman of Demetrios Poliorcetes, in fr. 25, cf. G. B. Philipp, *Gymnasium* 80 (1973) 505–9, A. Mastrocinque, *Athenaeum* N.S. 57 (1979) 266–7. Some have thought that Stratocles had tried to limit comedy's free speech, but it is perhaps more likely that he had made a personal attack upon Philippides, who now replied in kind. According to Polybios 12.13.7, the comic poet Archedicos mocked the politician Demochares in a way that recalls the Old Comedy (fr. 4). For further contemporary allusions in New Comedy cf. Webster [1970] 103–10.

32. Cf. L. R. Taylor, 'The opportunities for dramatic performances in the time of Plautus and Terence' *TAPA* 68 (1937) 284–304; there is a useful and brief account of Roman theatrical organisation in Gratwick [1982] 80–3.

33. *lictores* were attendants of the magistrate in charge of the festival and were partly responsible for order in the theatre.

34. The evidence for this is scanty, but perhaps sufficient, cf. Plaut. *Rudens* 86, Jocelyn [1967] 5–7.

35. On the *togata* see especially Leo [1913] 374–84, Beare [1964] Chap. xv.

36. This is a highly controversial subject and my account should be taken as schematic only; in addition to the standard books see R. G. Tanner, 'Problems in Plautus' *PCPS* N.S. 15 (1969) 95–105.

37. For the evidence cf. Duckworth [1952] 92–4, Jocelyn [1967] 22 n. 1, A. S. F. Gow, 'On the use of masks in Roman comedy' *JRS* 2 (1912) 65–77.

38. Cf. Sandbach [1973] 16–19, *id.* 'Menander and the three-actor rule' in *Le Monde Grec: Hommages à Claire Préaux* (Brussels 1975) 197–204, G. M. Sifakis, 'Boy actors in New Comedy' in *Arktouros: Hellenic Studies presented to Bernard M. W. Knox* (Berlin/New York 1979) 199–208. Although Roman poets did not observe the Greek limitation, the number of Roman scenes which require four or more speaking actors remains relatively small; this is presumably a sign of the difficulty of writing such scenes.

39. The bibliography is enormous; the best starting-points are Handley [1968] and D. Bain, '*Plautus uortit barbare*' in D. West and A. Woodman (eds.), *Creative Imitation and Latin Literature* (Cambridge 1979) 17–34.

40. The standard translation 'flute' is misleading, cf. K. Schlesinger, *The Greek Aulos* (London 1939) and S. Michaelides, *The Music of Ancient Greece* (London 1978) 42–6.

41. I exclude here *Casina* 64–6, which is normally taken as evidence for Plautine excisions in that play since, strictly interpreted, these verses need be no more than a pleasant joke by the *prologus* with no bearing on the Greek original. More important for the *Casina* is (i) our knowledge of the typical story-patterns of Greek comedy, and (ii) vv. 1012–14, which

acknowledge further elements in the story which the present performance will not include.

42. The problem of Plautine chronology is beyond the scope of this book; guidance will be found in C. H. Buck, *A Chronology of the Plays of Plautus* (diss. Johns Hopkins, Baltimore 1940), K. H. E. Schutter, *Quibus annis comoediae Plautinae primum actae sint quaeritur* (diss. Groningen 1952), Duckworth [1952] 54–5, Abel [1955] *passim*.

43. On the 'Artists' cf. Poland, *RE* 5A. 2473–558, Pickard-Cambridge [1968] 279ff.

44. Cf. E. J. Jory, 'Associations of actors in Rome' *Hermes* 98 (1970) 224–53, N. M. Horsfall, 'The Collegium Poetarum' *BICS* 23 (1976) 79–95.

45. Cf. especially Gentili [1979].

46. Cf. Ath. 14.621c–d, Wüst, *RE* 15.1735–8.

47. Cf. Bieber [1961] 129–46, A. D. Trendall, *Phlyax Vases*² (*BICS* Suppl. 19, 1967). For presentations of Greek New Comedy in Magna Graecia cf. Bernabò Brea *op. cit.* (n. 26 above).

48. *Epist.* 2.1.58 (*dicitur*) *Plautus ad exemplar Siculi properare Epicharmi* ('Plautus is said to hurry in the tradition of the Sicilian Epicharmus'). Brink is inclined to doubt the text, but it perhaps refers to the lack of polish of Plautine poetry (contrast v. 59 on Terence's *ars*), cf. Leo [1913] 138.

49. Cf. *Bacch.* 1088, where the *senex* Nicobulus says that he surpasses all *buccones* in stupidity. *Rudens* 535 seems to contain a reference to a character of farce called Manducus but unfortunately the very existence of this character is otherwise doubtful; what is, however, beyond doubt is that this scene of the *Rudens* is almost entirely a Plautine creation – the pimp and his friend are simply two comedians telling a series of jokes, and the Atellan farce was probably often like this.

50. On the literary *Atellana* cf. F. Leo, *Hermes* 49 (1914) 169–79 (= *Ausgewählte kleine Schriften* 1 257–67); there are also brief accounts in all standard works on Roman drama.

51. The betrothal ring (a Roman custom) at *Ad.* 347 would be a good example, if indeed that is a Terentian insertion, cf. Martin *ad loc.* The ring is something that a Roman audience would understand, but it is not obviously non-Greek. The absence of *pergraecari* ('to revel like a Greek') from Terence's plays is noteworthy; the word is, of course, incongruous in the mouth of an actor portraying a Greek, but this had not worried Plautus.

2 *The form of New Comedy*

1. Cf. D. Bain, 'Audience address in Greek tragedy' *CQ* N.S. 25 (1975) 13–25.

2. Cf. Kannicht *ad loc.* for further discussion.

3. Cf. Bain [1977] 186–7.

4. Cf. Ach. Tat. 4.4.2 where the narrator of a long excursus on elephants introduces his account with λέγοιμ' ἂν ὑμῖν...καὶ γὰρ ἄγομεν σχολήν ('I shall tell you...since we have plenty of time'), where one can see an attempt by Achilles to add realism to his story, or a joke about narrative technique, or both.

5. Cf. Men. fr. 152 K–T where sleeplessness is blamed as λαλίστατον ('most productive of chatter'), a situation which recalls the opening of *Clouds*, as Holzberg [1974] 48 notes.

6. I am not convinced by the suggestion of F. Skutsch, *RhM* 55 (1900) 272, that the speaker of this prologue is Fides; other divine prologists identify themselves explicitly. Verse 2 I take to be a simple linguistic joke of a common Plautine kind.

7. Cf. Wilamowitz [1925] 144–5, Abel [1955] 127 n. 292, Bain [1977] 188–9.

8. Cf. Pickard-Cambridge [1968] 67–8.

9. *Men.* 19–23, *ita forma simili pueri uti mater sua | non internosse posset quae mammam dabat, | neque adeo mater ipsa quae illos pepererat, | ut quidem ille dixit mihi qui pueros uiderat : | ego illos non uidi, ne quis uostrum censeat* ('the boys were so alike that not even the woman who gave them her breast could tell them apart, nor their own mother; I have this on the authority of someone who saw the boys – I didn't see them, and none of you is to think that I did'), is a nice joke on the convention of the omniscience of the *prologus*.

10. For πρᾶγμα cf. *Knights* 36 (with Neil's note).

11. Alexis fr. 108 seems to come from a postponed prologue delivered by the father of two sons, but we cannot tell whether he appeared with the sons in the scene preceding the prologue.

12. Cf. Hunter [1983] 23–30; it is, of course, not certain that the speaker of Antiphanes' prologue was a god, but it seems not unlikely.

13. The most obvious Plautine examples are the *Curculio* and the *Epidicus*, cf. E. Fantham, 'The *Curculio* of Plautus: an illustration of Plautine methods in adaptation' *CQ* N.S. 15 (1965) 84–100 (= Lefèvre [1973] 173–204) and ead. 'Plautus in miniature: compression and distortion in the *Epidicus*' *Papers of the Liverpool Latin Seminar* 3 (1981) 1–28.

14. Plautus does, however, give Palaestrio a passage (vv. 147–53) in which he foreshadows what is to happen in the play, in a manner which is very hard to envisage in a Greek play, cf. Abel [1955] 87–8. Diniarchus' foreshadowing of Phronesium's pretended childbirth (*Truc.* 84–8) seems to be another such example.

15. Cf. W. Ludwig, 'Die plautinische *Cistellaria* und das Verhältnis von Gott und Handlung bei Menander' in *Ménandre* 45–110. Whatever influences the Greek prologist exerted on the action of the *Synaristosai*, Plautus has made good use of the military associations of *auxilium* (cf. *Cist.* 197–202).

16. Cf. Hunter [1980] 216–27.

17. *Andria 5–7, nam in prologis scribundis operam abutitur, | non qui argumentum narret sed qui maleuoli | ueteris poetae maledictis respondeat,* ('for the poet

has to devote all his prologues not to explaining the plot but to replying to the slanders of a malicious old poet'), suggests that the Terentian practice was relatively novel.

18. Cf. W. Süss, 'Zwei Bemerkungen zur Technik der Komödie. 1. Der terenzische Prolog' *RhM* 65 (1910) 442–50, W. G. Arnott, 'Terence's prologues' *Papers of the Liverpool Latin Seminar* 5 (forthcoming).

19. Dover [1972] 56.

20. Cf. Ar. *Peace* 734–5 ~ Plaut. *Amph.* 64ff. (jokes about order in the theatre), Ar. *Birds* 786–9 ~ Plaut. *Poen.* 5–10 (hungry spectators).

21. Cf. esp. the opening of Aristeides' 'Hymn to Sarapis' (45 Keil), εὐδαιμόν γε τὸ τῶν ποιητῶν ἐστι γένος καὶ πραγμάτων ἀπήλλακται πανταχῇ. οὐ γὰρ μόνον αὐτοῖς ἔξεστι τὰς ὑποθέσεις τοιαύτας ὁποίας ἂν αὐτοὶ βουλη-θῶσιν ἑκάστοτε ἐνστήσασθαι κτλ. ('Happy and completely carefree is the tribe of poets. For not only can they make up any plots they like etc.'). If Antiphanes fr. 191 is not from a prologue, then the most plausible alternative is that the speech comes from an *agon* (between Tragedy and Comedy?).

22. It is worth noting the possibility that the object of this attack is the prologists of tragedy rather than comedy, although the latter seems more likely; for discussion of this fragment cf. C. Dedoussi, 'The New Comedy prologue of Pap. Argentor. Gr. 53: its interpretation and authorship' *Dodona* 4 (1975) 255–70.

23. Cf. F. Leo, *Ausgewählte kleine Schriften* (Rome 1960) I 135–49, H. Gelhaus, *Die Prologe des Terenz* (Heidelberg 1972) *passim*, S. M. Goldberg, 'Terence, Cato and the rhetorical prologue' *CP* 78 (1983) 198–211.

24. Cf. M. Pohlenz, 'Der Prolog des Terenz' *SIFC* N.S. 27/8 (1956) 434–43. With Terence's attack on the *obscura diligentia* of his rivals (*Andria* 21) perhaps compare the verses of Philip on pedantic scholars (*AP* 11. 347.5–6) γινώσκοιμ' ὅσα λευκὸν ἔχει στίχον· ἡ δὲ μέλαινα | ἱστορίη τήκοι τοὺς Περικαλλιμάχους 'I would know works whose lines are crystal-clear; let the darker learning sap the strength of our super-Callimachuses' (translation of Gow–Page, *The Garland of Philip* I p. 339).

25. With Terence's abuse of the uneducated (*Hec.* 4–5), *populus studio stupidus in funambulo | animum occuparat* ('the stupid people were wholly enthralled by a tightrope walker'), cf. Lucian's flattery of his audience at *Herodotus* (62 Macleod) 8, οἵ τε αὖ πανηγυρισταὶ οὐ συρφετώδης ὄχλος, ἀθλητῶν μᾶλλον φιλοθεάμονες κτλ. ('The audience gathered here is not some low rabble, more interested in athletes...'). I do not intend to imply that Terence's account is necessarily misleading; it may well be essentially correct, but the situation at least demands caution. The case for believing Terence is well put by D. Gilula, 'Who's afraid of rope-walkers and gladiators? (Ter. *Hec.* 1–57)' *Athenaeum* N.S. 59 (1981) 29–37.

26. Cf. Marti [1959] 102–6. Grumio's absence from most of the *Mostellaria* is adequately explained by his departure to the country at the end of the opening scene. I do not here count Acanthio in the *Mercator* as a

πρόσωπον προτατικόν, because his important role, coming after a human prologue, differs significantly from that of the other characters in this category.

27. On 'the Five-Act Law' of later literary theory cf. Brink on Hor. *AP* 189–90. A. Blanchard's detailed study of comic structure, *Essai sur la composition des comédies de Ménandre* (Paris 1983), came to me too late to be used in the preparation of this book.

28. Webster [1974] 73 wonders about the movement of Smicrines in the first act of the *Aspis*, but he seems to enter his own house at v. 96 from which he re-emerges at v. 149. I think it very likely that the consultations with his friends which he claims to have had (vv. 184–5) are imaginary; they are simply a useful screen for his greed. Austin *ad loc.* cites Plaut. *Aul.* 475–7, but a better parallel is *Stichus* 128, *mi auctores ita sunt amici, ut uos hinc abducam domum* ('my friends advise me to bring you home from here'), which is likely to be entirely fictitious.

29. Cf. W. G. Arnott, 'Time, plot and character in Menander' *Papers of the Liverpool Latin Seminar* 2 (1979) 343–60, esp. pp. 346–8.

30. Cf. K. Gaiser, *Wiener Studien* 79 (1966) 197–201 and Sandbach [1973] 326. The case of the *Epitrepontes* is difficult, cf. Sandbach *loc. cit.*, W. G. Arnott, *ZPE* 24 (1977) 17–18. Arnott argues that the movements of Syros are against the action spreading over two days, which would otherwise be the natural conclusion from αὔριον in 414–15; the background party which is going on is, however, not helpful in this regard, as it is clear that it has been going on for a few days (cf. vv. 136–7, 440–1). Elsewhere in Menander αὔριον seems always to mean 'tomorrow', although at *Periceir.* 983 it may have a vague, rather than a specific, reference to the future. Has Menander been less careful than usual in arranging the timing in this play, or does the incomplete state of the text (particularly in the first act) cloud our view of this issue?

31. Cf. Blundell [1980] 26–7.

32. *Poetics* 1455 b24–31; cf. Brink on Hor. *AP* 191 for later examples of this terminology.

33. Cf. *Andria* Praef. II.3, *Eun.* Praef. 1.5, Andrieu [1954] 41–4.

34. Cf. Beare [1964] 213; see also C. Questa, *T. Maccius Plautus : Bacchides*² (Florence 1975) pp. 27–30.

35. It may be that in vv. 882–4 Plautus is deliberately drawing attention to the unrealistic conventions of stage timing; for a full discussion of 'stage-time' in Plautus cf. Conrad [1915] 19–52.

36. For a full discussion see Hunter [1979] 25–8. The problem of Ter. *HT* 170–1 continues to excite much discussion, cf. D. Gilula, 'Menander's XOPOY, and where not to find it in Terence' *Latomus* 39 (1980) 694–701. Gilula argues that there is no real problem in Terence's play as Chremes does not leave the stage but merely stands at Phania's door and makes his enquiries; cf. also J. C. B. Lowe, *Hermes* III (1983) 450–1.

37. Cf. A. *Eum.* 33–4, ?Men. *Dysc.* 908–9, Hunter [1979] 24–5.

38. On this speech cf. G. E. Duckworth, 'Plautus and the Basilica Aemilia' in *Ut Pictura Poesis: Studia...P. Enk* (Leiden 1955) 58–65, Questa in *Ménandre* 223.
39. For what follows cf. W. Süss, 'Zwei Bemerkungen zur Technik der Komödie. II Der Komödienschluss' *RhM* 65 (1910) 450–60 and, for a recent account, Holzberg [1974] 121–73.
40. Cf., e.g., the common call for torches (W. G. Arnott, *Hermes* 93 (1965) 253–5) and the dancing challenge with which *Wasps* and *Stichus* end.
41. On the ending of the *Eunuchus* cf. above pp. 93–4.
42. Obvious examples are Plaut. *Amph.*, *Bacch.*, *Capt.*, *Curc.*, *Men.*, *MG*, *Pseud.*, *Trin.*, Ter. *Andria*, *HT*, *Hecyra*.
43. For the evidence cf. Jocelyn [1967] 29 n. 1, Pickard-Cambridge [1968] 165.
44. With Moschion's confidence in his sexual attractiveness (vv. 302–3, 308–9) cf. the boasting of the Cyclops at Theocr. 6.34–8; both lovers then take action to avoid the divine wrath which their words might arouse (*Periceir.* 304, Theocr. 6.39–40).
45. It would be nice to know whether Menander's technique evolved over time in this respect. The *Dyscolos* has many momentarily empty stages, the surviving part of the *Samia* only one (vv. 95–6). Unfortunately, the chronology of the plays is too uncertain to allow any conclusions.
46. Cf. Handley in *Ménandre* 10–12.
47. Diphilos fr. 1 and P. Mich. Inv. 4925 (cf. L. Koenen, *BASP* 16 (1979) 114–16, F. Perusino, *ZPE* 51 (1983) 45–9); Adesp. fr. 294 provides an example from Middle Comedy. For the doubtful cases cf. F. Perusino, *Il tetrametro giambico catalettico nella commedia greca* (Rome 1968) 158–60. For the 'colour' of this metre cf. Mar. Vict. VI p. 135 K (cited by Perusino p. 169) *est...iocosis motibus emollitum gestibusque agentium satis accommodatum*; the final scene of the *Dyscolos* is thus a very appropriate context for this metre.
48. Greek iambics and trochaics consist of the regular alternation of long (–), short (◡) and indifferent or *anceps* (×) syllables; in iambics the basic unit is ×–◡– and in trochaics –◡–×. Roman comedy substituted a simple alternation of long and *anceps* syllables, ×–×–×– etc. in iambics and –×–×–× etc. in trochaics. Helpful guidance in this area will be found in the metrical appendix to the edition of Plautus' *Casina* by W. T. MacCary and M. M. Willcock (Cambridge 1976).
49. Cf. H. H. Law, *Studies in the Songs of Plautine Comedy* (diss. Chicago 1922, repr. 1978) 103–5, Duckworth [1952] 373–4.
50. An exception is *Truc.* 209ff., on which cf. H. W. Prescott, *CP* 34 (1939) 10–11.
51. Cf. J. Collart, 'Le soldat qui ne chante pas' *REL* 47 bis, *Mélanges M. Durry* (1969) 199–208.
52. Cf. Fraenkel [1960] 406.

53. Havet, correctly in my view, identified this character as Diabolus, cf. Hunter [1980] 221.

54. Cf. Fraenkel [1960] 332–5, Gaiser [1972] 1089–91.

55. Cf. L. Braun, *Die Cantica des Plautus* (Göttingen 1970) 174–5 and, for the scene-type in general, Fraenkel [1960] 217–20.

56. I have not thought it worthwhile in a general book such as this to consider the question of whether particular lyric metres carry particular emotional colour; the matter is complex and, as far as I can tell, the results of previous investigations inconclusive. There is a useful collection of material in A. J. Tobias, *Plautus' Metrical Characterization* (diss. Stanford 1970), the value of which is, however, weakened by too heavy a reliance on the colometry of Lindsay's Oxford text. Further analyses of dramatic movement in terms of changing rhythms may be found in Taladoire [1956] 229–65.

57. For what follows I am much indebted to H. W. Bruder, *Bedeutung und Funktion des Verswechsels bei Terenz* (diss. Zurich 1970).

58. For bacchiacs marking a tipsy entry cf. above p. 48; for Terence's exploitation of theatrical convention here cf. above p. 78.

59. οὐ προέρχεται (v. 397, 'it doesn't move forward') puns on τὸ πρόβατον (v. 393, 'sheep, *lit.* forward mover'), and κατακέκομμ' ἐγώ (v. 398, 'I'm chopped up') varies the most common of all cook jokes (cf. e.g. *Dysc.* 410, *Aspis* 234, *Samia* 285). The vivid metaphor in 399, νεωλκῶν τὴν ὁδόν ('dragging [the sheep] like a ship over land'), is also part of Sicon's witty style, cf. Sandbach in *Ménandre* 119.

60. I am not persuaded that Getas appears with Sicon at v. 487, cf. Sandbach *ad loc.* and (*contra*) Blundell [1980] 53.

61. Cf. J. Diggle, 'Plautus, *Rudens*, Act 3 Scene 5 (780–838)' *RhM* 117 (1974) 86–94.

62. Cf. W. Steidle, *Studien zum antiken Drama* (Munich 1968) 42–3.

63. For this convention cf. Fraenkel [1960] 137–8, 155–6 and above p. 78.

64. Most of the dramatic inconsistencies gathered in P. Langen, *Plautinische Studien* (Berlin 1886) 89–232 and Marti [1959] are very instructive for students of ancient dramatic technique, but present in fact far fewer problems than Langen and Marti suppose.

3 *Plots and motifs*

1. For the *Epitrepontes* cf. Sandbach [1973] 293–4, Holzberg [1974] 62–3; for the *Hecyra* cf. D. Sewart, 'Exposition in the Hekyra of Apollodorus' *Hermes* 102 (1974) 247–60.

2. Cf. Webster [1970] 233, Hunter [1981] 42.

3. Cf. Fantham [1975] 69. This aspect of Pamphilus' character is given insufficient attention in the interesting discussion of the *Hecyra* in Konstan [1983] 130–41.

4. Cf. A. M. Young, 'The *Frogs* of Aristophanes as a type of play' *Classical Journal* 29 (1933/4) 23–32; for Old Comedy parallels with other scenes from *Frogs* cf. A. M. Wilson, *CQ* N.S. 24 (1974) 250–2.

5. Cf., e.g., Ar. *Clouds* 546–8, *Peace* 739–47, Metagenes fr. 14.

6. Cf. A. Traina, 'Plauto, Demofilo, Menandro' *La Parola del Passato* 9 (1954) 177–203, Webster [1970] 253–7. In his edition of the *Persa*, E. Woytek argues for particularly strong links between the *Persa* and the *Asinaria*, going well beyond the obvious similarities in the use of the motif of an agricultural sale (a motif also found in the *Truculentus*) and the 'low tone' of both plays. Woytek tentatively suggests that Demophilos was the author of the Greek original of the *Persa* as well as of the *Asinaria*.

7. Cf. Hunter [1981] 48 n. 44. In that article I sought to lend further weight to the arguments of those who caution that a Menandrian origin for the *Aulularia* should not be too readily assumed.

8. The fundamental discussion of this problem is that of G. Goetz, 'Dittographien im Plautustexte' *Acta societatis Lipsiensis* 6 (1876) 234–328, pp. 290–1. The main points are as follows: vv. 317–19 seem to prepare for a scene in which Astaphium uses her female wiles to win over the rustic slave; it is likely that in the Greek original this scene followed what is now v. 672, as there is no sign in vv. 669–71 that the slave's nature has already changed. Goetz ascribed the loss of this scene to a post-Plautine *retractator*, but Plautus himself might have been responsible, judging that the confrontation between Astaphium and the slave in II.2 sufficed for the play and that the slave's change of heart, which gives rise to scenes full of humour, did not require explicit motivation, cf. Marti [1959] 67. I suggest that vv. 692–3, *Strabacem hic opperiar modo, | si rure ueniat* ('I'll just wait here for Strabax to return from the farm'), is a final piece of defiance from the original scene of persuasion (cf. Demea's words at Ter. *Ad.* 852–3). For a recent discussion of this problem cf. G. Broccia, *Wiener Studien* 95 (1982) 154–7.

9. Cf. Donatus on v. 507, W. Ludwig, *Phil.* 103 (1959) 19–20 (= Lefèvre [1973] 378–9); an important ancestor of these scenes is the character of Iphigenia in E. *IA*, cf. Wilamowitz [1925] 135.

10. *Truc.* 531–2 is closely paralleled by *Eun.* 167–8, cf. Fraenkel [1960] 180.

11. Menandrian authorship is championed by P. Enk, 'Plautus' *Truculentus*' in C. Henderson (ed.), *Classical, Mediaeval and Renaissance Studies in Honor of B. L. Ullman* (Rome 1964) I 49–65 and P. Grimal, 'A propos du *Truculentus*' *REL* 47 bis, *Mélanges M. Durry* (1969) 85–98, but neither produces any convincing argument. Webster [1970] 147–50 suggests Philemon; Wilamowitz thought Menander a possible candidate, but preferred to ascribe the play to an imitator of Menander (*Kleine Schriften* I 229 n. 1).

12. Diphilos wrote a play called *Eunuch or Soldier* and this, together with the *Truculentus*, should be borne in mind when considering whether the rival

in Menander's *Eunouchos* was a soldier; for the motif in general cf. also Libanios, *Decl.* 32.38 (VII, p. 63 Foerster).

13. Cf., e.g., J.-M. Jacques, 'Le début du Misouménos et les prologues de Ménandre' in *Musa Iocosa: Festschrift Thierfelder* (Hildesheim/New York 1974) 71–9, G. Luck, 'Panaetius and Menander' *AJP* 96 (1975) 256–68. For the present state of the text of this scene cf. E. G. Turner's edition of Papyri 3368–71 in *Oxyrhynchus Papyri* Vol. XLVIII.

14. Such plays are known for Alexis, Anaxippos and Diphilos; for the motif cf. also Lysippos fr. 1 and Apollodoros of Gela fr. 1.

15. Cf. W. T. MacCary, 'Menander's characters: their names, roles and masks' *TAPA* 101 (1970) 277–90.

16. For other speculations cf. Bain [1977] 189. These verses are usually taken to refer to the giving of information in comic prologues, but they may rather be concerned with the unravelling of the plot at the end, cf. Ter. *Hec.* 866–7, *placet non fieri hoc itidem ut in comoediis | omnia omnes ubi resciscunt* ('I don't want it to be like in the comedies where everybody finds out everything').

17. Cf. Handley [1968] 9. A helpful discussion of the Plautine audience's familiarity with the stock techniques and themes of New Comedy is Handley's article entitled 'Plautus and his public: some thoughts on New Comedy in Latin' in *Dioniso* 46 (1975) 117–32.

18. A list of important texts would include the *Iliad*, Archilochos fr. 114 West and a number of tragedies; the pomposity of the soldier is associated with the pomposity of tragedy and the two are combined in the figure of the war-loving Aeschylus in *Frogs*. Observe, moreover, the similarity between S. *Aj.* 545–9 and Plaut. *Truc.* 505–11. On the comic soldier in general see Wehrli [1936] 101–13, W. Hofmann and G. Wartenberg, *Der Bramarbas in der antiken Komödie* (Berlin 1973), W. T. MacCary, 'Menander's soldiers: their names, roles and masks' *AJP* 93 (1972) 279–98.

19. Cf. *Periceir.* 985 ὡς κατὰ κράτος μ' εἴληφας ('How you have stormed me!').

20. Cf. *Mis.* fr. 2 παιδισκάριόν με καταδεδούλωκ' εὐτελές, | ὃν οὐδὲ εἷς τῶν πολεμίων ⟨οὐ⟩πώποτε ('a cheap little slave-girl has made me her slave; no enemy ever did that'). For an earlier expression of such sentiments cf. S. *Tr.* 1058–63 (the arch boaster Heracles).

21. Admittedly, it is not certain that the audience already knows the soldier's name at this stage, but it is not improbable that the opening scene had let this information drop; in our present text the name occurs only at v. 486.

22. Cf. J. A. Hanson, 'The glorious military' in T. A. Dorey and D. R. Dudley (eds.), *Roman Drama* (London 1965) 51–85.

23. Cf. *Persa* 470; these verses sound like a 'blasphemous' version of *Bacch.* 816–17 *quem di diligunt | adulescens moritur, dum ualet, sentit, sapit* ('Whom the gods love dies young, while he's strong, clever and wise'), on which see p. 139 above.

24. According to Hesychius, σάννιον is a term for the penis; cf. Ballio from βαλλός, a form of φαλλός.

25. Cf. the speech of Battaros in Herodas 2: there the real character of the pimp shines through his attempts to reproduce the rhetoric of an injured property-owner.

26. On these verses cf. Marti [1959] 98–9 and H. Lloyd-Jones, *CQ* N.S. 23 (1973) 280–1. Has it been suggested that *delibera* in 196 is a pun on *libera...liberali* in 194, a pun that would stress Aeschinus' confident superiority over Sannio?

27. For the dramatic illusion in ancient comedy see especially W. Görler, 'Über die Illusion in der antiken Komödie' *A&A* 18 (1973) 41–57 and Bain [1977] Chap. 12.

28. An interesting example is Xenarchos fr. 4.10–12, where a brothel-keeper's list of the difficulties in the way of adulterous affairs almost certainly relies on scenes familiar from contemporary comedies.

29. Cf. Bain [1977] 220–2, to which I should have referred in Hunter [1981] 46 n. 12.

30. For the links between Euripides' *Helen* and the *Miles Gloriosus* cf. Leo [1912] 165–7, K. Gaiser in Lefèvre [1973] 228–36.

31. I cannot agree with Handley, *Ménandre* 19, that 'once attention is drawn to the behaviour of the midwife, it needs some sort of naturalistic motivation [which H. finds in vv. 228ff.], or the audience will share the viewpoint of Simo and wonder why she is behaving like that'. The audience in fact knows why she does what she does – because this is drama and drama has its own convenient conventions. I am not sure that I understand the view of this scene taken by Gomme [1937] 260–1.

32. Cf. Men. *Dysc.* 1, Heniochos fr. 5, Plaut. *Rudens* 32–3 and, for human prologists, Ar. *Wasps* 54, *Peace* 50, Plaut. *Merc.* 1–8; on Men. *Samia* cf. above p. 25.

33. It seems likely that the word *tragicomoedia* was invented by Plautus for the *Amphitruo* prologue, cf. B. Seidensticker, *Palintonos Harmonia* (Göttingen 1982) 20–4.

34. For *seruus currens* as a technical term cf. Ter. *HT* 37, *Eun.* 36, Donatus on *Ad.* 299 and *Ph.* 179; note also Plaut. *Merc.* 109 *sed quid currentem seruom a portu conspicor*. On this character see G. E. Duckworth, 'The dramatic function of the *servus currens* in Roman comedy', in *Classical Studies Presented to Edward Capps* (Princeton 1936) 93–102, Denzler [1968] 112–17.

35. A Greek *seruus currens*, as we know this character in Roman comedy, seems likely enough, but has in fact not yet been proved. The most promising passage seems to be Adesp. fr. 244. 348–59 Austin (= 'Men. *Hydria*' 258–69 Gaiser, p. 338 of Sandbach's text of Menander), although Gaiser has a quite different explanation of that passage. At *Aspis* 399ff. a slave runs around the stage to fool another character (cf. Plaut. *Epid.* 192ff.), but he is not a *seruus currens* in the more technical sense

(*pace* W. S. Anderson, 'A new Menandrian prototype for the *servus currens* of Roman comedy' *Phoenix* 24 (1970) 229–36). Certain motifs of the Roman scenes do, of course, have Greek parallels. Breathlessness is found at S. *Ant.* 224, Ar. *Birds* 1122 and Men. *Dysc.* 96–7; it is noteworthy, however, that whereas Pyrrhias enters in breathless flight, like Amphitheos in the *Acharnians*, his nearest Roman relative, Curculio in Plautus' play named after him, is presented as a full-scale *parasitus currens*. A further development of some interest may be traced by comparing S. *OT* 1005–6 and *Tr.* 189–91 with the parasite's words at Plaut. *Capt.* 776–80. The other Greek fragments of possible relevance here are Men. fr. 690 K–T, Philemon fr. 58 (cf. Hor. *Sat.* 2.6.29–31) and Clearchos fr. 1 K–A.

36. Cf. *Persa* 465–6, *Poen.* 581, J. Blänsdorf, 'Die Komödienintrige als Spiel im Spiel' *A&A* 28 (1982) 131–54. For the dramatic connections of the trick in Menander's *Aspis* cf. above pp. 120–1.

4 Themes and conflicts

1. On this subject see especially Gomme [1937] 89–115, Fantham [1975] and D. Gilula, 'The concept of the *Bona Meretrix*: a study of Terence's courtesans' *RFIC* 108 (1980) 142–65. F. Della Corte, 'Personaggi femminili in Plauto' *Dioniso* 43 (1969) 485–97 is little more than a statistical survey, and I have not seen A. M. Mack, *Mulieres Comicae: female characters in Plautus and his predecessors* (diss. Harvard 1967), cf. *HSCP* 72 (1967) 395–7. L. A. Post, 'Woman's place in Menander's Athens' *TAPA* 71 (1940) 420–59 is a valuable collection of material, but has little to say about the comedies themselves.

2. For Athens cf. Pickard-Cambridge [1968] 264–5 and N. G. Wilson, *GRBS* 23 (1982) 158–9; Plaut. *Poen.* 28–35 and Ter. *Hec.* 35 seem to establish the presence of women (both slave and free) in the Roman audience, but men were almost certainly in the majority.

3. For other passages on the allegedly feeble intellect of women cf. Legrand [1910] 148 n. 3, Dover [1974] 99.

4. The whole passage in Aristophanes has a marked Euripidean colouring and v. 1124 is a quotation from Euripides' *Melanippe Sophe*, cf. Rau [1967] 201.

5. Cf. Xen. *Oec.* 7.42, [Arist.] *Oec.* 1.1343 b7–4 a8, 3.1–2 (*societas uitae*); for the extant marriage contracts cf. F. Preisigke, *Wörterbuch der griechischen Papyrusurkunden* (Berlin 1925–7) s.v. κοινωνία, E. G. Turner, *Chronique d'Égypte* 54 (1979) 123. For the idea in comedy cf. Diodoros fr. 3 (μέτοχος τοῦ βίου).

6. The jingle of πίνουσι ~ πεινῶσιν at the start of consecutive trimeters underlines the emotion of this speech.

7. For the grim plight of unwanted courtesans cf. also Ter. *HT* 388–91; so too the seriousness of their position shines through the jesting of the

opening scene of Plautus' *Cistellaria*, in which two courtesans and a *lena* gather for a meal.

8. Sandbach, *Ménandre* 131, points to her fondness for the parenthetic exclamation ὦ θεοί ('O gods').

9. My account of the legal position of women in Athens must necessarily be brief and simplified. In addition to the works listed in n. 1, fuller information may be sought in H. J. Wolff, 'Marriage law and family organisation in ancient Athens' *Traditio* 2 (1944) 43–95, Harrison [1968] *passim*, E. J. Bickerman, 'La conception du mariage à Athènes' *Bullettino dell'istituto di diritto Romano* 78 (1975) 1–28.

10. It has often been thought that the *Epitrepontes* establishes the right of a father to dissolve his daughter's marriage against her will and that of her husband, but E. G. Turner, *Chronique d'Égypte* 54 (1979) 120–2, points out that the legal position would have had to be established by a trial and the pressures upon a wife not to go against her father's wishes were enormous; this play should not, therefore, be used as evidence for a father's absolute right in this matter. For a judicious discussion of Menander's use of Attic law cf. P. G. McC. Brown, 'Menander's dramatic technique and the law of Athens' *CQ* N.S. 33 (1983) 412–20.

11. Cf. Alexis fr. 146, Antiphanes fr. 329, Men. frr. 579, 581–2, 593 K–T.

12. Cf. E. Schuhmann, 'Der Typ der *uxor dotata* in den Komödien des Plautus' *Phil.* 121 (1977) 45–65.

13. There are no grounds for Schuhmann's assumption (cf. previous note) that all henpecked husbands in Plautus are married *sine manu*, cf. Watson [1967] 25–31. Watson does not, however, convince me that *Asin.* 86 by itself establishes the marriage of Artemona and Demaenetus as *cum manu*; that verse may simply mean that Artemona's slave has got more money to play around with than her husband has, a sure sign of the weakness of the latter's position.

14. Cf. U. E. Paoli, 'L' ἐπίκληρος attica nella *palliata* romana' *Atene e Roma* 45 (1943) 19–29, E. Karabelias, 'L'épiclérat dans la comédie nouvelle et dans les sources latines' in H. J. Wolff (ed.), *Symposion 1971* (Cologne 1975) 215–54. Our clearest evidence for this transformation are the fragments of Menander's *Plocion* and Caecilius' translations preserved by Aulus Gellius 2.23.

15. Cf. Sandbach [1973] 296–8.

16. For these distinctions cf. Plaut. *Cist.* 331 and *Poen.* 265–70, where girls of one type look with contempt upon others whom they consider to be of a lower type; on the various words for 'prostitute' in these scenes cf. J. N. Adams, *RhM* 126 (1983) 329–32.

17. Cf. Fraenkel [1960] 136–42.

18. Cf. Fantham [1972] 82–91.

19. The basic discussion is W. Ludwig, 'Von Terenz zu Menander' *Phil.* 103 (1959) 1–38 (= Lefèvre [1973] 354–408).

20. Cf. notes on 110, 197, 292, 301, 584, 592, 604–5, 645–6. It is amusing to see in Chaerea's use of a picture of Jupiter and Danae to justify himself (vv. 583–91) an echo of the advice given to Pheidippides by the Ἥττων Λόγος (Ar. *Clouds* 1079–82).
21. Cf. Marti [1959] 23–4, A. J. Brothers, *CQ* N.S. 19 (1969) 314–19. There is now a full discussion by J. C. B. Lowe, 'The *Eunuchus*: Terence and Menander' *CQ* N.S. 33 (1983) 428–44.
22. Sandbach [1973] 32–4 has a clear account of the legal position of both parties after a rape.
23. Zoological inaccuracy (χοιρίον means 'little pig') is necessary to preserve the sense.
24. Cf., e.g., Plaut. *Asin.* 528–9. That Philocleon was previously tight with money is suggested by his association with the chorus, whose poverty is stressed (cf. vv. 248–53, 291–315), and by his rejection of carousing as leading to the payment of damages (v. 1255).
25. Cf. Wehrli [1936] 24.
26. Cf. A. C. Cassio, 'Motivi di agone epirrematico in commedia nuova' *Annali dell'istituto universitario orientale* (Naples) 1979, 1–22.
27. It is interesting, but presumably no more, that what Pheidippides calls out in his dream at v. 25, Φίλων, ἀδικεῖς. ἔλαυνε τὸν σαυτοῦ δρόμον ('Philon, that's wrong; keep to your own track') is very like the saying attributed to Pittacos on the wisdom of marrying a lady from your own social station, τὴν κατὰ σαυτὸν ἔλα ('Drive your own road') (Call. *Epigr.* 1 Pfeiffer, [Plut.] *De lib. educ.* 13f–14a).
28. A useful survey is Rissom [1971].
29. Dover [1974] 103.
30. The *topos* is turned back upon a young man by his father in Apollodoros fr. 7.
31. Cf. (most recently) H. Kemper, *Die im Corpus der Moralia des Plutarch überlieferte Schrift* περὶ παίδων ἀγωγῆς (diss. Münster 1971). Most of the treatise consists of simple commonplaces, but it is not unlikely that the author draws upon a lost peripatetic work on education.
32. The accounts of the *Heauton Timorumenos* which I have found most useful are E. Fantham, '*Hautontimorumenos* and *Adelphoe*: a study of fatherhood in Terence and Menander' *Latomus* 30 (1971) 970–98 and H. D. Jocelyn, '*Homo sum: humani nil a me alienum puto*' *Antichthon* 7 (1973) 14–46.
33. *non est mentiri meum* (v. 549, 'lying is not in my nature') seems to foreshadow Chremes' own disclaimer in v. 782.
34. Cf. Handley, *Ménandre* 175. We may compare the *Epidicus*, where in successive scenes first the son and then the father expresses *pudor* about their behaviour to a friend, cf. A. G. Katsouris, *Latomus* 36 (1977) 323.
35. A break in the papyrus leaves it unclear whether Moschion had fallen in love with this girl before the rape, but it is not unlikely.

36. Blundell [1980] 43. There is a good discussion of the character of Moschion by W. S. Anderson, 'The ending of the *Samia* and other Menandrian comedies' in *Studi classici in onore di Quintino Cataudella* (Catania 1972) II 155–79.
37. There is a valuable bibliography on the *Adelphoe* appended to Sandbach [1978].
38. This distinguishes Micio from Demaenetus in the *Asinaria*, whose only purpose in helping his son is the love he gains.
39. J. N. Grant, *CQ* N.S. 22 (1972) 326–7, proposes *illud quoi amicitia adiungitur* ('that [authority] to which friendship is joined').
40. Cf. Fantham [1972] 68–9. The whole of Demea's speech may be compared with the earnest platitudes of Isocrates' advice to a young man (*Ad Demonicum* 11–12).
41. Sandbach [1978] 139–40. This line of argument had already been suggested by V. Pöschl, *SB. Heidelberg* 1975, 11.
42. Cf. v. 880 *non posteriores feram* (I'll take the main part'), v. 896 *meditor esse adfabilis* ('I'm rehearsing to be nice'), v. 958 *suo sibi gladio hunc iugulo* ('I'm slitting his throat with his own sword').
43. We may compare Plaut. *Aul.* 150–2 where Plautus, rather than the Greek poet, seems to be responsible for the horror with which Megadorus greets the idea of marriage, cf. Marti [1959] 35–6, Fraenkel [1960] 98. Comedy had, of course, never looked sympathetically upon men who married late in life, cf. Ar. *Eccl.* 323–4.
44. Cf. A. E. Astin, *Cato the Censor* (Oxford 1978) 342.
45. For assessments of the fact that Cnemon's farm is worth 2 talents see Handley on *Dysc.* 842–4, Sandbach on v. 327; in general cf. J. K. Davies, *Wealth and the Power of Wealth in Classical Athens* (New York 1981). The most helpful accounts of Cnemon's character known to me are W. Görler, 'Knemon' *Hermes* 91 (1963) 268–87 and Schäfer [1965].
46. Of particular interest is the tantalising reference to Pherecrates' *Agrioi* ('The Wild Men') at Pl. *Prt.* 327c–d; the chorus of that play were misanthropes without 'education, law-courts, laws [cf. *Dysc.* 743–4] or any necessity to practise virtue', but unfortunately we cannot reconstruct Pherecrates' play in any detail.
47. *Wasps* 1320 is earlier than the revised version of *Clouds* which we possess; in that verse σκώπτων ἀγροίκως describes Philocleon as he breaks up a smart, urban party, and Philocleon is twice (vv. 1305–6, 1309–10) compared to phenomena of the countryside. The idea, of course, is much earlier than Aristophanes, cf. Alcman 16 Page, οὐκ ἦς ἀνὴρ ἀγρεῖος οὐ-|δὲ σκαιός κτλ.
48. Cf. Davies (n. 45) Chap. IV.
49. Cf. M. I. Finley, *Studies in Land and Credit in Ancient Athens, 500–200 B.C.* (New Brunswick 1951) 60–5; A. W. Gomme, *The Population of Athens in the Fifth and Fourth Centuries B.C.* (Oxford 1933) 37–48.

50. For the Greek 'bailiff' (ἐπίτροπος) in general see Xen. *Oec.* 12.3ff.; a *uilicus* also plays no part in the comedies of Terence.

51. Alexis fr. 108; the description of the second son as βῶλος, ἄροτρον, γηγενὴς | ἄνθρωπος ('a clod, a plough, a son of the soil') does not actually prove that he lived in the countryside, but it makes it very likely.

52. Cf. Sandbach *ad loc.*; W. Görler, Μενάνδρου Γνῶμαι (diss. Berlin 1963) 80–2 suggests that Daos' moralising is absurd, as Myrrhine will be well off after her daughter's marriage; it is true that Daos presents his news as a great piece of good fortune for Myrrhine, but Görler (like other critics) seems to overestimate Cleainetos' wealth, at least as far as our text allows us to judge. Myrrhine's good fortune consists in her daughter's desirable match, not in personal enrichment.

53. On these characters see W. S. Anderson, 'Chalinus *armiger* in Plautus' *Casina' ICS* 8 (1983) 11–21.

5 Comedy and tragedy

1. For this familiarity cf., e.g., Plaut. *Amph.* 41–4, *Rudens* 86.

2. Cf. Jocelyn [1967] 32–40.

3. Cf. Satyrus, *Vita Euripidis, POxy.* 1176 fr. 39 (Col. vii.8–22) and Quintilian 10.1.69 (= Menander, *Test.* 38 K–T).

4. Cf. Fraenkel [1964] I 487–502.

5. Cf. Haffter [1934] 104–7.

6. On the character of Hegio cf. especially E. W. Leach, 'Ergasilus and the ironies of the *Captivi' Classica et Mediaevalia* 30 (1969) 263–96. Particularly telling are vv. 146–50, in which the parasite's emotional and cynical declaration has the necessary effect upon Hegio – the parasite gets a dinner.

7. Vv. 61–2 are often invoked for the 'tragic' character of the play, but these verses refer merely to warfare as a characteristic of tragedy rather than comedy.

8. *tu mihi erus nunc es, tu patronus, tu pater,* | *tibi commendo spes opesque meas* ('You are now my master, you my patron, you my father: to you I entrust my hopes and my welfare'). This declaration is formulaic (cf. Ter. *Andria* 295, *Ad.* 456), but in the *Captivi* the presence on stage of the real *pater*, Hegio, adds an element of amusing irony to the melodrama. For another novel use of the formula cf. Ter. *Phormio* 496 where a young lover falls back upon this banality in a last-ditch effort to persuade a *leno* to relent.

9. A further example of this pattern is the opening of the *Curculio*, cf. Schäfer [1965] 45–6.

10. For the text of this passage see now *POxy.* 3433.

11. On λαλεῖν in Menander cf. Wilamowitz [1925] 60; a key passage is *Samia* 511–12, καθημένους δὲ πάντας ἐξ ἑωθινοῦ | περὶ ἐμοῦ λαλεῖν λέγοντας ὡς

ἀνήρ κτλ. Menander repeats the effect of fr. 740.8 at *Aspis* 240–1 (cf. above p. 120), where Smicrines' dazed reply to Daos' tragic utterance is entirely comic, ἀδελφός – ὦ Ζεῦ, πῶς φράσω; – σχεδόν τι σου | τέθνηκεν.::ὁ λαλῶν ἀρτίως ἐνταῦθ' ἐμοί;. Cf. also *Mis.* 210–11.

12. For κοινός in this phrase cf. Men. fr. 416.4 K–T (in an apparently 'serious' passage), fr. 737 K–T, G. Zuntz, *Proceedings of the British Academy* 42 (1956) 225–6. σπᾶν is a very rare verb in comedy, except in the sense 'to drink', and the more prosaic τὸν ἀέρα ἕλκειν occurs at Philyllios fr. 20.3 and Philemon fr. 119. The slave's argument in fr. 740 K–T is very reminiscent of the nurse's argument at E. *Hipp.* 433ff. (esp. 459–61), and cf. also *IA* 29–33. Barrett on *Hipp.* 460–1 cites Andocides 2.5, where the speaker quotes as a wise saying πάντες ἄνθρωποι γίγνονται ἐπὶ τῶι εὖ καὶ κακῶς πράττειν ('all human beings are subject to both good fortune and suffering').

13. With *Curc.* 591–2 cf. Adesp. fr. 296b. 1–3 Austin, εὖ γ' Εὐριπίδης | εἴρηκεν ⟨εἶναι⟩ τὴν γυναικείαν φύσιν | πάντων μέγιστον τῶν ἐν ἀνθρώποις κακῶν ('Euripides was right to say that womankind is man's greatest curse').

14. I am not convinced that the case for the influence of E. *Helen* has been successfully made, despite the similarity between *Helen* 1196 and *Aspis* 420–1, cf. D. B. Lombard, *Acta Classica* 14 (1971) 142–3.

15. About the Greek original of the *Casina* at this point we can say nothing; Leo [1912] 133 noted the close similarity of this scene to the narrative song of the Phrygian slave in E. *Or.* The similarity between the charades of Pardalisca and of Daos in the *Aspis* was noted by Fraenkel [1960] 330 n. 2.

16. Cf. Haffter [1934] 70.

17. To the commentaries of Austin and Sandbach add A. C. Cassio, 'Arte e artifici di Menandro (*Aspis* 1–18)' in *Studi in onore di Anthos Ardizzoni* (Rome 1978) 175–85 and Blundell [1980] 72–3. *Pace* D. del Corno, *Studi Classici e Orientali* 24 (1975) 29, I see no allusion in vv. 15–17 to Archilochos fr. 5 West.

18. With v. 195 cf. Ar. *Wasps* 314 ἀνόνητον ἄρα σ' ὦ θυλάκιον γ' εἶχον ἄγαλμα ('a useless ornament have I then carried you, O shopping-bag') and Ach. Tat. 3.10.6, μάτην σοι, ὦ θάλασσα, τὴν χάριν ὡμολογήσαμεν ('in vain, O sea, did we give you thanks').

19. It is generally assumed that *Bacch.* 933 is a direct parody of this verse of Ennius, but this would be a rash conclusion in the present state of our evidence, cf. H. D. Jocelyn, *HSCP* 73 (1969) 144 n. 54.

20. The most striking instances are *Persa* 341 ~ S. *El.* 597–8 (but cf. also Men. *Epitr.* 715, Ter. *Ad.* 76), *Persa* 350 ~ S. *Ant.* 719–20, *Persa* 371 ~ S. *Ant.* 685–6 (but cf. also Plaut. *Asin.* 514), *Persa* 647 ~ E. *IT* 500. The discussion between the parasite and his daughter may be traced back to the confrontations of Haimon and Creon in S. *Ant.* and of Neoptolemos and Odysseus in S. *Ph.*

21. Cf. Wilamowitz, *Kleine Schriften* II 271, Marti [1959] 68–9, Woytek's edition pp. 47–53.

22. Cf. G. W. Williams, *JRS* 48 (1958) 19.

23. The most notable examples are Pamphile in the *Epitrepontes* and the speaker of Pap. Didot I (printed on pp. 328–30 of Sandbach's Oxford text of Menander and cf. above pp. 83–4). For *tragicomoedia* in the *Amphitruo* cf. above p. 164 n. 33.

24. Cf. Sandbach [1973] 239. I am not convinced by J.-M. Jacques, 'Mouvement des acteurs et conventions scéniques dans l'Acte II du Bouclier de Ménandre' *Grazer Beiträge* 7 (1978) 37–56 (and see also Ş. Halliwell, *Liverpool Classical Monthly* 8 (1983) 31–2) that Chairestratos appears on the ἐκκύκλημα at *Aspis* 305. Apart from other objections, ἀγέτω in 387 does not seem the right word with which to conclude such a scene. I leave out of account here speculations about the possible role of this device in the Greek originals of certain Latin scenes, such as in the 'toilet-scene' of the *Mostellaria* or the party with which *Asinaria* concludes.

25. Cf. E. *IA* 2–3 and the commentaries of Handley and Sandbach on *Dysc.* 692.

26. Cf. the pun on the literal and transferred senses of ἄτοπος at Pl. *Phdr.* 230c6.

27. Cf. A. O'Brien-Moore, *Madness in Ancient Literature* (diss. Princeton, Weimar 1924) 155–62. Worthy of special note are vv. 824–5, which recall E. *HF* 952 παίζει πρὸς ἡμᾶς δεσπότης ἢ μαίνεται; ('Is the master teasing us or is he mad?'), and v. 865 which recalls the situation of E. *HF* and of the *Mercator*.

28. Dover, on *Clouds* 1478ff., compares *Peace* 661ff., where Hermes converses with the statue of Peace. Both Hermes and Peace, however, are gods and may reasonably be imagined to converse with each other; in the *Clouds* and the *Menaechmi* a mortal converses with a god. For such scenes in general cf. R. Kassel, 'Dialoge mit Statuen' *ZPE* 51 (1983) 1–12, and for the Roman stage-altar C. Saunders, 'Altars on the Roman comic stage' *TAPA* 42 (1911) 91–103, Duckworth [1952] 83–4.

29. Certain verses are, however, also strongly reminiscent of the *Hippolytos*, cf. 933 ~ *Hipp.* 1182–4, 931 ~ *Hipp.* 1188–9 and, outside this scene, 627 ~ *Hipp.* 1074–7 and 830–41 ~ *Hipp.* 1090–7. I would not be as confident as most critics that the *Heracles* is the direct model for the scene in the *Mercator*.

30. Cf. Rau [1967] 162–8. Ar. *Pl.* 632 φαίνει γὰρ ἥκειν ἄγγελος χρηστοῦ τινος ('it is likely that you are a messenger of some good news') looks like a joke on the convention of the messenger; cf. also *Acharnians* 1069–70.

31. Sandbach, *Ménandre* 129.

32. Cf. Rau [1967] 39–40.

33. Ar. *Knights* 1232ff., adduced in this context by Handley, *Ménandre* 41 and Goldberg [1980] 60, belongs to the rather different category of 'oracle revelation', cf. Rau [1967] 170–3. More relevant is the welcome to the eel at Ar. *Ach.* 885–7.
34. The word τέκνον itself is a mark of elevated style in the mouth of an Athenian male; the only other New Comedy examples known to me are the two possible instances in the mouth of Pataicos in the 'recognition-scene' of the *Periceiromene* (vv. 804, 813).
35. Cf. Bain [1977] 213.
36. I follow Sandbach's speaker distribution here; when H. W. Prescott, *CP* 13 (1918) 121, assigned these verses to 'the slave', this was presumably a slip of the pen or of the memory.
37. Cf. W. S. Anderson, 'Euripides' *Auge* and Menander's *Epitrepontes*' *GRBS* 23 (1982) 165–77. I am not persuaded by Anderson that the point of the quotation from the *Auge* is its inappropriateness, a feature which would serve to infuriate Smicrines all the more.
38. Before *Epitr.* 1121, ἀναγνώρισις/ -σμός is found only in the *Poetics*, where it seems to be used as a pre-existing technical term, and at Pl. *Tht.* 193c (of 'recognising' people whom one has seen at a distance).
39. For διαλλαγή cf. Hunter [1983] 27 n. 1.
40. λύσις occurs in comedy elsewhere only in a fragment of Epinicos (fr. 1.10) which apparently parodies the style of the historian Mnesiptolemos.

6 *The didactic element*

1. Cf. above p. 13 on *Dysc.* 741–5. Another good illustration is 'Apollodoros of Carystos' fr. 5 where utopian political advice is given to all the leading states, not just Athens. (For the authorship and dating of this fragment cf. Wilamowitz, *Kleine Schriften* II 261 n. 2.) For the specifically Athenian references in New Comedy cf. Webster [1970] 102–10. On Philippides fr. 25 cf. n. 31 to Chapter 1.
2. For the legal background to Saturio's speech cf. Woytek's commentary *ad loc.* (esp. p. 183). The extent of Plautus' debt to his Greek original here is exaggerated by Leo [1912] 123–5.
3. Cf. above pp. 99–100 with H. D. Jocelyn's article cited in n. 32 to Chapter 4.
4. Cf. Sandbach [1973] 74; in his work *On Fortune*, Menander's friend Demetrios of Phaleron (cf. above p. 3) saw the total destruction of Persian power and the startling rise of Macedon within the space of fifty years as the work of 'Fortune which makes no compacts with our way of life, whose constant innovations defeat our reasoning and which shows her own power in bringing to pass the things we don't expect' (*FGrHist* 228 F 39 = Demetrios fr. 81 Wehrli²).
5. Cf. Sandbach on v. 272 and *id., Ménandre* 116–19.

6. Particularly close to the fifth act of the *Dyscolos* is Plaut. *Trin.* 11.2; cf. also Men. *Epitr.* 919–22, Pap. Didot 1 (p. 328 in Sandbach's text of Menander), Plaut, *Asin.* 504–44, *Persa* 329–99. The forerunners of these scenes may be seen in the arguments between Haimon and Creon in Sophocles' *Antigone* and Neoptolemos and Odysseus in the *Philoctetes*.

7. There is an interesting parallel to this part of Cnemon's speech in Socrates' account of the origins of misanthropy at Pl. *Phaedo* 89d–e.

8. It seems certain that this is the sense, but the text of the beginning of v. 743 is problematic, cf. Sandbach *ad loc.*

9. Cf. Hom. *Od.* 9.112–15 τοῖσιν δ' οὔτ' ἀγοραὶ βουληφόροι οὔτε θέμιστες, | ἀλλ' οἵ γ' ὑψηλῶν ὀρέων ναίουσι κάρηνα | ἐν σπέεσι γλαφυροῖσι, θεμιστεύει δὲ ἕκαστος | παίδων ἠδ' ἀλόχων, οὐδ' ἀλλήλων ἀλέγουσι ('[The Cyclopes] have neither assemblies where advice is given nor laws, but they live in hollow caves on the peaks of lofty mountains, and each governs his children and his wives, and they have no concern for each other'). The contribution which Polyphemos makes to the depiction of Cnemon has perhaps received insufficient attention; the Homeric story certainly casts Cnemon's threat to eat Getas alive in a new light (v. 468, cf. v. 124).

10. To the commentaries of Handley and Sandbach on the present passage add Leo [1912] 113–22 and Kassel–Austin on Baton fr. 3.5.

11. Cf. in general Neumann [1958]; Neumann's approach is, however, far too schematic to account for the plays which we possess.

12. There are good reasons for believing that Plautus does not owe these passages to his Greek models, cf. Fraenkel [1960] 234.

13. On this speech cf. Hunter [1981] 40. Another speech which toys with these ideas is *Persa* 7–12.

14. Many are conveniently listed by Webster [1970] 110–12.

15. Diogenes Laertios 5.36; Alciphron, *Epist.* 4.19.14 Schepers.

16. It seems reasonable to assume that most of Demetrios' writing was done after he had retired to the court of Ptolemy in Egypt in the early years of the third century and may thus not be strictly contemporary with Menander's plays, cf. Cic. *De fin.* 5.54 and, for a general survey, F. Wehrli, *RE* Suppl. Bd. 11.514–22. For the scanty fragments of Demetrios' works cf. F. Wehrli, *Die Schule des Aristoteles*² Vol. IV (Basel 1968) and *FGrHist* 228.

17. In Theophrastos the flatterer laughs when his patron tells a bad joke (*Char.* 2.4), cf. Ter. *Eun.* 426–8 (based on Men. *Colax* fr. 3) where Gnatho pretends to find Thraso's hackneyed joke very amusing; for the motif cf. already Eupolis fr. 159.9–10.

18. For αὐθάδεια coupled with δυσκολία cf. Pl. *R.* 9.590a.

19. I give here the other parallels between comedy and *The Characters* which seem worthy of note (cf. also Legrand [1910] 324 and Barigazzi [1965] 69–86). The busybody (περίεργος) seeks to separate people he doesn't know who are fighting (*Char.* 13.5); cf. the action of the cook at Men.

Samia 383ff. The suspicious man (ἄπιστος) sends his slave in front of him so that he can't escape (*Char.* 18.8); cf. Plaut. *Curc.* 487 *i tu prod'*, *uirgo : non queo quod pone me est seruare* ('You go in front, girl; I can't watch what's behind me'). The arrogant (ὑπερήφανος) man acts as an arbitrator in an improper fashion (*Char.* 24.4, the text is badly corrupt); we may be reminded of *Epitr.* 224ff. – Syriscos' appeal to Smicrines 'not to scorn them' (v. 232) indicates the arrogance (ὑπερηφανία) of the latter. The coward (δειλός) has obvious general similarities to Sosia in the *Amphitruo*, and the oligarchic man might have links with *Sicyon.* 150ff., where the text is frustratingly incomplete. Finally, the impostor (ἀλαζών) reminds us of the *milites gloriosi* of Roman comedy; with *Char.* 23.3 cf. esp. Ter. *Eun.* 397–410.

20. For what follows see esp. Schäfer [1965] 94–5.
21. I have not thought it worthwhile to catalogue in the main text all of the passages from comedy where Theophrastos' influence has been suspected. Two commonly quoted examples are, however, worthy of note. Cnemon's denunciation of the motives of the sacrificers at Men. *Dysc.* 442–53 has seemed to many critics in keeping with the views expressed in Theophrastos' *On Piety*, as these can be reconstructed from Porphyry, *De abstinentia* II. It is, however, extremely unlikely that the verses are intended to have a 'philosophical' flavour. I am, in any case, not persuaded that Cnemon in fact makes a general plea for small, simple sacrifices as Theophrastos did, although Porphyry (*De abstinentia* II.17, p. 147 N²) cites vv. 449–51 to illustrate this theme. Those verses seem merely to be a sarcastic and specific reference to the present sacrifice. Secondly, close links have been seen between the denunciation of marriage at Plaut. *MG* 678–722 and the extract from Theophrastos' discussion of whether the wise man should marry, which is preserved by Jerome, *Adu. Iouinianum* 1.47 (*PL* xxiii.276–8 Migne). Certainly, there is much in this passage of Jerome which reminds us of the complaints of husbands and the presentation of wives in comedy, but the influence would seem to be all from comedy in general to Theophrastos and not vice versa, cf. Webster [1950] 214–16.
22. The specificity of ἀκούσιον...ἀτύχημα ('an involuntary misfortune') in v. 914 is nicely suggestive of a young man familiar with the distinctions of moral theory, cf. Arist. *EN* 5.1135 b11–25, *Rhet.* 1.1374 b6–9. It is often claimed that Menander follows strictly the Aristotelian analysis of ἀτύχημα ('misfortune'), ἁμάρτημα ('error') and ἀδίκημα ('sin'), but in fact his usage follows (i) the needs of plot and characterisation (cf. Gomme–Sandbach on *Epitr.* 891), (ii) ordinary Greek usage which itself appears to have changed during the course of the fourth century, cf. Dover [1974] 146–52.
23. A classic demonstration of careful analysis is Zuntz's discussion of fr. 416 K–T in *Proceedings of the British Academy* 42 (1956) 209–46; there is a useful survey in Gaiser [1967].

24. Cf. esp. *EN* 3.1110 b18ff., Barigazzi [1965] 135–60, W. W. Fortenbaugh, 'Menander's *Perikeiromene*: misfortune, vehemence and Polemon' *Phoenix* 28 (1974) 430–43.
25. Some guidance to this disagreement may be found in C. Lord, 'Aristotle, Menander and the *Adelphoe* of Terence' *TAPA* 107 (1977) 183–202. Scholarly agreement is, of course, an unrealistic hope as long as we are largely ignorant of how Menander's play ended.
26. This seems to me also true of the *Trinummus*, despite Elaine Fantham's important article, 'Philemon's Thesauros as a dramatisation of Peripatetic ethics' *Hermes* 105 (1977) 406–21.

Bibliography

This list contains works which are cited more than once in the notes, together with certain other important or influential modern studies. It is not intended as a bibliographical guide to New Comedy, but I hope that it will point anyone interested in 'Further Reading' in the right direction. Editions and commentaries on individual plays are not listed.

Abel, K. *Die Plautusprologe* (diss. Frankfurt 1955)
Andrieu, J. *Le Dialogue antique : structure et présentation* (Paris 1954)
Arnott, W. G. *Menander, Plautus and Terence* (*Greece & Rome* New Surveys 9, Oxford 1975)
Bain, D. *Actors and Audience* (Oxford 1977)
Barigazzi, A. *La formazione spirituale di Menandro* (Turin 1965)
Beare, W. *The Roman Stage*³ (London 1964)
Bieber, M. *The History of the Greek and Roman Theater*² (Princeton 1961)
Blundell, J. *Menander and the Monologue* (*Hypomnemata* 59, Göttingen 1980)
Conrad, C. C. *The Technique of Continuous Action in Roman Comedy* (diss. Chicago 1915)
Denzler, B. *Der Monolog bei Terenz* (Zurich 1968)
Dover, K. J. *Aristophanic Comedy* (London 1972)
    Greek Popular Morality in the Time of Plato and Aristotle (Oxford 1974)
Duckworth, G. E. *The Nature of Roman Comedy* (Princeton 1952)
Fantham, E. *Comparative Studies in Republican Latin Imagery* (Toronto 1972)
    'Sex, status and survival in hellenistic Athens: a study of women in New Comedy' *Phoenix* 29 (1975) 44–74
Fraenkel, E. *Elementi Plautini in Plauto* (Florence 1960)
    Kleine Beiträge zur klassischen Philologie (Rome 1964)
Friedrich, W. H. *Euripides und Diphilos* (*Zetemata* 5, Munich 1953)
Gaiser, K. 'Menander und der Peripatos' *A&A* 13 (1967) 8–40
    'Zur Eigenart der römischen Komödie: Plautus und Terenz gegenüber ihren griechischen Vorbildern' in H. Temporini (ed.), *Aufstieg und Niedergang der römischen Welt* I.2 (Berlin/New York 1972) pp. 1027–1113
Gentili, B. *Theatrical Performances in the Ancient World* (Amsterdam/Uithoorn 1979)
Goldberg, S. *The Making of Menander's Comedy* (London 1980)
Gomme, A. W. *Essays in Greek History and Literature* (Oxford 1937). See also under Sandbach, F. H.
Gratwick, A. S. 'The Early Republic' in *The Cambridge History of Classical Literature* Vol. II (Cambridge 1982; published separately 1983)

Haffter, H. *Untersuchungen zur altlateinischen Dichtersprache (Problemata* 10, Berlin 1934)

'Terenz und seine künstlerische Eigenart' *Museum Helveticum* 10 (1953) 1–20 and 73–102 (published separately, Darmstadt 1967)

Handley, E. W. *Menander and Plautus; a study in comparison* (Inaugural Lecture, University College, London 1968)

'Comedy' in *The Cambridge History of Classical Literature* Vol. 1 (Cambridge 1985)

Harrison, A. R. W. *The Law of Athens: the family and property* (Oxford 1968)

Holzberg, N. *Menander: Untersuchungen zur dramatischen Technik* (Nürnberg 1974)

Hunter, R. L. 'The comic chorus in the fourth century' *ZPE* 36 (1979) 23–38

'Philemon, Plautus and the Trinummus' *Museum Helveticum* 37 (1980) 216–30

'The *Aulularia* of Plautus and its Greek original' *PCPS* N.S. 27 (1981) 37–49

Eubulus: The Fragments (Cambridge Classical Texts and Commentaries 24, Cambridge 1983)

Jachmann, G. *Plautinisches und Attisches (Problemata* 3, Berlin 1931)

Jocelyn, H. D. *The Tragedies of Ennius* (Cambridge Classical Texts and Commentaries 10, Cambridge 1967)

Katsouris, A. G. *Tragic Patterns in Menander* (Athens 1975)

Konstan, D. *Roman Comedy* (Cornell 1983)

Kroll, W. *Studien zum Verständnis der römischen Literatur* (Stuttgart 1924)

Lefèvre, E. (ed.) *Die römische Komödie: Plautus und Terenz* (Wege der Forschung 236, Darmstadt 1973)

Legrand, P. *Daos* (Lyons/Paris 1910)

Leo, F. *Plautinische Forschungen*[2] (Berlin 1912)

Geschichte der römischen Literatur I: Die archaische Literatur (Berlin 1913)

Ludwig, W. 'The originality of Terence and his Greek models' *GRBS* 9 (1968) 169–82

Marti, H. *Untersuchungen zur dramatischen Technik bei Plautus und Terenz* (diss. Zurich 1959)

Ménandre = Entretiens sur l'antiquité classique publiés par Olivier Reverdin, Tome XVI, *Ménandre* (Vandoeuvres/Geneva 1970)

Neumann, M. *Die poetische Gerechtigkeit in der neuen Komödie* (diss. Mainz 1958)

Pickard-Cambridge, A. *The Dramatic Festivals of Athens*[2] (revised by J. Gould and D. M. Lewis, Oxford 1968)

Prescott, H. W. 'The antecedents of Hellenistic comedy' *CP* 12 (1917) 405–25, 13 (1918) 113–37, 14 (1919) 108–35

Rau, P. *Paratragodia: Untersuchungen einer komischen Form des Aristophanes* (*Zetemata* 45, Munich 1967)

Reinhardt, U. *Mythologische Beispiele in der neuen Komödie (Menander, Plautus, Terenz)* Teil I (diss. Mainz 1974)

Bibliography

Rieth, O. *Die Kunst Menanders in den Adelphen des Terenz*. Mit einem Nachwort hrsg. von K. Gaiser (Hildesheim 1964)

Rissom, H.-W. *Vater- und Sohnmotive in der römischen Komödie* (diss. Kiel 1971)

Sandbach, F. H. *The Comic Theatre of Greece and Rome* (London 1977) 'Donatus' use of the name Terentius and the end of Terence's *Adelphoe' BICS* 25 (1978) 123–45

Sandbach, F. H. and Gomme, A. W. *Menander: A Commentary* (Oxford 1973)

Schäfer, A. *Menanders Dyskolos: Untersuchungen zur dramatischen Technik* (Meisenheim am Glan 1965)

Taladoire, B.-A. *Essai sur le comique de Plaute* (Monaco 1956)

Trenkner, S. *The Greek Novella in the Classical Period* (Cambridge 1958)

Watson, A. *The Law of Persons in the Later Roman Republic* (Oxford 1967)

Webster, T. B. L. *Studies in Menander*[2] (Manchester 1960)
Studies in Later Greek Comedy[2] (Manchester 1970)
An Introduction to Menander (Manchester 1974)

Wehrli, F. *Motivstudien zur griechischen Komödie* (Zurich 1936)

Wilamowitz-Moellendorff, U. von *Menander: Das Schiedsgericht* (Berlin 1925)

Wright, J. *Dancing in Chains: the stylistic unity of the Comoedia Palliata* (Rome 1974)

Zagagi, N. *Tradition and Originality in Plautus* (*Hypomnemata* 62, Göttingen 1980)

Index of passages discussed

See also under individual play titles in Index of Subjects. Reference to notes is not made where a discussion can be found through the main text.

Index of passages discussed

Index of subjects

Reference to notes is not made where a discussion can be found through the main text.

Acharnians, 9, 109; Lamachos in, 8, 66
acts: five-act structure, 35–7; no act-divisions in Roman comedy, 37–40; role of fourth act, 40–1; role of fifth act, 41–2
Adelphoe, 105–9, 151; Sannio in, 55–6, 72
Alexis, 1, 3; *Kouris*, 111
altars, scenes involving, 115, 128
Ambivius Turpio, 26
Amphitruo: Alcumena in, 126–7; dramatic conventions in, 79–82; prologue of, 26, 79
Andria: dramatic conventions in, 77–9; Simo in, 34–5, 77–9, 101–2; Sosia in, 34–5
Apollodoros of Carystos, 4
M. Aristius Fuscus, 152 n. 3
Aristophanes: endings in, 41–2; parabases in, 30–3; prologues in, 24, 27; *Banqueters*, 110–11; *see also under play titles*
Aristotle, 37, 150–1
'Artists of Dionysus', 19
Asinaria, 62, 76–7
Aspis, 27, 28, 122–3; tragic parody in, 120–1
Atellan farce, 20–1
audience, composition of, 10, 83
Aulularia, 9, 148–9; and *Dyscolos*, 62
Aulus Gellius, 5, 18

Bacchides, 57–8, 68, 96–7, 106; and *Dis Exapaton*, 16–18
bomolochoi, 54
brothel-keepers, in comedy, 71–2

Caecilius Statius, *Plocion*, 18
Callimachus, 32
Captivi, 116–17; Greek original of, 155 n. 41
Casina, 41, 112–13; prologue of, 6, 157 n. 6

chorus, 9–10; size of, 10, 154 n. 21
Cistellaria, 63; prologue of, 25, 27, 32, 157 n. 15
Clouds, 33, 109–10; and *Adelphoe*, 97; and *Bacchides*, 96–7
comoedia togata, 15
contaminatio, 7, 30
cooks, in comedy, 54, 65, 76
costume, 11; *see also* masks
countryside, role of in comedy, 87–9, 92–5
Curculio, 48, 64

Demetrios of Phaleron, 3, 13, 148
Demophilos, comic poet, 162 n. 6
Diphilos, 1, 3, 55, 152 n. 1, 162 n. 12; *Paederasts*, 13
Dis Exapaton, 16–18
Donatus, 7, 38; on rape in *Eunuchus*, 94
dowries, in comedy, 90–2
Dyscolos, 40, 44–5, 111, 142–5; Chaireas in, 34; Cnemon in, 9, 65, 109, 127–8, 144–5, 148–9; Getas in, 54–5; prologue of, 29; Sicon in, 29, 54–5

ekkyklema, 127
Epicharmus, 20
Epicurus, 3
Epitrepontes, 59–61, 85–7, 134–6, 149–50; family law in, 166 n. 10; Habrotonon in, 60, 89–90; time covered by, 159 n. 30
Eunuchus, 64, 88–9, 92–5; and *Truculentus*, 63
Eupolis, *Flatterers*, 9
Euripides: influence on New Comedy, 25, 28, Chap. 5 *passim*; prologues of, 25, 28

Fortune, role of in New Comedy, 11, 141–4
Frogs, 61–2
C. Fundanius, 152 n. 3

182